CHOICE ✓ C0-BXS-309

DATE DUE

SEP 22 1989		

University of London Classical Studies

VIII

THE ARATUS ASCRIBED TO
GERMANICUS CAESAR

The Aratus ascribed to Germanicus Caesar

Edited with an introduction, translation & commentary

by

D. B. GAIN

Lecturer in Classics,
University of the Witwatersrand, Johannesburg

Aratus Solensis,

UNIVERSITY OF LONDON
THE ATHLONE PRESS
1976

Published by
THE ATHLONE PRESS
UNIVERSITY OF LONDON
at 4 Gower Street, London W C I

Distributed by Tiptree Book Services Ltd
Tiptree, Essex

U.S.A. and Canada
Humanities Press Inc
New Jersey

© *University of London* 1976

ISBN 0 485 13708 9

Printed in Great Britain by
WESTERN PRINTING SERVICES LTD
BRISTOL

VXORI
ANNAE

PREFACE

This book originated as a thesis submitted for the degree of Doctor of Philosophy at the University of London in 1971. It has been extensively revised.

My thanks go firstly to Professor F. R. D. Goodyear (who supervised the original thesis) and Professor G. P. Goold, both of whom read a draft of the book. For their suggestions, and, particularly, correction of errors, I am very grateful. I would also like to thank Professors O. Skutsch and E. J. Kenney, Dr J. Diggle and Mr E. Courtney for offering suggestions and discussing difficulties with me.

My final thanks go to the University of the Witwatersrand, for subsidizing the cost of publication, to the University of London for funds to purchase microfilms of manuscripts, and to the librarians who provided me with these microfilms.

Johannesburg,   D. B. GAIN
July 1974

CONTENTS

PREFACE   vii

INTRODUCTION   I

1. The Manuscripts, 1
2. Editions, 8
3. The form of the present edition, 10
4. Bibliography, 11
5. Sources of the poem, 13
6. Identity of the author and date of the poem, 16

TEXT AND APPARATUS CRITICUS   21

TRANSLATION   53

COMMENTARY   80

INDEX   141

STAR MAPS

Hemisphaerium Boreale   18

Hemisphaerium Australe   19

INTRODUCTION

I. THE MANUSCRIPTS

i. *Description of the Manuscripts*

I give a *stemma codicum* below.

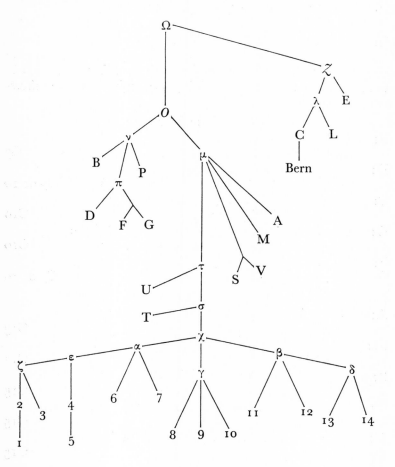

The Greek letters and the symbols O and Z represent lost manuscripts. The other symbols represent the manuscripts or early printed editions whose name, location (in the case of a manuscript) and exact or approximate date is given below. C9 means 9th century, C10 10th, etc.

Z family

Bern:	Codex Bernensis 88 (Bürgerbibliothek, Bern)	C10
C:	Codex Bononiensis 188 (Bibliothèque de Boulogne-sur-mer)	C10
E:	Codex Einsidlensis 338 (Stiftsbibliothek, Einsiedeln)	C10
L:	Codex Leidensis Voss. Lat. Q 79 (Universiteits-Bibliotheek, Leiden)	C9

L = the agreement of the majuscule and minuscule texts in the manuscript. Where they differ, L = majuscule, l = minuscule.

O family: ν branch

B:	Codex Basileensis A.N. iv 18 (Universitätsbibliothek, Basel)	C9
D:	Codex Berolinensis Phillippicus 1832 (Deutsche Staatsbibliothek, East Berlin)	C9 or 10
F:	Codex Parisinus Lat. 5239 (Bibliothèque Nationale, Paris)	C10
G:	Codex Argentoratensis Lat. 275 (Bibliothèque Universitaire et Regionale de Strasburg)	C10
P:	Codex Parisinus Lat. 7886 (Bibliothèque Nationale, Paris)	C9 or 10

O family: μ branch

A:	Codex Arundelianus 268 (British Museum Library, London)	C13
M:	Codex Matritensis 19 (Biblioteca Nacional, Madrid)	C12
S:	Codex Strozzianus 46 (Biblioteca Medicea Laurenziana, Florence)	C15
T:	Codex Egertonensis 1050 (British Museum Library, London)	C15
U:	Codex Vat. Barb. Lat. 76 (Biblioteca Apostolica Vaticana)	C15

V: Codex Vat. Lat. 3110 (Biblioteca Apostolica
     Vaticana)   C15
1:   Edition of Pisanus, Venice   1488
2:   Codex Montpesulanus 452 (Bibliothèque de
     l'école de médecine, Montpellier)   C15
3:   Codex Matritensis 8282 (Biblioteca Nacional,
     Madrid)   C15
4:   Codex Vat. Barb. Lat. 77 (Biblioteca Apostolica
     Vaticana)   C15
5:   Codex Monasterii Sanctae Mariae apud Scottos
     521, Vienna   C16
6:   Codex Vat. Urb. Lat. 1358 (Biblioteca Apostolica
     Vaticana)   C15
7:   Codex Laur. Gad. 89 suppl. plut. 43 (Biblioteca
     Medicea Laurenziana, Florence)   C15
8:   Codex Vat. Lat. 3293 (Biblioteca Apostolica
     Vaticana)   C15
9:   Editio Princeps (ed. Bonincontrius, Bologna)   1474
10: Codex Vat. Lat. 1653 (Biblioteca Apostolica
     Vaticana)   C15
11: Codex Additional 15819 (British Museum Library,
     London)   C15
12: Codex Panormitanus 2QQ.E.11 (Biblioteca
     Comunale, Palermo)   C15
13: Codex Berolinensis Lat. Oct. 149
     (Staatsbibliothek der Stiftung Preussischer
     Kulturbesitz, West Berlin)   C15
14: Codex Vat. Reg. Lat. 1801 (Biblioteca
     Apostolica Vaticana)   C15

The following, omitted from the *stemma codicum* as being heavily contaminated, are derived from χ: the edition of Aldus (Venice, 1499) and Codex Etonensis 88 (Eton College Library, Windsor), C 15 or 16.

I have seen A, 11, T and Codex Etonensis. I have collated the other manuscripts in microfilm.

There also exists a Codex Ambros. D 52 inf. (15th cent.) of the Collegio Ambrosiano, Milan (described in Holder's *Avienius*, p. xii). I have not been able to obtain a microfilm. There may also exist a certain Codex Fribergensis, a collation

of which was incorporated into his edition by Orelli. Both
contain lines 1–430 and iv 52–163, and are thus copies of σ. I
have also not seen certain early editions mentioned in Hartley's
Catalogus Universalis Librorum Insignium et Rarissimorum (1699),
one of 1497, 8vo, Venice, another of 1500, 4to, Venice, another
of 1503, Rhegium, impressum expensis et labore Francisci
Mazalis calcographi diligentissimi. The last two are probably,
like many later editions, based on the Aldine.

ii. *Differences between O and Z*

Where *O* or *Z* present an impossible reading which seems
merely a corruption of the reading of the other branch of the
tradition, which must surely be correct, I have usually sup-
pressed the variants. *Z* omits 35, 65–70, 83, 97, 143, 267, 343,
555, 568–71 and fragment iv (all contained in *O*), has 90–5
after 64, after 146 a verse made up from 148 and Avienius 370,
then Avien. 371–4, 376–8, Germ. 147, Germ. 148/Avien. 383,
Avien. 384, 388–90; it has Germ. 387–93 before 286, after 341
Avien. 749, after 342 Avien. 747–8 and 750, after 464 one, after
472 two spurious verses. At the end it has Avien. 1741–62,
1769–70, 1773, 1870, 1877–8 (the numeration of Avienius is
Holder's). *O* contracts 207–8 into one verse, omits 248–50,
255–7, 270–2, 278–80, 284–6, 289–90, 315–17, 321–3, 328–30,
333–5, 341, 344–6, 356–8, 363–5, 379–81, 393–5, 414–16, 426–8,
431–2, 434–6, 440–2, 459–61, 532–4, 583–725 and fragments ii
and iii. *O* omits 253 verses contained in *Z*, *Z* 180 contained in
O, they have 499 verses in common. E alone contains 4 verses,
A alone 9, 1½ are known only from a quotation by Priscian.
Total verses extant is 946½. Three of these are spurious. Thus
the total of genuine verses is 943½.

iii. *Division of the poem into sections in Z*

Many of the above omissions and transpositions can be ex-
plained by the fact that in both *O* and *Z* (as can be seen from
B and M, C and L, respectively) the text of much of the poem
was divided into sections, illustrated by pictures of the con-
stellations etc. L has a text written in majuscules (and minus-
cules, neglected in the following description) in a deluxe

format. A picture page is followed by pages of text illustrating it. In C text and pictures are on the one page; E has no pictures.

The following is the format of L; that of Z must have been very similar, as we shall see in the next section. Column A gives the figure, column B the number of lines of text in the pages following it, column C the line numbers.

A	B	C
Nil	8, 8	1–8, 9–16
Draco et Vrsae	11, 11, 11, 14	17–27, 28–39, 40–50, 51–64
Bootes	3, 3	90–2, 93–5
Corona	2, 2	71–2, 73–4
Ophiuchus	7, 7	75–81, 82–9
Virgo	15, 15, 15	91–111, 112–26, 127–41
Gemini	4, 4	148 + verses of Avienius
Cancer	3, 3	147 + Avien.
Leo	4, 4	149–52, 153–6
Auriga	9, 8	157–65, 166–73
Taurus	5, 5	174–8, 179–83
Cepheus	5, 4	184–8, 189–92
Cassiepia	4, 4	193–6, 197–200
Andromeda	4, 4	201–4, 205–8
Pegasus	8, 7	209–16, 217–23
Aries	6, 5	224–9, 230–4
Triangulum	3, 3	235–7, 238–40
Pisces	4, 3	241–4, 245–7
Perseus	4, 4	248–51, 252–5
Pleiades	6, 6	256–61, 262–8
Lyra	4, 3	269–72, 273–5
Cycnus	5, 5	276–80, 281–5
Aquarius	4, 3	387–90, 391–3
Capricornus	10, 10	286–95, 296–305
Sagittarius	5, 4	306–10, 311–14
Aquila	3, 3	315–17, 318–20
Delphin	4, 3	321–4, 325–7
Orion	3, 2	328–30, 331–2
Canis (Maior)	4, 4	333–6, 337–40
Lepus	4, 3	341–2, 344 + Avien.
Argo	6, 5	345–50, 351–5

A	B	C
Cetus	4, 3	356–9, 360–2
Eridanus	8, 8	363–70, 371–8
Piscis Aust.	4, 4	379–82, 383–6
Ara	10, 10	394–403, 404–13
[Centaurus]	6, 6	414–19, 420–5
Hydra	4, 3	426–9, 430–2
Procyon (CMi)	2, 2	433–4, 435–6
The planets	5, 4	437–41, 442–5
Equator, ecliptic and tropics	16 pp. of 15 each, 11, 15, 12	446–725
Celestial spheres	15, 13; 15, 1	Fr. iii 1–15, 16–28 Fri. ii 1–15, 16
Nil	15, 13	Avien. 1741–55, 1756–1878

I have put *Centaurus* in square brackets, as the figure has been lost from L (it is found in C) with the loss of a leaf, which also contained the minuscule text of 404–13. Note that 142–6 is not contained in the majuscule text of L. The minuscule text, C and E have it, thus Z must have had it.

iv. *Explanation of Z's peculiarities*

Many of Z's peculiarities can be explained from the above table. I go through them in order. Line 35 was probably omitted through *homoeomeson* (the similarity of letters in the middle of two lines, on which see Housman's Lucan p. xix). Below the *cum* of 35 comes the *cumbala* of 36. Lines 90–5 are the text after the figure of Bootes. The figure and its text have been transposed, deliberately or accidentally. 65–70 illustrate Engonasin. Either this was supplanted by the transposition of Bootes or, as *non ulli nomen, non cognita causa laboris* (66), no figure was drawn and so the text was simply omitted. 83 was omitted either because both 82 and 83 start with *in* or because *dextera* is the 2nd last word in each, or for both of these reasons. The omission of 97 is hard to explain, unless the similarity of *spica* in 97 and *diua* below it in 98 was sufficient cause. Line 143 was omitted as *quique* starts both 142 and 143. Line 267 was probably omitted from Ω due to the similarity of *tempora* in 267 and *teporadmonet* below it in 268 and then placed in the margin. *O* put it back into the text, *Z* dropped it altogether. On the omission of 343 see below, on interpolations. I can see no explanation for the omission of 555.

Now let us turn to interpolations. The editor felt that what the author said on Gemini and Cancer (lines 147–8) was inadequate to illustrate his plates and so he made a suitable number of verses by interpolation from Avienius. He also felt that 284–5, with their brief mention of Aquarius, were not sufficient to illustrate his plate, and so transposed 387–93 to add to the text. He also felt 341–3 were inadequate to describe Lepus and so he interpolated from Avienius, dropping 343 as unnecessary, as his interpolations gave Lepus' position. The motive for the interpolation of a verse after 464 and two after 472 is expansion of the account.

v. *Explanation of O's peculiarities*

O had virtually the same pictures as *Z*, but the sections of text were sometimes somewhat different. All the omissions in *O* up to and including that of 532–4 are omissions of the initial lines of sections (e.g. 248–50 are the first three lines of the section on Perseus, and so on). M carries the process further, omitting an additional line at the start of sections. Lines 207–8 are contracted into one verse, as the scribe's eye slipped from *Andromeda* in 207 to the same word in 208. *O* also omits 583–725 and fragments ii and iii. *Z* has ii and iii in the wrong order. Fragment iv follows on iii without a break in the sense. The simplest explanation of all this is that in the archetype 583–725, ii and iii occupied one quaternion (i.e. a gathering of four sheets or eight leaves, sixteen pages, the most common gathering). The last two leaves of it became detached. When *Z* was copied from it, the last two leaves had been replaced in the wrong order, and were so copied. Later, these leaves and the rest of the quaternion, weakened by their removal, were lost and hence all the verses were omitted by *O*. Note that fragments iii and iv both occupy two pages in L: I believe each similarly occupied a leaf in the archetype. The archetype had fourteen or around fourteen verses per page; 583–725 occupied eleven pages, a figure of the celestial spheres one (as in L) and fragments ii and iii two each.

Note that with fourteen lines per page fragment iii (28 lines) occupies exactly two pages; the next quaternion thus began with iv 1, the verse immediately following on iii 28 in the poem.

vi. *Relationships of the Z manuscripts*

The evidence for the *stemma codicum* I have given for the Z manuscripts is as follows. OE sometimes agree against CL. OCL often agree against E. E sometimes occupies an intermediate position between O and CL, CL one between O and E. L never agrees with O against CE or occupies an intermediate position, nor does C ever occupy an intermediate position between O and EL. The only evidence against it is that C agrees with O against EL once (470 hirsutis OC hirsuti EL, rightly—but the preceding *clunibus* could easily have changed *hirsuti* to *hirsutis* independently in O and C) and may agree in another place (230 nitere O, correctly, niteret EL, C now reads nitere, but its second hand may have erased the final t. Dahms reports erasures in C which I have not been able to detect on microfilm). *Bern* follows C as corrected by the second hand. These corrections could be, and probably are, entirely conjectural.

vii. *Relationships of the O manuscripts*

The μ, ν division is seen in many readings, and in the fact that ν omits 224, 400, 402 and 513 (found in μ and Z) and iv 3–4 (found in μ. Z omits the whole fragment). The π manuscripts only contain 1–146. P contains many conjectures, thus, unless B and P agree, μ is not recoverable after 146. The μ, ν division is often meaningless, as only M of the μ manuscripts conforms completely to its stemmatic position. M always omits the first line after a section of scholia and also lines 1–17 and 522–31. V omits everything after 439. τ omitted 70,96 and iv 1–51. U omits 515–82, σ 431–514 as well. The remainder of the stemma is of no significance in establishing the text.

2. EDITIONS

On the 15th-century editions of our poem (Bonincontrius, Valla and Aldus) cf. the beginning of the previous section. I have collated all the 16th-century editions in the British Museum (almost all that exist). All are based on Aldus, only that of Morel (1559) having any conjectures of merit. I have obtained microfilm copies of the conjectures of the 16th-century scholars Turnebus and J. J. Scaliger and quote those I consider worth mentioning. Most of what survives of our poem was printed in 1600 by Grotius in his *Syntagma Arateorum*. (Earlier editions, deriving ultimately from χ alone, printed only what it contained.) Grotius used Morel's edition and the manuscript L, thus his edition lacks the lines missing in both these sources (70, 555, 568–71, ii 17–20, iv 1–51, v and vi). The next editor, Schwartz (1715), printed many of the conjectures Grotius had proposed in his commentary but not put in his text and as well several conjectures of his own. He was the first to print fragment vi, found only in Priscian. He added to Grotius' commentary, which he reprinted, notes of his own, citing other authors on various myths or expressing disagreement with Grotius on textual matters. I have not seen the edition of Schmidt (1728), but use Breysig's reports of it. Orelli states that it is based on Schwartz, and it seems to have little original material. iv 1–51 was edited for the first time in 1769 by Iriarte (from M). It was edited from P in 1773 by Burman the younger. Iriarte's performance is much the better. Burman repeats some of his emendations. I ascribe these to Iriarte, as the earlier. Orelli (1832) collated the three Swiss manuscripts (B, Bern and E) and hence was able to perceive the OZ division. He constructed the first *apparatus criticus* and first printed 70, 555 and 568–71 (from B). In his 1st edition (1867, reprinted 1967), Breysig first used P for the whole poem and cited selected readings of S and a few χ manuscripts. Fragment v was printed for the first time by Baehrens in RhM for 1877, p. 323 and it and ii 17–20 were included in his text in the first volume of *Poetae Latini Minores* (1879), although ii 17–20 were only printed in the *apparatus*. Baehrens used Dahms' collation of C and first collated A, which alone contains fragment v. Breysig produced his 2nd edition in 1899 (in the Teubner series).

The text of all these editions is very unsatisfactory and in many places incomprehensible and a new edition is badly needed.

3. THE FORM OF THE PRESENT EDITION

First, the text. When I have been unable to decide between the readings of O and Z I have printed that of O, recording Z's reading in the *apparatus criticus*, with the remark *nihilo deterius*. This is because where both O and Z are present O is more often right than Z. Excluding doubtful cases, in 1–221 Z is right 40 times against 50 for O. Moreover, O has far fewer detectable interpolations. Where more than one attractive emendation has been proposed, I have printed the one I consider best, mentioning in the *apparatus* ones I consider nearly as likely. Other emendations are mentioned only in the commentary.

In spelling I have preferred assimilated forms. Where I print *is* accusative plurals, one or both branches of the tradition exhibit them. No conclusions should be drawn from silence in the *apparatus* about the spellings transmitted in any place, for I have often altered or corrected the spellings transmitted. In constructing the *apparatus* I have given only one entry for manuscripts which have the same word, but in different spellings.

In the *apparatus criticus* I usually only mention the sub-variants of what is the archetype at a particular point. I mention the readings of individual manuscripts only when I consider them true or possibly true or where conjecture and/or contamination have made it impossible to discover the sub-variants. Where Z only is present, I have often ignored individual errors of E, which are very numerous. I have mentioned only the earliest author of a conjecture. As some conjectures were repeated several times, the mention of everyone who proposed every conjecture would encumber the *apparatus* with a lot of information which may be of interest for the history of scholarship, but is of no value for the establishment of the text. Sometimes the spelling assigned to a conjecture in the *apparatus* differs from that in the text. In that case, the spelling in the *apparatus* is that which was used by the author of the emendation.

The commentary defends the text I have printed and discusses the astronomy of the poem and its uses of and divergences from Aratus. Other information is included occasionally. I have only discussed conjectures where I believe the transmitted text is corrupt or where there is evidence for supposing that it may be corrupt. If I consider my translation is not an adequate demonstration that the transmitted text makes good sense in other places, I attempt to explain the text in the commentary. I have usually ignored impossible or very improbable conjectures (many are mentioned in Breysig's and Baehrens' editions).

4. BIBLIOGRAPHY

Editions used of frequently quoted authors (rp. = reprinted).
Aratus, Maass (1892, rp. Berlin, 1955, 1964).
Aratus scholia, Maass (1898, rp. Berlin, 1958).
Avienius, Holder (1887, rp. Hildesheim, 1965).
Cicero's Aratus, Buescu (1941, rp. Hildesheim, 1966).
Eratosthenes (*Catasterismorum Reliquiae*), Robert (1878, rp. Berlin, 1963).
Germanicus scholia, Breysig (1867, rp. Hildesheim, 1967).
Hipparchus, Manitius (Leipzig, Teubner, 1894).
Hyginus (*Poetica Astronomica*), Bunte (Leipzig, 1875).
Manilius, Housman (1903–30, rep. Hildesheim, 1971).

I mention the following editors of our author:
Baehrens, E. (*Poetae Latini Minores*, Vol. 1, Leipzig, 1879).
Bonincontrius, L. (*M. Manlii ... Astronomicon ... Arathus Germanici ad Augustum*, Bologna, 1474).
Breysig, A. (*Germanici Caesaris Aratea*, Ed. 1 1867 (rp. Hildesheim, 1967), Ed. 2 Leipzig, 1899).
Buhle, I. ('Αράτου Σολεως Φαινομενα, Vol. 2, Leipzig, 1801).
Grotius, H. (*Syntagma Arateorum*, Leiden, 1600).
Halma, N. ('Αράτου Σολεως Φαινομενα, et *Germanici Caesaris Phaenomena*, Paris, 1821).
Iriarte, J. (*Regiae Bibliothecae Matritensis Codices Graeci MSS*, Madrid, 1769) (pp. 203–12).
Morel, G. ('Αράτου Σολεως Φαινομενα, Paris, 1559).
Orelli, J. (*Phaedri Fabulae ... accedunt Germanici Aratea*, Zurich, 1832).
Schwartz, J. (*Carmina ... Familiae Caesareae*, Coburg, 1715).

The following is a list of other books and articles mentioned, in alphabetical order of author.

Barth, C. von, *Aduersariorum Libri LX*, Frankfurt, 1624.

Bentley, R., *M. Manilii Astronomicon*, London, 1739.

Burman (the elder), MSS conjectures, published by Baehrens in his edition.

Courtney, E., 'Some Passages of the Aratea of Germanicus', *CR n.s.*, 20, 2 (1969), 138–41.

——, 'Poetae Latini Minores', *CR n.s.*, 22, 2 (1972), 173–4.

Dahms, R., 'Ad Germanicum Caesarem', *JKPh*, 99 (1869), 269–75.

Ellis, R., 'Ad Aratea Germanici' in *Noctes Manilianae*, Oxford, 1891, pp. 234–48.

Frey, J., 'Zu Germanicus', *RhM n.f.* 13 (1858), 409–27.

Gronouius, J., *Obseruationum Libri IV*, Leipzig, 1755.

Haupt, M., 'Analecta' in *Opuscula* 3, 2 (1876), 406–7.

Heinsius, N., MSS conjectures, published by Baehrens in his edition.

Housman, A. E., 'The Aratea of Germanicus', *CR* 14 (1900), 26–39 (rp. in *The Classical Papers of A. E. Housman*, Cambridge, 1972, vol. 2 pp. 495–515. Dual references are given).

Kroll, W., 'Randbemerkungen', *RhM n.f.* 60 (1905), 556–557.

——, 'Zu den Fragmenten des Germanicus', *WKPh* 35 (1918), 304–11.

Le Boeuffle, A., 'Les Aratea de Germanicus', *RPh* 47 (1973), 61–7.

Lachmann, K., *T. Lucreti Cari de Rerum Natura Libri Sex*, Berlin, 1850.

Maybaum, J., *De Cicerone et Germanico Arati interpretibus* (dissertation), Rostock, 1889.

Morel, W., 'Germanicus' Aratea', *CR* 57 (1943), 106–7.

Muncker, T., *Mythographi Latini*, Amsterdam, 1681.

Panske, P., Pp. 506–9 of *Commentationes philologicae Ribbeckio oblatae*, Leipzig, 1888.

Sabbadini, R., 'Sallustius ... Germanicus ... cum nouis codicibus conlati atque emendati', *Museo Italiano di Antichità classica*, 3 (1890). Our author is discussed on pp. 87–96.

Schaubach, J., Conjectures published by Breysig, ed. 2.

Stahl, F., *Dissertatio de Ausonianis studiis poetarum Graecorum* (dissertation), Kiel, 1886

Steinmetz, P., 'Germanicus, der römische Arat', *Hermes*, 94 (1966), 450–82.

Thierfelder, A., 'Adnotationes in poetas Latinos minores. 2: in Germanicum', *RhM n.f.* 91 (1942), 209–16.

Voss, J., *Des Aratos Sternerscheinungen und Wetterzeichen*, Heidelberg, 1824.

Wakefield, G., *T. Lucreti Cari de Rerum Natura Libri Sex*, London, 1796–7.

Winterfeld, P. de, *De Rufi Festi Auieni metaphrasi Arateorum recensenda et emendanda* (dissertation), Berlin, 1895.

——, 'De tribus Germanici locis', *Hermes*, 30 (1895), 557–63.

In the commentary and *apparatus* the names of those who published their conjectures in books or articles are followed by the page number of their work. Those whose names are not followed by a page number are either editors, whose conjectures will be found in their text and/or commentary at the relevant place, scholars who have communicated their conjectures to me personally (mentioned in the preface) and Scaliger and Turnebus, whose conjectures I have discovered in manuscript. Those of Turnebus are contained in the edition of Aratus etc. by Morel (Paris, 1559) numbered Rés.v 980, in the Bibliothèque Nationale, Paris. They are in the same handwriting as Turnebus' signature in the front of the book. The catalogue falsely assigns them to Johannes Curterius. The conjectures of Scaliger are found on fols. 149 sqq. of Codex Scalig.61 of the Bibliotheek der Rijks-universiteit, Leiden, in the margins of a collation of L.

5. SOURCES OF THE POEM

Lines 1–725 of the poem are based on lines 1–731 of Aratus' *Phaenomena*, but with many omissions, expansions, contractions or additions. The author usually paraphrases; he seldom follows Aratus almost word for word. Fragments ii–vi, all that remain of the rest of his poem, are not based on the second half of Aratus, the weather signs. Whether they are based on another writer, or are a compilation of several sources, and whether there are original elements in them or not, is unknown. I have noted in the commentary the main divergences from Aratus, quoting or giving references to authors who have similar material.

Hipparchus' commentary on Aratus seems to be the source of some of our author's many modifications of Aratus, but whether it was used directly or indirectly, there is no way of telling. Sometimes the author follows Aratus, not Hipparchus. Sometimes Hipparchus corrects serious errors of Aratus; some of his corrections are very petty. Sometimes he reads too much into Aratus. He never takes account of the fact that Aratus sometimes assigns different stars to parts of constellations from the ones he assigns himself. Our author has some modifications of Aratus' astronomy not found in this treatise of Hipparchus. Their source is not clear. The statement in 60–2 seems to come from Attalus, probably via Cicero's *Aratus*.

I list below the passages where Hipparchus criticizes Aratus. Column A gives the lines of Aratus he discusses, column B the corresponding lines of our author, column C gives various symbols (H means our author agrees with Hipparchus, A that he agrees with Aratus, A & H that he agrees partly with the one, partly with the other. If one of the symbols is bracketed, this means that the agreement is by implication only, or is partial. A blank means that he agrees with neither, a question mark that the matter cannot be determined. The passages where our author does not agree with Aratus are discussed in the commentary). Column D gives the reference to Hipparchus (ed. Manitius).

A	B	C	D
46	50		1.4.3
47–8	48–9		1.4.3
52			1.4.2
60	58	A	1.4.4
69–70	69	H	1.2.6
77–80	75–9	(A)	1.4.16–17
84	81–2	H	1.4.15
147–8	147–9	A	1.5.1–13
177–8	181–3	(H)	1.5.14–18
184–5	188–91	H	1.2.12; 1.5.19
188			1.5.20

A	B	C	D
188–90	194	H	1.5.21
228–30	229–30	A	1.6.5–7
239	241–3	H	1.6.8–9
254–5	255–6	(A)	1.6.12–13
258; 261	259–60	A	1.6.14
270	271–2	A	1.5.20
276–7	279–81	(H)	1.6.15
308–10	313–14	A & H	1.7.1–18
349–50	352–5	(A)	1.8.1
367–9	371–4	H	1.8.2–3
405	395	(A)	1.8.14–17
431–5	423–5	A	1.8.18–19
436–8	414–18	H	1.8.21–2
439–40	418–20	A	1.8.23
479	451	?	1.9.14–15
481–2	461–2	(H)	1.10.1–3
483	462	(H)	1.10.5
484–5	463–4	(H)	1.10.6
487	464–5	A	1.10.7
487–8	465–6	H	1.10.7
488–9		(H)	1.10.9
497–9	473–5	(A)	1.3.5–7
505–6	490–1	A	1.10.16
515–16	501–2	A	1.10.18
519–20	504–6	A & (H)	1.10.19
520	507	A	1.10.20
521	508	(H)	1.10.20
559–68	573–88	H	2.1.2–14
572	591	A	2.2.7
575–6			2.2.8
578	593	H	2.2.10
581; 721–2	594–9	H	2.2.11–29
590–1	604–6	A	2.2.31–2
591–3	608–9	A	2.2.33
594	610	A	2.2.34
595	610–11	(A)	2.2.35
598	614	A	2.2.37

A	B	C	D
600	617	A	2.2.38
625–6	637	A	2.2.47
629	640	A	2.2.48
629–30	640–1	A	2.2.49
633	642–3	A & H	2.2.50
649–52	642–3	H	1.7.19–22
662–3	671–2	A	2.2.54
665–8	676	(H)	2.2.55
672–3	673; 677–8	(A)	2.2.58
674–5	680	(H)	2.2.59
687–8	685	H	2.2.60
688–9	683–4	A	2.2.61
691	679; 690	H	2.3.2–3
693–4	693–4	A	2.3.5
693	693	A	2.3.6–9
697–8	698	(H)	2.3.5
	691	H	2.3.10
699–700	699	A	2.3.14–15
701–3	701–3	A	2.3.16
704–9	704–5	H	2.3.17
710–11	707–8	?	2.3.26
714–19	710–16	A	2.3.34
719–20	717–18	A	2.3.35
721–3	718	H	2.3.36

6. IDENTITY OF THE AUTHOR AND DATE
OF THE POEM

Lactantius (*Inst.* 1.21.28 & 5.5.4) quotes verses from this poem, calling the author Germanicus Caesar. Jerome (*Comment. in Ep. Tit* 1.12) says that one of those who translated Aratus into Latin was Germanicus Caesar. Firmicus Maternus 2 *praef.* 2 mentions a translation of Aratus by Iulius Caesar. The poem was anonymous in ΖπΑτ. M has lost the beginning. Its title in BP is *Claudii Caesaris Arati Phaenomena*, in SV *T(iberii) Claudii Caesaris Arati Phaenomena*. I suggest the original was something like *x Claudii x, postea Germanici Iulii Caesaris Aratus: Phaenomena*.

This reconciles the testimony of the manuscripts with that of Lactantius, Jerome and Firmicus. The title of the poem was then *Aratus* (the title given by Priscian in quoting fragment vi— *Caesar in Arato*). Cicero similarly used *Aratus* (the title *Aratea* has no authority for either author). I suggest *Phaenomena* is a subtitle, the subtitle to fragments ii–vi being lost.

The author could be either the emperor Tiberius or his nephew Germanicus. Germanicus' *nomen gentilicium* before adoption was Claudius (his full name being unknown), after adoption he was Germanicus Iulius Caesar. Suetonius, in his eulogy at the beginning of his *Caligula*, talks of Germanicus' Greek and Roman oratory and learning (3.1) and of Greek comedies, left among other fruits of his studies (3.2).

Secondly, the claims of Tiberius. His name after adoption by Augustus and after Augustus' death is given as Tiberius Iulius Caesar Augustus (Dessau 3.1.262). This fits Firmicus' Iulius Caesar. Dio Cassius says of Tiberius after Augustus' death (57.8.2) 'He was generally styled Caesar, sometimes also Germanicus (from Germanicus' exploits). He was called *princeps senatus* in accordance with the ancient custom—and that even by himself.' Thus Jerome's and Lactantius' Germanicus Caesar could refer to Tiberius. His name before adoption was Tiberius Claudius Nero (Dessau 3.1.261; Suet. *Tib.* 6,4). This fits the Tiberius Claudius of S and V. The poem fits Tiberius' interests well. Suetonius says at 69.1 that he was addicted to astrology (cf. 558–60 and the astrological fragments iii and iv), at 70.3 that his special aim was a knowledge of mythology (cf. the frequent mythological additions to Aratus, in particular the long passage 531–64), that he spoke Greek readily and fluently (hence would have had no trouble with Aratus), at 71.1 that he did not like using too many Greek words in Latin (cf. fragment vi, where the author says that Greek may be a rich language, but there is nothing wrong with the Latin word *triangula*, which he proposes to use instead of the Greek). At 70.1 Suetonius says that he was greatly devoted to literary studies in both languages (what better evidence than writing a Latin poem based on a Greek?), that he composed a *Conquestio de morte L. Caesaris* and wrote Greek poems in imitation of Euphorion, Rhianus and Parthenius, whose poems he greatly admired (70.2). Euphorion

Hemisphaerium Boreale

These maps are reproduced with certain simplifications from the edition of
Aratus by Buhle (Leipzig, 1793–1801) who took them from Schaubach's
edition of the Catasterismi of Eratosthenes.

Hemisphaerium Australe

and Rhianus were Alexandrian poets like Aratus. Suetonius also says that he delivered a eulogy of his father when he was nine (6.4). Moreover, during his long stay at Rhodes he would have had ample leisure to study astronomy, to which the Rhodians Attalus, Hipparchus and Geminus had contributed, in particular Hipparchus, of whose work the author makes extensive use.

We now come to verses 1–16 and 558–60. Verses 1–16 address the emperor, the writer calling himself his son. If Tiberius is the author, the emperor is Augustus, if Germanicus, Tiberius. Lines 558–60 refer to the death and deification of Augustus, hence, if Tiberius is the author, 1–16 are an apostrophe to the dead and deified Augustus. As such, the tone, deriving inspiration from a god (*numen* 16), as Aratus did from Zeus, is entirely appropriate. As an apostrophe to the living Tiberius by Germanicus, they are less appropriate, as Tiberius tended to avoid honours, and would hardly have welcomed being called a god, as the recipient of 1–16 is. Manilius calls him *lumen mundi* in 4.766, but this stops short of calling him a god. The assertion that peace was restored under Augustus' leadership is entirely appropriate, that it was restored under Tiberius' less appropriate. But in lines 3–4 the author calls the poem *doctique laboris/primitias*, i.e. his first work. But Tiberius' *Conquestio de morte L. Caesaris* must surely have been written soon after Lucius' death, i.e. many years before the death of Augustus. But it is conceivable that Tiberius composed most of the poem many years before and added lines 1–16 and 558–60 (1–16 presumably replacing a previous introduction closer to Aratus) only after Augustus' death, thus producing a sort of second edition.

My opinion is that the evidence does not allow one to say whether the author was Tiberius or Germanicus.

TEXT

Ab Ioue principium magno deduxit Aratus.
carminis at nobis, genitor, tu maximus auctor,
te ueneror tibi sacra fero doctique laboris
primitias. probat ipse deum rectorque satorque.
quantum etenim possent anni certissima signa,   5
qua Sol ardentem Cancrum rapidissimus ambit
diuersasque secat metas gelidi Capricorni
quaue Aries et Libra aequant diuortia lucis,
si non parta quies te praeside puppibus aequor
cultorique daret terras, procul arma silerent?   10
nunc uacat audacis ad caelum tollere uultus
sideraque et mundi uarios cognoscere motus,
nauita quid caueat, quid scitus uitet arator,
quando ratem uentis aut credat semina terris.
haec ego dum Latiis conor praedicere Musis,   15
pax tua tuque adsis nato numenque secundes.
  Cetera quae toto fulgent uaga sidera mundo
indefessa trahit proprio cum pondere caelum.
axis at immotus semper uestigia seruat
libratasque tenet terras et cardine firmo   20
orbem agit. extremum geminus determinat axem
quem Grai dixere polon: pars mersa sub undas
Oceani, pars celsa sub horrifero Aquilone.
  Axem Cretaeae dextra laeuaque tuentur
siue Arctoe seu Romani cognominis Vrsae   25
Plaustraue, quae facies stellarum proxima uerae:
tres temone rotisque micant, sublime quaternae.
si melius dixisse feras, obuersa refulgent
ora feris; caput alterius super horrida terga
alterius lucet; pronas rapit orbis in ipsos   30

9 parta μΖ: tanta ν   11 ad Ζ: in O   12 cognoscere O: agnoscere Ζ 15
conor Ζ: cogor O   26 ue Grotius: que OΖ   uerae Barth 47.18: uera O:
uero Ζ   30 orbis O: axis Ζ nihilo deterius

declinis umeros. ueteri si gratia famae,
Cresia uos tellus aluit, moderator Olympi
donauit caelo. meritum custodia fecit,
quod fidae comites prima incunabula magni
fouistis Iouis, attonitae cum furta parentis 35
aerea pulsantes mendaci cymbala dextra,
uagitus pueri patrias ne tangeret auris,
Dictaeis texere adytis famuli Corybantes.
hinc Iouis altrices Helice Cynosuraque fulgent.
dat Grais Helice cursus maioribus astris, 40
Phoenicas Cynosura regit. sed candida tota
et liquido splendore Helice nitet; haud prius ulla,
cum Sol Oceano fulgentia condidit ora,
stella micat caelo, septem quam Cresia flammis.
certior est Cynosura tamen sulcantibus aequor, 45
quippe breuis totam fido se cardine uertit
Sidoniamque ratem nunquam spectata fefellit.
    Has inter medias abrupti fluminis instar
immanis Serpens sinuosa uolumina torquet
hinc atque hinc supraque illas (mirabile monstrum). 50
cauda Helicen supra tendit; redit ad Cynosuran
squamigero lapsu. qua desinit ultima cauda
hac caput est Helices; flexu comprenditur alto
Serpentis Cynosura; ille explicat amplius orbes
sublatusque retro maiorem respicit Arcton. 55
ardent ingentes oculi, caua tempora claris
ornantur flammis, mento sedet unicus ignis.
tempus dexterius quae signat stella Draconis
quaeque sedet mento.....................
.................lucetque nouissima cauda
extremumque Helices sidus micat. hac radiatur 60
Serpentis decline caput, qua proxima signa
occasus ortusque uno tanguntur ab ore.

---

31 ueteri *Grotius*: ueteris *OZ*
35 *om.* Z   fouistis *Housman* p. *36/511*: fouerunt *O*   **38** dictaeis texere adytis
Heinsius: dictei texere datis *Z*: dictae aetexere dei ν: dicta exercere deae μ   **40**
cursus *O*: cursum *Z nihilo deterius*   **49** torquet *O*: uersat *Z nihilo deterius*   **51**
supra *Z*: superat *O*   redit *Z. om. O*   **59** *inter* mento *et* lucetque *lacunam
indicauit Courtney p. 139*   **60** hac *Turnebus*: ac *OZ*   **61** qua *Grotius*: quae *OE*:
utque L *de* C *non liquet*

Oceani tumidis ignotae fluctibus Arctoe,
semper inocciduis seruantes ignibus axem.
Haud procul effigies inde est defecta labore.   65
non ulli nomen, non cognita causa laboris:
dextro namque genu nixus diuersaque tendens
bracchia, suppliciter passis ad numina palmis,
Serpentis capiti figit uestigia laeua.
Tum fessi subter costas atque ardua terga   70
clara Ariadnaeo sacrata est igne Corona;
hunc illi Bacchus thalami memor addit honorem.
Terga nitent Sertis; at qua se uertice tollit
succiduis genibus lapsum et miserabile sidus,
hac Ophiuchus erit. longe caput ante notabis   75
et uastos umeros, tum cetera membra sequuntur.
illis languet honos; umeris manet integer ardor,
luna etiam mensem cum pleno diuidit orbe.
lux tenuis manibus, per quas elabitur Anguis,
pressus utraque manu, medium cingens Ophiuchum.   80
Scorpios ima pedum tangit, sed planta sinistra
in tergo residet, uestigia dextera pendent.
impar est manibus pondus: nam dextera paruam
partem Anguis retinet, per laeuam attollitur omnis
quantumque ab laeua distantia Serta notantur,   85
erigitur tantum Serpens atque ultima mento
stella sub aetheria lucet crinita Corona.
at qua se dorso sinuabit lubricus Anguis
insigni caelum perfundent lumine Chelae.
Inde Helicen sequitur senior baculoque minatur,   90
siue ille Arctophylax seu Bacchi ob munera caesus

65–70 om. *Z, in quo uersum 64 sequuntur 90–5, quos*
excipiunt 71–89   **65** effigies *G. Morel*: effigiem *iam* S: efficiens *O*   inde *G.*
Morel: unde *O*   **66** ulli *Postgate apud Housman p. 31/502*: illi *O*   nomen *G.*
Morel: numen *O*   cognita *Housman p. 31/502*: magni *O*   **68** passis v: pansis μ
69 laeua *Grotius*: seua *O*   **70** subter *Orelli*: suter B: *aut* supter *aut* super B²:
super *O*   **73** sertis *Breysig*: stellis *OZ*   at qua se *Turnebus*: adquas se *Z*:
aquas e v: aqua se μ   **74** lapsum *O*: lassum *Z nihilo deterius*   sidus *Z* om. *O*
75 hac *Z*: hic *O*   notabis E: notabilis Ecλ: nitendo *O*   **78** mensem cum
pleno *O*: pleno mensem cum E *nihilo deterius*: pleno mense cum λ   **83** om. *Z*
nam μ: iam v   paruam Aτ: parua *O*   **87** lucet *O*: fulget *Z nihilo deterius*
crinita *O*: crinata *Z*   **89** insigni *Z*: insignis *O*   **90** inde *O*: ipsam *Z nihilo*
deterius   baculo *O*: iaculo *Z*   **91** bacchi ob munera *Grotius*: bacchio munere
Z: brachio munera *O*

Icarus, ereptam pensauit sidere uitam.
non illi obscurum caput est, non tristia membra,
sed proprio tamen una micat sub nomine flamma:
Arcturum dixere, sinus qua uincula nodant.   95
 Virginis inde subest facies, cui plena sinistra
fulget Spica manu maturisque ardet aristis.
quam te, diua, uocem? tangunt mortalia si te
carmina nec surdam praebes uenerantibus aurem
exosa heu mortale genus, medio mihi cursu   100
stabunt quadrupedes et flexis laetus habenis
teque tuumque canam terris uenerabile numen.
 Aurea pacati regeres cum saecula mundi
Iustitia inuiolata malis, placidissima uirgo,
siue illa Astraei genus es, quem fama parentem   105
tradidit astrorum, seu uera intercidit aeuo
ortus fama tui, mediis te laeta ferebas
sublimis populis nec dedignata subire
tecta hominum et puros sine crimine, diua, penatis
iura dabas cultuque nouo rude uulgus in omnem   110
formabas uitae sinceris artibus usum.
nondum uesanos rabies nudauerat ensis
nec consanguineis fuerat discordia nota,
ignotique maris cursus, priuataque tellus
grata satis, neque per dubios auidissima uentos   115
spes procul amotas fabricata naue petebat
diuitias, fructusque dabat placata colono
sponte sua tellus nec parui terminus agri
praestabat dominis, sine eo tutissima, rura.
 At postquam argenti creuit deformior aetas,   120
rarius inuisit maculatas fraudibus urbis
seraque ab excelsis descendit montibus ore
uelato tristisque genas abscondita rica,
nulliusque larem, nullos adit illa penatis.
tantum, cum trepidum uulgus coetusque notauit,   125

---

92 sidere uitam Z: munere ripam µ: munera ripam ν
97 *om.* Z 100 cursu O: curru λ: currum E   103 regeres G. *Morel*: regeret OZ
105 es *Grotius*: est OZ 109 penatis *om.* O 110–11 omnem ... usum O:
omnes ... usus Z *nihilo deterius*   112–13 attulit Lact. Inst. *5.5*   116 petebat P:
petebant OZ 119 sine eo *Lachmann p. 38*: signo OZ 121 inuisit AE: inuasit
$OE^{c}λ$ 122 descendit *scripsi*: descendens OZ 123 rica *Scaliger*: ripa OZ

increpat 'o patrum suboles oblita priorum,
degeneres semper semperque habitura minoris,
quid me, cuius abit usus, per uota uocatis?
quaerenda est sedes nobis noua; saecula uestra
artibus indomitis tradam scelerique cruento'.   130
haec effata super montis abit alite cursu,
attonitos linquens populos grauiora pauentis.
    Aerea sed postquam proles terris data, nec iam
semina uirtutis uitiis demersa resistunt
ferrique inuento mens est laetata metallo,   135
polluit et taurus mensas assuetus aratro,
deseruit propere terras iustissima uirgo,
et caeli sortita locum, qua proximus illi
tardus in occasu sequitur sua plaustra Bootes.
    Virginis at placidae praestanti lumine signat   140
stella umeros. Helicen ignis non clarior ambit,
quique micat cauda quique armum fulget ad ipsum
quique priora tenet uestigia quique secunda,
clunibus hirsutis et qui sua sidera reddit.
    namque alii, quibus explentur ceruixque caputque,   145
uatibus ignoti priscis, sine honore feruntur.
    Qua media est Helice, subiectum respice Cancrum;
at capiti suberunt Gemini. qua posterior pes,
horrentisque iubas et fuluum cerne Leonem.
    hunc ubi contigerit Phoebi uiolentior axis,   150
accensa in Cancro iam tum geminabitur aestas.
    tunc lymphae tenues, tunc est tristissima tellus,
et densas laetus segetes bene condet arator.
ne mihi tum remis pulset uada caerula puppis;
dem potius uentis excusso uela rudente   155
excipiamque sinu Zephyris spirantibus auras.
    Est etiam Aurigae facies, siue Atthide terra

127 semper semperque 𝑍: semperque 𝑂   uocatis 𝑂: precatis 𝑍   **137** attulit
Lact. Inst. 5.5 propere L𝑐V: proprie 𝑂𝑍 Lact. codices   **143** om. 𝑍, post 134 et post
142 habet 𝑂   **144** qui 𝑂: qua 𝑍   **145** alii Grotius: aliae 𝑂𝑍   explentur Breysig
ed. 2 p. xxx: expletur iam C²: expletum 𝑂𝑍   u.**146** finitur π, uersum 146 sequuntur
in 𝑍 ad capiti suberunt gemini prolemque tonantis ex 148 et Auieni 370 (ed. Holder)
confictus, Au. 371–4, 376–8, tum 147, tum qua posterior pes et duro concaua dorso
ex 148 et Au. 383 confictus, Au. 384, 388–90, tum 149 sqq.   **149** horrentis 𝑂: ora
horrentis 𝑍   **152** tunc 𝑂: hinc 𝑍   lymphae τ: nymphae 𝑂𝑍   **155** rudente
𝑂E: rudenti λ   **157** atthide terra 𝑍, om. 𝑂

natus Ericthonius, qui primus sub iuga duxit
quadrupedes, seu Myrtoas demersus in undas
Myrtilos. hunc potius species in sidere reddit: 160
sic nulli currus, sic ruptis maestus habenis
perfidia Pelopis raptam gemit Hippodamian.
ipse ingens transuersus abit laeua Geminorum
maiorisque Vrsae contra delabitur ora.
numina praeterea secum trahit; una putatur   165
nutrix esse Iouis (si uere Iuppiter infans
ubera Cretaeae mulsit fidissima Caprae),
sidere quae claro gratum testatur alumnum.
    hanc Auriga umero totam gerit, at manus Haedos
ostendit, nautis inimicum sidus, ubi illos   170
orbis ab Oceano celsus rapit; haud semel Haedi
iactatam uidere ratem nautasque pauentis
sparsaque per saeuos morientum corpora fluctus.
    Aurigae pedibus trux adiacet ignea Taurus
cornua fronte gerens et lucidus ore minaci.   175
quamlibet ignarum caeli sua forma docebit
et caput et patulas naris et cornua Tauri.
fronte micant Hyades. quae cornus flamma sinistri
summa tenet, subit haec eadem uestigia dextra
Aurigae mediaque ligat compagine diuos.   180
Myrtilos exoritur summo cum Piscibus ore,
totus cum Tauro lucet; ruit Oceano Bos
ante, super terras cum fulget Myrtilos ore.
    Iasides etiam caelum cum coniuge Cepheus
ascendit totaque domo, quia Iuppiter auctor   185
est generis; prodest maiestas saepe parentis.
ipse breuem patulis manibus stat post Cynosuran
diducto passu. quantum latus a pede dextro
Cepheos extremam tangit Cynosurida caudam,
tantundem ab laeuo distat; minor utraque iungit   190
regula Cepheos uestigia. balteus ambit

                                    165 una putatur—*168 attulit*
Lact. Inst. 1.21   169 totam gerit at manus *O*: portans inmanibus *Z*   171
ab τ: ad *O*, *om. Z*   176 quamlibet *Grotius*: quemlibet *Z*: quem liber *O*   180
ligat *Turnebus*: ligant *OZ*   181 piscibus *O*: fluctibus *Z*   182 totus *O*: tutus *Z*
190 tantundem *O*: tantumque *Z*

qua latus, ad flexum sinuosi respicis Anguis.
Cassiepia uirum residet sublimis ad ipsum,
clara etiam pernox caelo cum luna refulsit,
sed breuis et paucis decorata in sidere flammis.   195
qualis ferratos subicit clauicula dentes
succutit et foribus praeducti uincula claustri,
talis disposita est stellis. ipsa horrida uultu
sic tendit palmas, ceu sit planctura relictam
Andromedan, meritae non iusta piacula matris.   200
  Nec procul Andromeda, totam quam cernere nondum
obscura sub nocte licet; sic emicat ore,
sic magnis umeris candet nitor ac mediam ambit
ignea substricta lucet qua zonula palla.
sed poenae facies remanet districtaque pandit   205
bracchia, ceu duri teneantur robore saxi.
  Andromedae capiti Sonipes supereminet ales.
uertice et Andromedae radiat quae stella, sub ipsa
aluo fulget Equi; tres armos et latera aequis
distinguunt spatiis. capiti tristissima forma,   210
et ceruix sine honore obscuro lumine sordet.
spumanti mandit sed qua ferus ore lupata,
et capite et longa ceruice insignior exit
stella nitens, armis laterique simillima magno.
nec totam ille tamen formam per singula reddit.   215
primo praestat equum, medio rupta ordine membra
destituunt uisus, rudis inde assurgit imago.
Gorgonis hic proles in Pierio Helicone,
uertice cum summo nondum decurreret unda,
Musaeos fontis dextri pedis ictibus hausit.   220
inde liquor genitus nomen tenet: Hippocrenen
fontes nomen habent; sed Pegasus aethere summo

192 ad flexum L: adflexum $O\mathcal{Z}$ respicis
Maybaum p. 38: respicit $O\mathcal{Z}$ **194** pernox V: pernix O: nox $\mathcal{Z}$ caelo cum O:
cum stellas $\mathcal{Z}$ **195** sed breuis et O: est breuis $\mathcal{Z}$ **198** disposita est $\mathcal{Z}$:
dispositis O **199** sit ζ: si $O\mathcal{Z}$ **201** andromeda μ: andromedam $\mathcal{Z}$: andro-
medae P: andromede B   nondum PVτ: nodum μ: notum B: posse $\mathcal{Z}$ **203** ac
O: hanc $\mathcal{Z}$ mediam *Panske p. 508*: media $O\mathcal{Z}$ **204** lucet $\mathcal{Z}$v: fulget μ
uersum **207** Andromedae . . . **208** uertice et *om.* O **208** radiat quae AC[2]:
radiatque $O\mathcal{Z}$ **211** et O: est E: ast λ   **212** sed qua *G. Morel*: sed quae $\mathcal{Z}$:
seque $\mathcal{Z}$ lupata *Grotius*: lupato $O\mathcal{Z}$ **221** hippocrenem O: hippocrenes $\mathcal{Z}$
222 habent O: habet $\mathcal{Z}$

uelocis agitat pennas et sidere gaudet.

Inde subest Aries, qui longe maxima currens
orbe suo spatia ad finem non tardius Vrsa   225
peruenit et quanto breuiore Lycaonis Arctos
axem actu torquet, tanto pernicior ille
distantis cornu properat contingere metas.
clara nec est illi facies nec sidera possunt,
officiat si luna, sua uirtute nitere.   230
sed quaerendus erit zonae regione micantis
Andromedae; terit hic medii diuortia mundi,
ut Chelae, candens ut balteus Orionis.

Est etiam propiore deum cognoscere signo,
Deltoton si quis (donum hoc spectabile Nili   235
diuitibus generatum undis) in sede notabit.
tres illi laterum ductus, aequata duorum
sunt spatia, unius breuius, sed clarior ignis.
hunc Aries iuxta. medium Deltoton habebit
inter Lanigeri tergum et Cepheida maestam.   240

Hunc ultra gemini Pisces, quorum alter in Austrum
tendit, Threicium Borean petit alter et audit
stridentis auras, niueus quas procreat Haemus.
non illis liber cursus, sed uincula cauda
singula utrumque tenent uno coeuntia nodo.   245
nodum stella premit. Piscis, qui respicit auras
Threicias, astra Andromedae cernantur ad ulnam.

Subter utrumque pedem deuotae uirginis ales
Perseos effigies, seruatae grata puellae.
moles ipsa uiri satis est testata parentem: 250
tantus ubique micat, tantum occupat ab Ioue caeli.
dextera sublatae similis prope Cassiepiam
sublimis fulget: pedibus properare uidetur
et uelle aligeris purum aethera findere plantis.

---

224 *om.* ⱽ*M*   currens Ƶ: torrens µ   **225** suo *om. O*
ursa *Grotius*: ursae Ƶ: uram *O*   **226** breuiore lycaonis E: breuior helycaonis λ:
grauiore lycaonis *O*   **232** medii *O*: summi Ƶ   **234** propiore AU: propriore
OƵ   signo *O*: motu Ƶ   **238** breuius *Bentley ad Manil. 1.359*: breuior *OƵ*
239 *attulit Mico Leuita u.124*   hunc ⱽ *Miconis codices*: huc µ: huic Ƶ   **241**
austrum *O*: austros Ƶ *nihilo deterius*   **247** astra *Housman p. 31/503*: dextram *OƵ*
248-50 *om. O*   **252** sublatae Ƶ: sublata *O*   cassiepiam *O*: cassiepia Ƶ   **254**
findere Ƶ: tangere *O*

Poplite sub laeuo, Tauri certissima signa,   255
Pleiades suberunt. breuis has locus occupat omnis,
nec faciles cerni, nisi quod coeuntia plura
sidera communem ostendunt ex omnibus ignem.
septem traduntur, numero sed carpitur una,
deficiente oculo distinguere corpora parua.   260
nomina sed cunctis seruauit fida uetustas:
Electra Alcyoneque Celaenoque Meropeque
Asteropeque et Taygete et Maia parente
caelifero genitae (si uere sustinet Atlas
regna Iouis superosque atque ipso pondere gaudet).   265
lumine non multis Plias certauerit astris,
praecipuo sed honore ostendit tempora bina,
cum primum agricolam uernus tepor admonet agri
et cum surgit hiemps portu fugienda peritis.
Quin etiam Lyra Mercurio dilecta, deorum   270
multum accepta epulis, caelo nitet ante labore
deuictam effigiem | torti subiecta Draconis   273b
tempora laeua premit | cui planta erectaque dextra.   272b
Contra spectat Auem, uel Phoebi quae fuit olim   275
Cycnus uel Ledae thalamis qui illapsus adulter
furta Iouis falsa uolucer sub imagine texit.
inter defectum sidus Cycnumque nitentem
Mercurialis habet sedem Lyra. multa uidebis
stellarum uacua in Cycno, multa ignea rursus   280
aut medii fulgoris erunt. penna utraque laeta,
dexterior iuxta regalem Cepheos ulnam,
at laeua fugit instantem sibi Pegason ala.
Piscibus interlucet Equi latus; ad caput eius
dextra manus, latices qua fundit Aquarius, exit.   285

255–7 *om. O*   **256** *has* Kenney: est Z: et C², *fortasse at*
uel sed   **264** uere *O*: uero Z **267** *om.* Z **268** uernus tepor admonet
Haupt p. 406: uentus super immouet *O*: uentus super imminet Z agri Z: atri *O*
269–75 *om.* E   **269** *post 272* λ   **269** portu *O*: ponto λ   **270–2** *om. O*   **271**
multum *Haupt p. 407*: plurimulum λ   accepta Grotius: accepte λ   epulis
Burman: prohs λ   **272** diuellit Housman eique medio inseruit 273, hemistichiis inuersis
273b torti C²: tortis λ: porti *O*   **272b** cui *add.* Baehrens   **274** *post 628 trans-
posuit Housman*   **275** quae *O*: qui λ *nihilo deterius*   **276** illapsus Grotius: lapsus
OZ   **278–80** *om. O*   **280** cygno Grotius: cycnum E: cignum λ   **284–6**
om. O   **285** latices qua Grotius: laticesque Z uersum 285 sequuntur 387–93 in
Z, quos excipiunt 286 sqq. in λ

quo prior Aegoceros semper properare uidetur
Oceano mersus sopitas condere flammas.
tum breuis occasus ortusque intercipit hora,
cum Sol ambierit metas gelidi Capricorni.
nam neque perficiet cursus et uota breuis lux,   290
et cum terrores auget nox atra marinos,
multum clamatos frustra speculaberis ortus.
tunc rigor est; rapidus ponto tunc incubat Auster;
pigra ministeria, et nautis tremor alligat artus.
sed rationem anni temeraria pectora soluunt: 295
nulla dies oritur, quae iam uacua aequora cernat
puppibus, et semper tumidis ratis innatat undis.
in terra temptare undas iuuat; aspera sed cum
assultat lateri deprensae spuma carinae,
tunc alii curuos prospectant litore portus   300
inuentasque acie terras pro munere narrant;
ast alii procul a terra iactantur in alto: 303
interea exanimat pauidos instantis aquae mons.   302
munit eos breue lignum et fata instantia pellit,
nam tantum a leto, quantum rate fluctibus, absunt.   305
   Belligerum Titan etiam cum contigit Arcum
ducentemque ferum sinuato spicula neruo,
iam clausum ratione mare est, iam nauita portu
infestam noctem fugitat longasque tenebras.
signum erit exoriens nobis tum nocte suprema   310
Scorpios: ille micat supra freta caerula cauda;
insequitur grauis Arcus et in lucem magis exit.
tunc alte Cynosura redit, tunc totus in undas
mergitur Orion, umeris et uertice Cepheus.
   Est etiam, incertum quo cornu missa, Sagitta   315
quam seruat Iouis Ales. habet miracula nulla,
si caelum ascendit Iouis armiger. hic tamen ardens

286–314 om. E   286 quo prior Grotius: cum
primum λ   aegoceros Grotius: egochero L: ego chero C   289–90 om. O
292 speculaberis Baehrens: spectaueris λ: spectauerat O   293 rigor O: rigora λ
est Dahms p. 273: aut Oλ   rapidus Oλ: rabidus Baehrens   294 alligat O: occupat λ
nihilo deterius   295 sed λ: et O   299 post 301 habet L   300 om. λ   alii
Grotius: alti O   301 acie Housman p. 32/504: alii Oλ   302 & 303 inter se
transposuit Grotius   303 a λ: e O   alto λ: altum O   306 etiam O: magnum λ
307 ducentem O: lucentem λ   313 redit Grotius: repit O: regit λ   314
mergitur O: uergitur λ   315–17 om. O   317 ardens scripsi: ardum Ƶ

unguibus innocuis Phrygium rapuit Ganymeden
et telo appositus custos quo Iuppiter arsit
in puero, luit excidio quem Troia furorem. 320
Delphin inde breuis lucet iuxta Capricornum
paucis sideribus: tulit hic Atlantida nymphen
in thalamos, Neptune, tuos, miseratus amantem.
Sidera quae mundi pars celsior aethere uoluit
quaeque uident Borean uentis assueta serenis 325
diximus, hinc alius decliuis ducitur ordo,
sentit et insanos obscuris flatibus Austros.
Primus in obliquum rapitur sub pectore Tauri
Orion. non ulla magis uicina notabit
stella uirum, sparsae quam toto corpore flammae. 330
tale caput magnique umeri, sic balteus ardet,
sic uagina ensis, pernici sic pede lucet;
talis ei custos aderit Canis ore timendo:
ore uomit flammam, membris contemptior ignis.
Sirion hanc Grai proprio sub nomine dicunt. 335
cum tetigit Solis radios, accenditur aestas,
discernitque ortu longe sata: uiuida firmat,
at quibus astrictae frondes aut languida radix,
exanimat. nullo gaudet maiusue minusue
agricola et sidus primo speculatur ab ortu. 340
Auritum Leporem sequitur Canis, et fugit ille:
sic utrumque oritur, sic occidit in freta sidus.
tu paruum Leporem rimare sub Orione.
At qua cauda Canis languenti desinit astro,
fulgent Argoae stellis aplustria Puppis; 345
puppe etenim trahitur, non recto libera cursu,
ut cum decurrens inhibet iam nauita remos

321–3 *om. O* **321–7** *om.* E **321** delphin *Scaliger*: delphini λ **324** quae *om. O*
326 decliuis *O*: declinis λ *nihilo deterius* ducitur *O*: dicitur λ **328–30** *om. O*
328 obliquum *Grotius*: obliquo Z **331** humeri C²: humeris OZ ardet *O*:
exit Z **332** *attulit Mico Leuita u.303* lucet *O*: ludit Z **333–5** *om. O*
333 ei C²: et Z **335** hanc *Breysig*: hunc Z proprio sub E: priosum C:
priosuum L: prios suum *l* **336** aestas *O*: aestus Z *nihilo deterius* **338** ad-
strictae *Baehrens*: adstete *O*: adsuetas Z radix *O*: cernis Z **341** *om. O*
uersum 341 sequitur Auieni 749 in Z *uersum 342 sequuntur Auieni 747, 748, 750 in Z*
343 *om. Z* rimare *Burman*: primare *O* **344–6** *om. O* **345** *attulit Prisc.*
GLK. 2.351.5 **347** remos *OZ*: remis *Gronouius 4.60* ora *Sabbadini p. 92*: ore
OZ

auersamque ratem uotis damnatus ab ora
praeligat, optatam cupiens contingere terram.
sed quia pars uiolata fuit, coeuntia saxa   350
numine Iunonis tutus cum fugit Iason,
haec micat in caelo; lateri non amplior auctus
qua surgit malus; qua debet reddere proram,
intercepta perit nulla sub imagine forma;
puppis demisso tantum stat lucida clauo.   355
  At procul expositam sequitur Nereia Pristis
Andromedan. media est Solis uia, cum tamen illa
terretur monstro pelagi gaudetque sub axe
diuerso posita et Boreae uicina rigenti:
Auster Pristin agit. duo sidera praelegit unum,   360
namque Aries supra Pristin Piscesque feruntur.
Belua sed ponti non multum praeterit Amnem,
Amnem qui Phaethonta suas defleuit ad undas,
postquam patris equos non aequo pondere rexit,
uulnere reddentem flammas Iouis; hunc, noua silua,   365
planxere ignotis maestae Phaethontides ulnis.
  Eridanus medius liquidis interiacet astris:
huius pars undae laeuum ferit Orionis
lapsa pedem. procul amotis qui Piscibus unus
uincula conectit nodus cristam super ipsam   370
aequoreae Pristis radiat. sunt libera caelo
sidera non ullam specie reddentia formam,
sub Leporis latus, auersam post denique puppim,
inter et Eridani flexus clauumque Carinae
atque haec ipsa notes nullam praebere figuram.   375
sunt etiam toto sparsi sine nomine mundo
inter signa ignes, quibus etsi propria desit

349 praeligat *Muncker p. 50*: perlegit *OZ*   **350** quia *O*: quae *Z*   **351**
cum fugit *Z*: confugit *O*   **352** amplior *O*: amplius *Z*   auctus *Orelli*: actus *O*:
aucta *Z*   **353** qua surgit σ: quam surgit *OZ*   malus *O*: maius *Z*   **355**
lucida *O*: roscida *Z*   **356-8** *om. O*   **359** rigenti *Housman p. 32/505*: legenti *O*:
legente *Z*   **360** praelegit *Schwartz*: perlegit *OZ*   **363-5** *om. O*   **366** maestae
Z: adaestae ν: adesie μ   **367** astris *O*: undis *Z*   **368** laeuum ferit *O*: medium
tenet *Z*   **369** unus *Grotius*: usus *OZ*   **370** connectit *AU*: coniectit *O*: coniecit *Z*
371 aequoreae *Grotius*: aequore *OZ*   radiat *Breysig*: adiat ν: adit μ: radians *Z*
72 sp ecie *O*: caelo *Z*   **374** eridani *Scaliger*: eridanum *OZ*   **375** notes *scripsi*:
notas *iam Goodyear*: nota est *Z*: nota si *O*   **376** mundo *Bᶜ*: mundi *OZ*

forma, per appositi noscuntur lumina signi.
Est etiam a Geminis diuersus Piscibus unus,
qui Borean fugitat, totus derectus in Austros,   380
uentre sub Aegoceri, Pristin conuersus ad imam.
infimus Hydrochoos sed qua uestigia figit,
sunt aliae stellae; qua caudam Belua flectit
quaque caput Piscis, media regione locatae
nullum nomen habent nec causa est nominis ulla: 385
sic tenuis cunctis iam paene euanuit ardor.
nec procul hinc dextra defundit Aquarius undas
atque imitata cadunt errantis signa liquoris.
e quibus una magis sub cauda flamma relucet
squamigerae Pristis, pedibus subit altera signi   390
fundentis latices. est et sine honore Corona
ante Sagittiferi paulum pernicia crura.
   Scorpios erecta torquet qua spicula cauda,
Turibulum uicinum Austris sacro igne uidebis,
Arcturum contra; sed quanto tardius ille   395
Oceanum occasu tangit, tanto magis artae
Turibulo metae; uix caelum suspicit et iam
praecipiti tractu uastis demittitur undis.
multa dedit natura homini rata signa salutis
uenturamque notis cladem depellere suasit.   400
inter certa licet numeres sub nocte cauenda
Turibulum; nam si sordebunt cetera caeli
nubibus obductis, illo splendente, timeto
ne pacem pelagi soluat uiolentior Auster.
tum mihi substricto spissentur cornua uelo   405
et rigidi emittant flatus per inane rudentes.
quodsi deprensae turbauit lintea puppis
incubuitque sinu laxo, uel mergitur undis
prona ratis sorbetque inimicum Nerea prora,

378 appositi *O*: oppositi *Z*   **379-81** *om. O*   **379** diuersus *Grotius*: diuersis *Z*
380 fugitat *Grotius*: fugiat *Z*   **382** qua τ: quae *OZ*   **387-93** *post 285 habet Z*
392 paulum E: paululum λ: nullum *O*   **393-5** *om. O*   **394-413** *om.* E   **396**
tanto *Grotius*: tanto et *O*λ   **397** turibulo *O*: turibuli λ *nihilo deterius*   **398**
demittitur *Schwartz*: dimittitur *O*λ   **400 & 402** *om.* ν   **402** cetera μ: tempora λ
403 splendente timeto *O*: splendenti metuendum λ   **405** substricto spissentur
Housman pp. 32-3/505: spissentur substricto *iam Grotius*: siccentur subscricto L:
siccentur subsricto C: siccentur abstricto *O*   **409** sorbet *Grotius*: soluet *O*:
seruet λ

uel si respexit seruator Iuppiter, aegre 410
ultima persoluunt iactati uota salutis.
nec metus ante fugit quam pars effulserit orbis
quae Borean caelum spectantibus indicet ortum.
Sunt etiam flammis commissa immania membra
Centauri, capite atque hirsuto pectore et aluo 415
subter candentis hominem reddentia Chelas;
inde per ingentis costas, per crura, per armos,
nascitur intacta Sonipes sub Virgine. dextra
seu praedam e siluis portat seu dona propinquae,
placatura deos, cultor Iouis admouet Arae. 420
hic erit ille pius Chiron, iustissimus omnis
inter nubigenas et magni doctor Achillis.
hic, umero medium scindens iter aetheris alti
si tenuem traxit nubem stellasque recondit,
toto clarus equo, uenientis nuntiat Euros. 425
Nec procul hinc Hydros trahitur, cui cauda superne
Centaurum mulcet; tractu subit ille Leonem,
peruenit ad Cancrum capite et tria sidera tangit.
huic primos tortus Crater premit, ulterioris
uocali rostro Coruus forat. omnia lucent, 430
et Coruus pennis et paruo pondere Crater
et spatio triplicis formatus sideris Hydros.
Sub Geminis Procyon fulgenti lumine surgit.
Hic caelo ornatus trahitur noctemque diemque.
sors sua cuique data est, semel assignata tuentur 435
immoti loca nec longo mutantur in aeuo.
Quinque aliae stellae diuersa lege feruntur
et proprio motu mundo contraria uoluunt
curricula exceduntque loco et uestigia mutant.
haud equidem possis alio contingere signo 440

410 respexit λ: perspexit O   **411** iactati *Grotius*: iactatae Oλ
412 effulserit orbis O: perfulserit omnis λ   **413** ortum O: orbem λ   **414–16**
om. O   **419** e μ, *om.* νZ   **421** iustissimus S: tutissimus OZ **423** hic O:
hinc Z scindens ζ: scandens O: scandit Z **426–8** *om.* O   **426** superne
Grotius: superni Z **427** mulcet *Housman p. 33/505*: lucet Z tractu C²:
tractus Z **428** capite C²: capiti Z tria *Scaliger*: tristia Z **429** huic C²:
hic OZ primos PU: primo est Z: primo O   tortus *Grotius*: ortus OZ
431–2 *om.*O   **432** triplicis *Grotius*: triplici Z **433** fulgenti lumine O: fulgentia
lumina Z surgit OZ: pandit E^c **434–6** *om.* O   **440–2** *om.* O   **440**
possis *Grotius*: possim Z

quae diuis sedes. hinc atque hinc saepe uidentur
occasus ortusque. neque anfractus breuis illis,
annosasque uias tardus uix perficit orbis.
hoc opus arcanis an credam postmodo Musis,
tempus et ipse labor, patiantur fata, docebit.   445
Signorum partes, quorum est praedicta figura,
annum expleturi praecidunt quattuor orbes.
interualla trium transuersus colligat unus.
nec par est illis spatium: duo namque feruntur
inter se aequales, est quorum maxima forma;   450
et totidem . . . . praedictis ante minores.
hi semper distant, illos communia signa
committunt. qua se tangunt, pars aequa rotarum
diuiditur, binos ut si quis desecet arcus.
dissimilis quintus liquida sub nocte uidetur: 455
sidera cum reddunt sinceros eminus ignis,
lactis ei color et mediis uia lucet in umbris;
lacteus hic orbis nullo minor orbe rotatur.
Celsior ad Borean qui uergit circulus, altos
et peragit tractus uicinis haud procul Vrsis,   460
per Geminos currit medios, uestigia tangit
Aurigae plantamque terit Perseida laeuam;
transuersae Andromedae latera utraque persecat actus
et totam ex umero dextram; summa ungula pulsu
acris Equi ferit orbis iter. tum candidus ora   465
Cycnus habet iuxta, cubito lucet super ipsum
nixa genu facies et primis ignibus Anguis.
effugit at Virgo; totus Leo, totus in ipso
Cancer. ab aduersis omnem secat ille Leonem
clunibus hirsutique iubam per pectoris exit.   470
Cancro fulgentes oculi, ceu regula currat

441 quae diuis sedes E: que diuisa dies *l*: quediui sa di
es L: quae diuisa die C   **446** est *om.* λ, *post* figura *ponit* E   **447** praecidunt
Scaliger: praedicunt *OZ*   **449** illis U: illi *OZ*   **450** est quorum *scripsi*: quorum
est EL: quorum est et *O*: quorum extat C   **451** inter se *OZ*: *fortasse* pariter
454 quis *Z*: qui *O*   **457** et *O*: est *Z*   **459–6ı** *om. O*   **462** terit *O*: tegit *Z*
463 latera utraque persecat actus *O*: secat utraque latera tactu *Z*   **464** ex
Orelli: ab *OZ*   pulsu *O*: cursu *Z*   *post uersum 464* diuidit et (atque CL^c)
sagittiferi medium pernicia crura *habet Z*   **465** acris equi ferit *O*: hinc alius
rapit *Z*   **47ı** fulgentes *O*: qui fulgent *Z nihilo deterius*   currat *O*: currit *Z*

per medios, sic diuidui latera utraque tangunt.
hunc octo in partis si quis diuiserit orbem,
quinque super terras semper fulgere notabit,
abdi tres undis breuibusque latere sub umbris.   475
hoc Cancrum tetigit cum Titan orbe, timeto
aestatem rapidam et soluentis corpora morbos.
tunc habet aeterni cursus fastigia summa
erectoque polo propius non applicat umquam
candentis currus. aduerso nititur orbe   480
dum tangat metas; pronus deuoluitur inde.   481
Aegoceros metas hiemis glacialibus astris   483
aestatisque tenet flagranti sidere Cancer: 484
hic Boreae propior, contrarius excipit Austros.   482
hoc medium sidus findit deuexior orbis,   485
fundentis latices genua implicat, alligat illum
intorta Pristis cauda; uelocia crura
contingit Leporis, Canis aluum desecat imam.
desecat et sacrae speciosa aplustria Puppis
Centaurique umeros et Scorpion ultima cauda   490
spicula torquentem; magnus micat Arcus in illo.
inde Austro propior Sol est Aquilone relicto
et gelidas hiemes hebetato lumine portat.
huius tres caelo partes assurgere cernes,
quinque latent undis et longa in nocte feruntur.   495
    Hos inter medius nullo minor orbis agetur,
in quo cum Phoebus radiatos extulit ignis,
diuidit aequali spatio noctemque diemque.
bis redit haec facies, librat quae sidera mundi,
cum uer fecundum surgit, cum deficit aestas.   500
signa Aries Taurusque aequo tanguntur ab orbe
sed princeps Aries totus fulgebit in illo;
Tauri armum subit et flexi duo sidera cruris.

472 diuidui *Scaliger*: diuidit *OZ*   *post uersum 472 et geminis humeros et tauri
ungula dextra/radit ophyuci humeros uastos fulgere notabis add.* Z   **475** abdi
tres *Grotius*: abdit tres Z: adiutrix ν: adultrix μ   **476** timeto Z: timete *O*   **479**
propius *Orelli*: breuius *O*: breuibus Z   **480** currus ABᶜEPSU: cursus λ BM
483 astris S: austris *OZ*   **484** flagranti sidere E: fraglanti sidera λ: flagrantia
sidera *O*   **482** *post 484 transposuit Housman p. 33/506*   **482** hic *Grotius*: hinc
OZ   **494** cernes Z: cernis *O*   **495** in *om.* Z   **497** radiatos extulit Z: radios
intulit *O*   **499** librat quae *anon. apud Breysig*: librato Z: libato *O*   sidera *O*:
sidere Z

at medium Oriona secat spiramque priorem
Hydri, tum Cratera leuem Coruique forantis   505
ultima, deficiunt nigra qua sidera cauda.
illic et Chelas transuerso lumine quaeres
et celsi mediam partem Anguis et........
.....................a medio Ophiuchum
nec procul inde Aquilam; toto capite incubat ardens
Pegasus et longae spatio ceruicis inhaeret.   510
hos orbis, quorum tractus et signa notamus,
rectus per medios percurrens traicit axis.
tres interuallis paribus sine fine rotantur
nec mutare uias possunt nec iungere sulcos.
quartus in obliquum tres unus colligat orbis,   515
partibus extremis diuersos implicat; unum
inter utrumque secat medium desectus ab illo.
non si Palladia doctus formaret ab arte,
distantis orbis melius religasset ab uno.
sed tribus idem ortus omni nascuntur ab aeuo   520
atque eadem occasus remanent certissima signa.
   Quartus ab Oceano tantum uestigia mutat,
obliquo currens spatio, quantum Capricornus
aestifero distat Cancro; quam latus ad auras
aetherias surgit, tam sacris mergitur undis.   525
[nec tamen humanos uisus fugit ultimus orbis.]   530
haec uia Solis erit bis senis lucida signis.
nobilis hic Aries aurato uellere, quondam
qui tulit in Tauros Phrixum, qui prodidit Hellen,
quem propter fabricata ratis, quem perfida Colchis
sopito uigile incesto donauit amori.   535
corniger hic Taurus, cuius decepta figura
Europe, thalamis et uirginitate relicta,
per freta sublimis tergo mendacia sensit,

505 tum *Courtney p. 140*: et *OZ*   cratera *O*: crateram *Z*   forantis
Frey p. 412: ferentis ν: ferentes μ: querentis *Z*: sedentis *Baehrens*   **508** *inter* et *et* a
lacunam indicaui   a medio *Z*: medio *O*   **509** aquilam *O*: aquila *Z*   **511**
tractus *Grotius*: actus *ZASU*: aptus M: apius B: apices P   notamus *O*: docemus
Z   **512** percurrens *O*: decurrens *Z* *nihilo deterius*   **513** *om.* ν   rotantur
Grotius: notantur μZ   **515** colligat *Grotius*: colligit *OZ*   **522–35** *om.* M
526–9 *huius loci non esse uidit Housman p. 33/506, post 567 transposui*   **530** *huius loci
non est*   **532–4** *om.* O   **535** uigile *Grotius*: uigili *Z*: uigiles *O*   amori *Grotius*:
amore *OZ*

litore Cretaeo partus enixa marito.
sunt Gemini, quos nulla dies sub Tartara misit,   540
sed caelo, semper nautis laetissima signa,
Ledaeos statuit iuuenis pater ipse deorum.
te quoque, fecundam meteret cum comminus Hydram
Alcides, ausum morsu contingere uelle,
sidere donauit, Cancer, Saturnia Iuno,   545
nunquam oblita sui, nunquam secura nouerca.
hinc Nemeaeus erit iuxta Leo, tum pia Virgo;
Scorpios hinc duplex quam cetera possidet orbe
sidera, per Chelas geminato lumine fulgens,
quem mihi diua canet dicto prius Orione.   550
inde Sagittifero lentus curuabitur Arcus,
qui solitus Musas uenerari supplice plausu
acceptus caelo Phoebeis ardet in armis.
cochlidis inuentor, cuius Titania flatu
proelia commisit diuorum laetior aetas,   555
bellantem comitata Iouem, pietatis honorem
ut fuerat, geminus forma, sic sidere, cepit.
hic, Auguste, tuum genitali corpore numen
attonitas inter gentis patriamque pauentem
in caelum tulit et maternis reddidit astris.   560
proximus infestas, olim quas fugerat, undas
Deucalion paruam defundens indicat urnam.
annua concludunt Syriae duo numina Pisces
tempora. tunc iterum praedictus nascitur ordo.
[Lanigeri et Tauri, Geminorum, postea Cancri,   565
tunc Leo, tunc Virgo, tunc Scorpios, Arcitenensque
et gelidus Capricornus et imbrifer et duo Pisces.]
in sex signiferum si quis diuiserit orbem   526
aequales partes, succumbet regula binis
inferior signis, spatii tantumque tenebit

539 creteo Z: acretae O **544** ausum morsu Z: ausus morsus O
uelle *Housman p. 34/507*: bello OZ, *fortasse* coniungere bellum   **545** cancer
Scaliger: cancrum OZ **546** nouerca L^c: nouercae OZ **547** hinc Z: hic O
nemeeus *Scaliger*: nemeus OZ **550** *dedi ex* O quae mihi dicta canat (E canant λ)
magnum sidus orionis Z **552** plausu Z: plausus O **554** cochlidis *Scaliger*:
cochitis B *ante corr.* coclitis O: poplitis Z **555** *om.* Z **561** infestas O: infectas Z
562 paruam E: parum $Oλ$ **565–7** *deleuit Grotius*   **567** gelidus Z: geminus O
526–9 *post 567 transposui*   **527** partes *Grotius*: aries OZ succumbet *Grotius*:
succumbit Z: occumbit O

lunatus lateris quantum a tellure recedit.　　　　529
huius quantum altas demergitur orbis in undas　　　　568
Oceani, tantum liquidum super aera lucet.
nullaque nox bis terna minus caelo trahit astra,　　　　570
nullaque maior erit, quam quanto tempore in auras
orbis perfecti diuisus tollitur arcus.
Saepe uelis quantum superet cognoscere noctis
et spe uenturae solari pectora lucis.
prima tibi nota Solis erit, quo sidere currat;　　　　575
semper enim signo Phoebus radiabit in uno.
cetera tum propriis ardentia suspice flammis,
quod cadat aut surgat summoue feratur in orbe,
quantoue exiliant spatio, cum caerula linquunt;
namque aliis pernix saltus, maiore trahuntur　　　　580
mole alia, Oceanum tardo linquentia passu.
quodsi nube caua Solis uia forte latebit,
occulet aut signum conscendens uertice caelum
altus Athos uel Cyllene uel candidus Haemus
Gargaron aut Ides superisue habitatus Olympus,　　　　585
tum dextra laeuaque simul redeuntia signis
sidera si noris, nunquam te tempora noctis
effugient, nunquam ueniens Tithonidos ortus.
　Cum primum Cancrum Tethys emittit in auras,
excipit Oceanus Minoae serta Coronae,　　　　590
occidit et dorso Piscis, caudaque priore.
mergitur in totos umeros Ophiuchus, at Anguis
ultima cauda micat; tortus habet unda timendos.
nec multo Arctophylax his longius hic iacet astris,
lumine qui primo cum Scorpios occidit undis　　　　595
occulitur pedibus; durat tamen arduus ore

529 lunatus *Housman p. 33/506*: una tui *O*: una suis Z
568-71 *om.* Z　　**571** auras *Orelli*: au v: austros μ　　**572** orbis *O*: aeui Z
arcus *O*: orbis Z　　**576** signo phoebus *O*: phoebus signo Z *nihilo deterius*　　**578**
quod *Orelli*: quid *O* Z　　**579** ue μ Z: que v　　**580** saltus *Orelli*: saltu *O*: alius Z
582 si AP^c: sine *O* Z　　nube *O*: fine Z　　*uersum 582 excipit fr. iv in O*　　**585** Ides
Le Boeuffle p. 63: idens λ: iden E: ingens *Housman p. 34/507*　　habitatus *Heinsius*:
agitatus Z　　**588** ueniens *Grotius*: uentus Z　　tithonidos *scripsi*: tithonius Z
589 primum *Grotius*: primo Z　　**590** minoae *Grotius*: minoiae Z　　**591** dorso
Grotius: dorsus Z　　**593** unda *Thierfelder p. 213*: illa Z　　**594** longius hic iacet
scripsi: longe subiacet Z

dum rigidum Aegoceri signum freta lucida terret.
siderea uix tum satiatus luce Bootes
in terras abit et noctis plus parte.............
.............................relinquit.
at contra, nullo defectus lumine, totus   600
Orion umeris splendebit magnaque diui
uagina et claro caelatus balteus igni,
cornua et Eridanus liquido feret utraque caelo.
    At cum prima iuba radiarit flamma Leonis,
quicquid parte micat, Cancro nascente, sub undas   605
omne abit atque feri uenientis defugit ora.
tota Iouis mersa est pennis stellantibus Ales,
quique genu posito defessus conditur undis
crure tenus; redit in caelum uasti caput Hydri
et pernix Lepus et Procyon et Sirius ipse   610
totiusque Canis rapidi uestigia prima.
    Accipe quae uitent exortae Virginis ora:
Delphinus notis iam tum defluxerit undis
et Lyra dulce sonans et flammis cincta Sagitta
et niueus Cycnus properarit tangere fluctus;   615
utraque penna uolans caudam uix lucet ad ipsam;
nigrescitque Padus, terrae qui proximus amnis;
tum caput abscondet Sonipes, tum tota latebit
ceruix; at contra sublimior Hydra feretur
Creterra tenus et surgent aplustria Puppis   620
Argoae totusque Canis; pede cum pia Virgo
nascitur, illa ratis media plus arbore lucet.
    Surgentes etiam Chelas sua signa notabunt:
exilit Oceano tum toto crine Bootes,
quem claro ueniens Arcturus nuntiat ore,   625
celsaque Puppis habet, cauda minus attamen Hydra.

597 aegocheri E: aegocheris L: aego cheris C   599
inter parte *et* reliquit *lacunam indicaui*   605 cancro *Schaubach*: caelo Z   606 feri
Grotius: fert Z   ora *Scaliger*: hora Z   611 rapidi LᶜCE: rabidi L *nihilo
deterius*   612 exortae *Burman*: exorsae Z   613 notis *Grotius*: motis Z   de-
fluxerit *Grotius*: deflexerit Z   618 abscondet *Grotius*: abscondit Z   tum
Grotius: cum Z   620 cratera tenus et surgent aplustria *Grotius*: terra tenus
traxit surgentia plustria Z: creterra *primus scripsit Kinch, Quaestiones Curtianae
Criticae, Hauniae 1883, p. 29*   621 pede *Housman p. 34/507–8*: sed Z   624
exilit *Grotius*: exilem Z   tum *Baehrens*: nunc Z   626 habet *suspectum*   hydra
Grotius: illa Z

nixa genu species flexo redit ardua crure.

partibus haud aliis noctem eluctata supremam,   628

summa genus subuersa tenet qua se Lyra uoluit.   274

bis solet illa una caelo se ostendere nocte,   629

nam si Phoebeos currus, dum longa uenit nox,   630

occasu sequitur, rursus fugit Oceanum ortu.

crure simul Chelae fulgent; cum Scorpios exit

tergo obstipa suo caelo profertur imago.   635

at Philyra cum natus auitis surgit ab undis   634

iam totis radiat membris miserabile sidus.   633

imperfecta redit caelo tum torta Corona

et Chiron pius ad caudam cognoscitur imam;

Pegasus abscondit toto cum corpore pennas

nec lucet cauda praemersus pectore Cycnus.

abdit et Andromeda uultus et maxima Pristis   640

occasu insequitur uementi uirginis ora:

crista super caelo fulget. caput abditur ipse

regalis Cepheus alias intactus ab undis.

Non prius exoriens quam clarus fluxerit Amnis,

Scorpios Oriona fugat; pauet ille sequentem.   645

sis uati placata, precor, Latonia Virgo;

haec ego non primus, ueteres cecinere poetae,

uirginis intactas quondam contingere uestes

ausum hominem diuae sacrum temerasse pudorem.

deuotus poenae tunc impius ille futurae   650

nudabatque feris augustas stipite siluas

---

628 eluctata *Grotius*: fluctuata Z supremam Z: suprema Lᶜ
274 *post 628 collocauit Housman p. 32/504*   *uersum 274 om.* E   uoluit O: uersat λ
nihilo deterius   **629** illa *Grotius*: ille Z **631** occasu *Grotius*: occasus Z *ordinem*
uersuum **633–5** *mutauit Housman p. 35/509, 633 post 635 iam Grotius*   **635** tergo
obstipa *Housman p. 35/509*: argosipia Eᶜλ: argosiria E   profertur *Housman*:
refertur EL: referetur CLᶜ   **634** philyra cum natus auitis *Housman*: cum tantus
abit quantum lyra Z (*loco* lyra li*ra C, *b ut opinor in ras.*)   surgit C: surgat EL
633 iam EL: tum C   **636** tum *Grotius*: cum Z torta *Ellis p. 240*: tota Z
637 pius *Grotius*: prius Z imam *Grotius*: ima Z **638** cum corpore *Maybaum*
p. 49: tunc pectore Z **640** abdit et andromede *Schwartz*: abditur andromedae
iam *Grotius*: ardet et andromedae Z **641** occasu *Schwartz*: occasum Z inse-
quitur *Grotius*: sequitur Z uementi *Housman p. 35/510*: uenienti E *marg.*:
uentis et E: uenientis et λ   **642** ipse *Voss p. 111*: ipsi Z **643** alias *Voss*: altis Z
644 non prius *Housman p. 35/510*   scorpios EL: scorpion C   fluxerit
Steinmetz p. 472: fulserit Z **646** sis *Grotius*: si Z **647** haec *scripsi*: non Z
651 augustas *Housman pp. 35–6/510*: angusto Z

pacatamque Chion dono dabat Oenopioni.
haud patiens sedenim Phoebi germana repente
numinis ultorem media tellure reuulsa
scorpion ingenti maiorem contulit hostem.   655
parcite, mortales, nunquam leuis ira deorum.
horret uulnus adhuc et spicula tincta ueneno
flebilis Orion et tamquam parte relicta
poenae tela fugit; tamen altis mergitur undis,
Scorpios ardenti cum pectore contigit ortus.   660
nil super Andromedae, nil Pristis luce fruetur;
in caput atque umeros rapit orbis Cassiepiam
declinemque trahunt aeterni pondera mundi
corruptaque cadit forma, certauerat olim
qua senis aequorei natis, cum litore Canchli   665
Doridos et Panopes spectasset stulta choreas.
illa abit Oceano; totius serta Coronae
in caelum redeunt, totum se liberat Hydros.
cruribus expectat Chiron obscurior Arcum,
corpore iam toto, iam toto uertice clarus.   670
tum fera, quam dextra portat Centaurus, in auras
exilit et claris aperitur flexibus Anguis
innixusque genu laeua minus aequora linquit.
    At cum prima subit facies remeabilis Arcus,
iam sicca Oceano Chiron pernicia crura   675
extulit et celsis Ophiuchus fulget in astris.
nil trahit obscurum Serpens et trunca recepta
desinit esse manu membris deformis imago.
iam Lyra cum superis et Cycni dextera penna;
radit tellurem rediens tum sidere Cepheus;   680
tum Canis abscondit totius corporis ignis

653 haud *Grotius*: at E: ad λ   **658** tamquam *scripsi*: quamquam *Z*   **659** poenae tela *scripsi*: teli paene *iam Grotius*: coeli poene *Z*   **662** cassiepiam *Grotius*: cassiepia *Z*   **663** aeterni pondera *Grotius*: aeterno pondere *Z*   **664** cadit *Grotius*: cadunt *Z*   certauerat *Grotius*: certauerit *Z*   **665** senis *Grotius*: sinus *Z* canchli *Grotius*: cancri *Z*   **667** totius ... coronae *Grotius*: totiensque ... corona *Z*   **669** arcum *Grotius*: arcu *Z*   **670** iam toto iam toto *Baehrens*: iam uasto iam toto *iam Grotius*: iam toto uastus et *Z*   **673** linquit *Grotius*: linquunt *Z*   **674** arcus *Grotius*: arcu *Z*   **676** extulit et *Orelli*: expulit *Z*: expellit Eᵉ: expulerit Cˣ: expulit et *man. 2 in Bernensi*   **677** et *Breysig*: sed *Z*   **678** manu *Grotius*:manum *Z*   membris *Breysig*: mediis *Z*   **680** tum *scripsi*: cum *Z*

et latet Orion et semper tutus in undis
est Lepus Argoaeque ratis, qua flexile signum
in puppim formatur, adhuc aplustria lucent.
mergitur et Perseus et Caprae nobile lumen.   685
   Aurigam totum abscondit ueniens Capricornus
atque omnem ornatum uenerandae numine Puppis.
tum Procyon obscurus abit; redit armiger uncis
unguibus, ante omnis gratus tibi, Iuppiter, Ales.
omnibus et stellis Cycnus redit et leue Telum   690
et paruus Delphinus et apta Altaria sacris;
et minus exsurgit Minoa nota Corona.
   Hydrochoos caelum scandens simul euocat ore
et ceruice tenus fidentem Pegason alis.
auersum Chirona trahit nox atra sub undas,   695
Oceanus caudam tinguit, nondum capit ora,
non uastos umeros, non pectora tristia saetis.
Hydram plus mediam condit, pars tertia lucet.
   Hanc Pisces abdunt orti totumque biformem.
cum geminos Pisces Aquilonis prouocat aura,   700
ille etiam surgit, qui tristes respicit Austros;
Piscibus ille simul surgit, et liberat ortus
cum pernix Aries in caelum cornua tollit.
Pisces educunt Cepheida; laetior illa
Nereidas pontumque fugit caeloque refertur.   705
   Ortus Lanigeri properabunt condere sacrum
Turibulum; patrio fulgebit in aethere Perseus
· ·
   Persea cum pennae reddunt, iam Plias ab undis
effugit et dextro Tauri cognoscitur armo.
fixus et in cornu trahitur sine curribus ullis   710
Myrtilos. haud totum cernes; non integer ipse
in caelum rediit; pars dextera mergitur undis;

692 et minus
Winterfeld p. 33: eminus *Z*   minoa *Winterfeld*: minoia EL: *aut* minori *aut* minom
C   **697** non pectora *Grotius*: tum pectora *Z*   setis *Grotius*: sertis *Z*   **699**
totum *Grotius*: tum *Z*   biformem *Grotius*: biformes *Z*   **702** et liberat ortus
suspectum: se liberat ortu *Goodyear*   **705** nereidas pontumque fugit *Grotius*:
nereidos pontoque fugam *Z*   *post* **707** *lacunam indicaui*   **708** reddunt *Scaliger*:
redeunt *Z*   **709** tauri *Grotius*: tauri et *Z*   **710** cornu *Dahms*: curru *Z*   **711**
haud *Grotius*: aut *Z*   non integer ipse *Grotius*: cum interit ipsum *Z*   **712**
rediit Eᶜ: redit *Z*   dextera C: dextra EL

uertice lucebit, teneros manus efferet Haedos
laeua, Iouis nutrix umero radiabit in ipso;
proxima telluri nascetur planta sinistra: 715
cetera cum Geminis perfecto sidere surgent.
Tauro Pistricis pariter cristaeque refulgent
caudaque; uicinum terris iam cerne Booten.
At cum se genibus demisit pars Ophiuchi,
signum erit Oceano Geminos remeare relicto.   720
totaque iam Pristis lucebunt squamea terga;
Eridani et primos deprendat nauita fontes,
caelum conspiciens, dum claro se mouet ortu
Orion; habet ille notas quae tempora noctis
significent, uentosue truces fidamue quietem.   725

Fragmentum ii

Vna uia est Solis, bis senis lucida signis.
hac rapitur Phoebe, per idem Cythereius ignis
fertur iter, per idem cristatus uertice Mauors
Mercuriusque celer, regno caelique uerendus
Iuppiter et tristi Saturnus lumine tardus.   5
omnibus his gemini motus, quorum alter ab ipsis
nascitur et proprios ostendit sidere nisus
(tum mundum subeunt lento pede), concitus alter
inuitos rapit et caeli circumrotat orbem.
annua Sol medius designat tempora, Phoebe   10
menstrua, namque anno Solem remeare uidebis,
mouerit unde suos currus per signa uolantis.
hoc peragit spatium breuiore citatior orbe
mensem expleturis Phoebe contenta diebus.

713 efferet *Grotius*: effugit Z
714 radiabit *Grotius*: radiauit Z **716** surgent *Grotius*: surget Z **717** pistricis
Scaliger: pistrices Z **719** at *scripsi*: et Z demisit *Grotius*: dimisit Z   **720**
geminos *Scaliger*: gemino Z **721** pistris *Grotius*: piscis Z terga ELᶜ: terra λ
722 primos *Grotius*: primo Z **724** noctis *Grotius*: noctes Z **725** significent
Grotius: significet Z fidamue *Grotius*: fidamque Z *uersum 725 excipit
fragmentum iii in Z, tum fr. ii; fragmenta solus praebet* Z **ii 2** hac *Grotius*: ac Z
phoebe *Grotius*: phoebee Z **4** caeli *Schwartz*: caelo Z **8** concitus *om.* E   **9**
circumrotat *Grotius*: circum notat Z **10** tempora ELᶜ: tempore λ   phoebe
Grotius: phoebee Z **11** namque *Grotius*: namqua E: nam qua λ   **13** spatium
breuiore *Grotius*: spatio breuior Z **14** contenta *Grotius*: contemta E: con-
tempta λ

annuus est Veneri cursus neque tardior illa   15
Mercurius, bimos Gradiuus perficit orbis.
per duodena pater superum dum signa feretur,
bis senos Phoebus iam tum compleuerit annos
. . . .
cursus inaequalis cunctis: nunc igne citato
festinare putes, nunc pigro sidere sumpto.   20

Fragmenta iii & iv

Grandine permixtos Aries niuibusque caducis   iii 1
uicina aspergit tristis supra iuga nimbos.
Taurus portat aquas et uentos excitat acres;
fulmina tum crebro iaculatur Iuppiter et tunc
intonat emissis uiolentior ignibus aether.   5
at Geminis leuiter perstringunt caerula uenti,
rarus et in terras caelo demittitur umor.
omnia mitescunt tranquillo sidere Cancri.
siccus erit Leo, praecipue cui pectora feruent.
Virgo refert pluuias et permouet aera uentis.   10
lenius est Librae signum; uix rorat in illo.
Scorpios assidue caelo minitabitur ignis   12
atque truces uentos; densa niue saepe rigebunt.   14
rara Sagittifero descendunt flamina terris;   15
lentior in pluuias, magis inuenit arua quieta.   13
Aegoceros alias parcit, sed frigora durat,
instabilita gelu falli uestigia passus.
Qui fundit latices caelo quoque permouet imbris.
omnia miscentur cum Piscibus; aspera uentis

16 bimos *Stahl p. 47*: binos *Z*   *uersum 16 sequuntur Auieni uersus*
1741–62, 1769–70, 1773, 1870, 1877, 1878 ed. Holder, tum in E uersus 17–20, quos non
habent CL   **17** per *Baehrens*: er E   feretur *Baehrens*: feruntur E   **18** com-
pleuerit *Baehrens*: compleferat E   *post* **18** *lacunam indicaui*   **19** inaequalis
cunctis *Baehrens*: inequatis cuncti E   **20** sumpto E: sompno *Baehrens*   **iii 1**
permixtos *Ellis p. 241*: permixtus *Z*   **2** uicina aspergit *scripsi*: aspargit uicina
iam Ellis: spargunt uicina *Z*   nimbos *scripsi*: piscis λ: pisces E   **3** acres
Grotius: aries *Z*   **5** emissis *Scaliger*: emissus *Z*   **6** perstringunt *Housman p.*
34/507: perstridunt *Z*   **11** rorat Lᶜ: rore *Z*   **12** caelo *Z fortasse* caeli   **13–14**
om. C   *uersum* **13** *post* **15** *transposuit Courtney p. 174*   **14** uentos *Z*: uenti *Grotius*
rigebunt *Z fortasse* rigebit   **15** rara sagittifero *Grotius*: rara sagittiferi ELᶜ:
sagittiferique rara λ   descendunt *Grotius*: descendit *Z*   flamina *Skutsch*:
pluuia *Z*   **13** quieta L: ctu E   **16** alias E: alia λ   parcit *Grotius*: spargit *Z*
sed *Grotius*: et *Z*   **17** instabilita *scripsi*: instabilique *Z*   falli *Z*: fallit Lᶜ

aequora turbatos uoluunt ad sidera fluctus;   20
imbribus incumbit caelum solemque recondit;
grandine pulsatur tellus, niue condita dura est.
  Haec ut quisque deus possedit numine signa
adiungunt proprias uires. torpere uidentur
omnia Saturno; raros ille exprimit ignis   25
et siccas hiemes astrictis perficit undis.
grandine durantur pluuiae, niue grando putrescit
et rigor accedit uentis. lentissimus ille: 28
Iuppiter est illo laetus magis. hic ubi Solis   iv 1
uitauit flammas proprio bene lucidus ore
. . . .
commissas Cereri fruges spectabis in herbis
pomaque purpureo primum nascentia flore;
nec pecus in fetu fallet, noua turba repente   5
mugiet e stabulis; alto balabit ouili.
idem, ne tellus nimium siccata tepore
destituat sata, cum tetigit fera cornua Tauri
dat pluuias, sorbetque datas cum Pliada fugit
atque adiit Geminos. Cancro placidissimus idem   10
dat modicas uires, rapidos et temperat aestus.
et Leo terribilis sub te, pater, ipse repellit
instantis morbos et Ditis limina claudit.
incipis agricolis in Virgine soluere uota.
iam tum maturae segetes et spicea pendet   15
ante larem primum perfecta messe corona.
Libra tumescentis musto bene percoquit uuas.
Scorpion ingrediens tua, Liber, munera condit;
iamque Sagittiferum scandens sua frigora reddit
nunquam laetae hiemi, modice tamen in Capricorno.   20
Hydrochoon Piscesque agitat saeuissimus idem.

---

22 condita dura est *scripsi*: moenia durant ζ **24** torpere L^c: torpore ζ **28**
lentissimus *Housman p. 36/511*: mitissimus ζ *fr. iv solus praebet O (ABMPS 1–51;*
ABMPS τ 52–163) fr. iii & iv iunxit Housman p. 36/510   **iv 1** laetus *Iriarte*:
laeto *O*   solis P: solus *O*   **2** proprio P: proprior *O*   *post uersum 2 lacunam*
indicaui   **3–4** *om.* ν   **5** fallet *Iriarte*: falet B: falit M: fallit APS   **6** balabit
Iriarte: balauit P: ualebit *O*   ouili AMP: obili BS   **7** tepore *Iriarte*: repente *O*
8 destituat *Iriarte*: destituit A: distituat *O*   **9** pliada *Orelli*: pliade *O*   **10** adiit
Iriarte: adit AP: adid BM: ad id S   **14** incipis *Housman p. 36/511*: incipit *O*
soluere AS: sorbere Mν   **15** pendet *Iriarte*: pendent *O*   **16** corona *Iriarte*:
coronam *O*   **19** frigora *Housman*: munera *O*

si statuit currus quocumque in sidere fessos,
Lanigero tonat et Poeni per terga Leonis
omniaque hibernis permiscet mensibus astra.
At cum Phoebeos Mauors effugerit ignes,   25
siue Aries Geminique deum siue acre Leonis
sidus et aequatae librato pondere Chelae
aut arcu pollens aut imbris fusor habebit,
spissatis caecus nebulis hebetabitur aer
nullaque praecipites agitabunt aequora uenti.   30
his idem lentos signis cum supprimet ignis
Belliger et pigra cursus statione tenebit,
tum crebro magnus tonitru pulsabitur aether,
tum resoluta dabit nimbos cum grandine nubes;
sed magis, hibernae steterit cum sidere partis,   35
ecfundet totas uiolento numine uires.
at modicos imbres, proni cum cornua Tauri
frugiferamque Deam uel brumalem Capricornum
attigerit, liquido non saeuus ab aethere fundet.
inuectus Cancro, terras cum letifer ortu   40
Sirius afflauit, nocituros temperat aestus.
Scorpios at rimans qua tollit acumina caudae
frigidaque extremi iam claudunt sidera Pisces,
Martia non illos turbabit stella neque imbre
aut ulla condet nitidos caligine soles.   45
sed si forte diem uictus mutauerit aer
et uentos ecfundet aqua, gelidissimus undae
tum rigor et toto Boreas dominabitur orbe.
At faciles glebas astringit frigore uerno
alma Venus, pecudis claro cum uellere fulsit   50
sub lucem exoriens, eademque, ubi tempore eodem
aetherium uenit Taurum super, imbribus atris
et tonitru crebraque abscondit grandine terras.
temperat in Geminis annum. nec crede sereno,

24 hibernis *Iriarte*: hiberni *O*
27 *bis habet* ν   **29** spissatis *Orelli*: siocatis BM: siccatis APS   **31** supprimet
Iriarte: supprimit AMP: suprimit BS   **32** pigra *Housman p.* *36/511–12*: nigra *O*
tenebit Bᶜ: tenebat *O*   **40** inuectus *scripsi*: incertus *O*   **42** rimans *scripsi*:
primae *O*   tollit *Iriarte*: colit *O*   caudae A: cauda *O*   **44** imbre *Iriarte*:
imbres *O*   **47** effundet *Goodyear*: aut fundet *O*   **48** tum *Iriarte*: rim Mν: *aut*
uim *aut* rim S: uim A   **52** *incipit* τ   atris *Grotius*: astros *O*

nubila nec diuturna puta, cum sidere Cancri   55
fulserit ardentis: nil hoc in tempore certum.
flagrantis placide lucens haec temperat aestus
cum posuit sedem Nemeaei finibus astri.
Virgineque et Libra semper pendentia tantum
nubila continua magis in statione manebunt.   60
tum quoque nulla fides caelo, cum Scorpion acrem
stat super, incerta namque omnia lege feruntur.
heu quantis terras tum Iuppiter imbribus omnis
obruet! aut glomerata cadet quam densa per auras
immitis grando! caelum quam saepe sonabit!   65
cum spatium attigerit tendentis spicula signi,
non terris imbres, ponto non flamina deerunt.
et caeli terret sonitus mortalia corda
cum sedem Aegoceri Cythereius attigit ignis.
umidus at gelidos portendit Aquarius imbris,   70
hibernaeque cadunt pluuiae concretaque grando
Piscibus a geminis, ubi prima recurrit in astra.
Phosphoros haec tibi signa dabit cum Aurora....
ingrediens Venus alma polum; sed ubi Hesperos ignes
prouocat aetherios et noctem inducere terris   75
incipit, exoriens haec te Cytherea monebit.
uere cauere imbres et fulgura torta memento.
Phrixeae rutilo pecudis radiauerit astro,
nubila erunt mixtusque fragor pluuialibus undis
flaminaque assiduo terris instantia pulsu   80
et dirae caelo deiecti grandinis ictus.

---

56 nil *ante* hoc
add. Baehrens, *post* hoc *iam* Grotius   tempore *scripsi*: litore *O*   **57** haec *Breysig*
ed. 1: hic *O*   estus S^c: testus S, *om. O*   **58** nemeaei *Grotius*: nemeis *O*   astri
Grotius: astris *O*   **59** et τ, *om. O*   **61** tunc *Grotius*: nunc *O*   caelo *Grotius*:
caelum *O*   acrem *Grotius*: acer *O*   **63** tum *G. Morel*: cum *O*   imbribus β:
ignibus *O*   **64** auras *Housman p. 37/512*: astras BMPS (*fac. ex* astraa B?): astra
Aτ   **66** spicula signi *Grotius*: singula signis *O*   **70** imbres *Grotius*: ignis *O*
72 ubi *Ellis p. 244*: sub *O*   recurrit *Housman p. 37/512*: recurret *O*   **73**
phosphoros *Schaubach*: hesperos *O*   cum *Courtney p. 140*: cum lucifer *O*   aurora
P: curora M: cur ora B: orta A: ora τ: hora S: lucifera Aurora *Housman p. 37/512*
75 inducere *Orelli*: ducere *O*   **76** haec te *falso Parisino attribuit Breysig*: haecte P:
haec cae B: ecce AM: ecce haec Sτ   monebit P: mouebit *O*   **77** torta me-
mento *Ellis*: comamenalto *O, fortasse* crebra memento   **79** erunt mixtus *Housman
p. 37/512*: cum mixtus BM: commixtus APS τ   **80** instantia *Grotius*: tum stantia
O **81** et *add. Grotius*   *post 82 lacunam indicaui*

uere magis nitido Tauri cum sidere fulsit

. . . .

apponi Geminis eadem inconstantia perstat:
cum dederit soles, inducet nubila caelo;
nubila cum fuerint, subitos mirabere soles   85
et modo de uento, gelido modo protinus imbre
lucet et alterna uariabit nube serena.
sin leuis ingressa est spatiosi sidera Cancri,
pacem mundus habet: non ulli corpora soles
pestiferi incendunt, non sidera densa solutos   90
astringunt artus; alieno tempore lenis
omnia pacato tum sidere temperat aer.
at rapidis eadem ne solibus aestuet orbis
efficiet, magni signo conspecta Leonis.
Virgine erunt pluuiae plenique in nube fragores,   95
concaua quos reddunt incluso nubila uento.
detrahet autumno pluuias eademque replebit
nubibus assiduis, Chelae dum frigore primo
extremum autumni superent glaciante teporem.
Scorpios at raris, ne quid caua terra grauetur,   100
horrebit pluuiis. at diris omnia nimbis
continuisque ruet, cum per sinuosa feretur
cornua Centauri rapida distincta sagitta.
Aegoceros imbres et crebro fulmine ruptis
nubibus elidet sonitus tremuloque nitore   105
flagrantis teli mortalia lumina uincet.
haec eadem fundens praedicet Aquarius imbrem.
extremi saeuis maria increbrescere uentis
ostendent Pisces, Veneris cum stella notarit.

83 apponi AMTU: adponi BP^c:
adpone P: ad poni S: appota χ   inconstantia *Grotius*: constantia *O*   **84**
nubila τ: nebula *O*   **86** de *Schwartz*: te *O*   gelido modo μ: gelido ν   **87**
alterna uariabit *Iriarte*: alternabit M: altern. a A: alter nauit B: alternauit P:
alternat S: alterna superabit τ   **88** ulli *Bonincontrius*: nulli *O*   **95** plenique
Grotius: plerique *O*   **97** detrahet *Orelli*: detrahit *O*   **98** chele *Grotius*: caelum *O*
dum *Housman p. 37/513*: ob *O*: ad P   primo *falso Matritensi attribuit Iriarte*:
prima *O*   **99** glaciante teporem *Housman p. 37/513*: glaciante rigore *iam Baehrens*:
glaciaterrore *O*   **100** quid *Grotius*: quis *O*   **101** nimbis *Grotius*: nimbos *O*
102 feretur *Schwartz*: tenetur *O*   **106** lumina *Schwartz*: numina *O*   **109** quom
Baehrens: quae AMP: que BS: quos τ

Est quoniam certis ea iam tibi cognita signis,   110
accipe quid moueat mundo Cyllenius ignis
si modo Phoebei flammas effugerit axis,
matutina ferens solitos per sidera cursus.
cum pecudis uillis auratae fulserit astro
uentorumque graues et dirae grandinis irae   115
non intermisso patiendae tempore surgent.
quin aliqua pluuias etiam in regione notabis
adfore; non omni namque est tunc imber in aruo.
ast ubi se Tauri sinuatis cornibus affert,
grandine significat. Geminis tranquilla serenti   120
et placidum nautis spondet caelumque fretumque
. . . .
nubilaque atque imbres, aestus ac frigora miscet.
certus at ardor erit, quamuis iuuet aura Fauoni,
cum uasti calida radiabit sede Leonis.
templa sed Astraei simul ac possederit ignis,   125
omnia mixta feret, pluuias tantum modo Libra.
Scorpios et pluuias meditabitur; undique uenti,
undique grando uenit, rumpuntur fulmina nimbis.
Centauri attigerit cum iam Cyllenius Arcum,
idem ubi consurget Capricorni sede biformis,   130
aut subitos caelo deducet crebrius imbres
fulminis aut iactu magnum perrumpet Olympon.
nulla serenato Phryx rorans nubila caelo
comparat, at gelidos flatus caelique fragores
non alio melius signo praedicere possis,   135
Piscibus haec eadem quamuis cognoscere detur.

110 ea iam tibi *Housman p. 38/513*: ratiuiam *O*: paphie iam *Courtney*   114 pecudis *Grotius*: pecudum *iam* τ: pecum μ: pricum ν   auratae *scripsi*: aurati *O*   117 aliqua *scripsi*: alias *O*   118 aruo P: aruis μ: arui B   119 affert *falso Basileensis correctori attribuit Breysig*: afert B^c: effert *O*   120 serenti *Schwartz*: sereni *O*: serena U   *uersum excidisse suspicatus est Schwartz, sed utrum ante an post 122 non indicauit. quem secutus lacunam ante 122 indicaui. lacunam post 122 indicauit Baehrens, nihilo deterius.*   123 at *add. Orelli*   125 astraei *Schwartz*: extraeis *O*: astraeae *Grotius*   128 fulmina nimbis *Wakefield ad Lucr. 1. 1013*: culmina nimbis μ: culminant imbres B: fulmina et imbres P   129 arcum *Grotius*: arcus *O*   130 idem *Baehrens*: aut idem *O*: aut SUχ consurget *Grotius*: consurgit *O*   capricorni sede biformis *Baehrens*: capricornisetde biformis P: capricornisetdebi formis M: capricornius sede biformi S: capricornis et debiformis AB: capricornus et ipse biformis τ   133 phryx rorans *Housman p. 38/514*: capricornus *O*   134 at *Grotius*: aut *O*: au B

quandoquidem exoritur ignis dum Cyllenaeus
quid faceret primo docui cum lumine Solis,
tempus, et occasu moueat quid, discere, Phoebi:
uer erit hibernis totum exsecrabile nimbis   140
et crebro tonitru; uincet florentia rura
spesque nouae segetis quatientur grandinis ictu
urenturque gelu, magni cum regna Tonantis
ingrediens pecudis conscenderit aurea terga.
hinc et Agenorei stellantia cornua Tauri   145
quidue ferant Gemini, rabido quid sidere Cancer,
si penitus quaeres, Taurum saeuire uidebis
grandine nec contra ferri ratione probanda
aut Cancro aut Geminis. | saeuisque caloribus ardet   150b
hic qua ficta Leo | calidus uestigia seruat.   149b
flatibus at gelidis miscet tranquilla serena
spicifera Dea iusta manu, nec Libra tenenti
dissentit diuae, sed, ut haec, uentura serena
nuntiat; a uentis cessat mare, cessat et aer.
Scorpios in pluuias rarus, sed nubibus atris   155
creber agit nimbos et saeua tonitrua portat,
clara Sagittiferi tetigit cum lumina signi.
Aegocero semper caelo leuis excidit imber;
frigidus at rabidis horrebit Aquarius Euris
brumalesque dabit pluuias atque igne perenni   160
cum sonitu quatiet nubes. si cura sagacem
non frustrata animum certo me limite ducit,
haec eadem tibi signa dabunt non irrita Pisces.

Fragmentum v

Astrorumque globos et sidera maximus Atlas

137 dum *scripsi*: quoque
O   **138** docui *Schwartz*: modo cui *O*   **139** occasu *Grotius*: occasus *O*   moueat
Baehrens: moneat *O*   quid *Housman p. 38/514*: que *O*   **141** uincet *scripsi*:
uinget S: iunget *O*   **143** gelu *Baehrens*: caelum *O*   **146** rabido *Orelli*: rapido *O*
149 *diuelli eique medio inserui 150 hemistichiis inuersis*   **150** hic μ: hinc ν   qua
scripsi: quo *O*   ficta *Baehrens*: dicta *O*   **151** flatibus *Grotius*: flatus *O*   serena
Iriarte: serenis *O*   **152** iusta *Housman p. 38/515*: aut mita *aut* muta B: nuta μ:
nuda P   libra *Iriarte*: libera *O*   tenenti *Housman*: tendenti *O*   **154** a
Iriarte: ad *O*   **159** rabidis *scripsi*: rapidis *O*   **161** si cura *Grotius*: secura ν:
securas μ   **162** frustrata *Iriarte*: frustrat AS: frustat BM: frustratum P: frustrans τ
fr. v sine interstitio post iv 163 solus praebet A   **1** que *add. Baehrens*

protulit in populos, numeris uersutus, et omnes
stellarum motus certa ratione notauit;
quae Pharii Tyriique uiri commenta sequentes
aequora uere nouo......................   5
...................uentos et flamina cuncta
Aeolus in partes diuisi rettulit orbis:
quo premeret Boreas, Notus unde attolleret imbres
quaque Eurus Zephyrusque domo procederet undis
et circumpositos armaret in aequora fratres.

Fragmentum vi

quidni te diuite lingua,
Graecia, praecurram potiusque triangula dicam?

2 numeris
uersutus *Baehrens*: humeris uirtutis A   4 tyrii *Baehrens*: syrii A   5 *inter* nouo *et*
uentos *lacunam indicauit Baehrens*   uentos et *Baehrens*: uento sed A   6 rettulit
Baehrens: retulit A   8 procederet *Baehrens*: proce**** A   *fr. vi debetur Prisc.*
GLK 3.417   1 quidni te *Housman p. 39/515*: cur *libri*

TRANSLATION

Aratus began with mighty Jupiter. My poem, however, claims you, father, greatest of all, as its inspirer. It is you that I reverence; it is to you that I am offering sacred gifts, the first fruits of my literary efforts. The ruler and begetter of the gods himself approves. (5) What power would there be in the points which mark for certain the seasons of the year, the one where the violent sun turns around in the sign of the burning Crab, the one where he grazes the opposite turning post in chill Capricorn, or those where the Ram and the Balance make the two divisions of the day equal, if the gaining of peace under your leadership had not allowed ships to sail the level sea, (10) the farmer to till the land and the sound of arms to recede into distant silence? At last there is an opportunity to lift one's gaze boldly to the sky and learn of the celestial bodies and their different movements in the heavens and discover what the sailor and the canny ploughman should avoid, when the sailor should entrust his ship to the winds and the ploughman his seed to the soil. May your presence and the peace you have won aid your son; grant your divine power, (15) to favour me as I attempt to tell of this in Latin verse.

The stars which gleam throughout the heavens move ceaselessly, never tiring, for the sky causes them to rotate along with its own mass. The axis, however, does not move, but always stands in the one place, (20) holding the earth in equilibrium and making the sky rotate about its steady pivot. Twin poles, as the Greeks call them, bound it at each end; part of the axis is sunk in the waters of the Ocean, part is high up under the terror-bringing North Wind.

(25) The Bears of Crete, called Arctoe, or, in Latin, Ursae, guard it on the right hand and on the left. They are also called Ploughs, and the shape of a plough is the closest to the real shape formed by their stars: each has three stars at the pole and the wheels, four in the upper part. If you prefer to call them

animals, these gleaming animals face away from each other; the head of one shines above the shaggy back (30) of the other; the sky carries them down headfirst, their bodies pressing upon their shoulders. If the old tale is acceptable, the land of Crete nurtured them; the ruler of Olympus granted them a place in the sky. They earned this by guarding him, for they faithfully tended great Jupiter in his earliest infancy. (35) His terrified mother had stolen him from his father's jaws and the Corybantes, her servants, hid him in a cave on mount Dicte and clashed bronze cymbals together with their hands to distract his father and prevent the sound of the baby wailing from reaching his ears. Because they were the nurses of Jupiter, Helice and Cynosura shine in the sky. (40) The Greeks set their course by Helice, its stars being brighter; the Phoenicians are guided by Cynosura. All of Helice is shining and gleams with a clear radiance; no constellation begins to shine after the sun has hidden his gleaming countenance in the Ocean before seven-starred Cretan Helice. (45) Cynosura, however, is the surer guide for those cleaving the level sea, since it is short and all of it turns around at the pole, a reliable guide. It has never been known to deceive Phoenician sailors guided by it.

In the middle of them, like a portion of a river, a monstrous Snake twists its winding coils (50) in this direction and that and above them, a strange portent. Its tail extends above Helice; it stretches its scale-bearing body towards Cynosura. The head of Helice lies where the tip of its tail ends; Cynosura is contained within a high coil of the Snake, which then stretches out further, and, (55) sweeping back and up, looks back at the larger Bear. Its huge eyes and hollow temples are illuminated by bright stars; only one star sits on its chin. ⟨The line joining⟩ the star which marks the Snake's right temple to the one which sits on its chin ⟨points to the place where⟩ (60) the tip of Helice's tail and her last star shine. Where the head of the setting Serpent gleams, the nearby points of rising and setting are touched by the one head. The Bears are unknown to the rolling waves of the Ocean and guard the pole continually with their never-setting stars.

(65) Not far from her is a being worn out with toil. No one knows his name or the cause of his toil. He kneels on his right

knee and stretches out his arms in different directions, his palms stretched out in supplication to the gods. His left foot treads the Serpent's head.

(70) Beneath the sides and lofty back of this weary being lies the bright Garland, placed in the heavens on account of Bacchus' passion for Ariadne. He granted her this honour because of their marriage.

This wretched constellation is sunk on failing knees. His back is lit by the Garland; the Snake-Bearer lies where his head is uplifted. (75) You will notice the head and monstrous shoulders of the Snake-Bearer long before the rest of him, in which there is little to please. The shoulders' radiance, however, remains undiminished, even when the moon's orb is full at the middle of the month. The light in his hands is feeble. The Snake slithers through them; (80) he grasps the Snake in both hands; it coils around his middle. The Scorpion lies near the soles of his feet. His left foot lies on its back, his right foot being unsupported. The weight borne by his hands is unequal. His right hand holds only a small part of the Snake; it is entirely lifted up by his left hand. (85) It rears up from the left hand of its Bearer as far as the Garland. Its last star gleams on its chin, its rays like hairs, just below the Garland of the sky. But where this slippery Snake writhes around its Bearer's back, the Claws pour forth their clear light into the sky.

(90) An old man, threatening his animals with a goad, follows Helice. He is either the Guardian of the Bears or Icarus, slain because of his services to Bacchus and rewarded for the loss of his life with a place among the stars. His head is by no means faint, nor is his body gloomy; only one of his stars, however, has its own name. (95) Men call it Arcturus. It lies where his garment is fastened by a knot.

Then comes the Maiden. A full and ripe ear of wheat shines in her left hand. What shall I call you, Goddess? If you are affected by the poems of mortals and do not, (100) in hatred of the human race, turn a deaf ear to those who venerate you, I will halt my steeds in mid career and, rejoicing in my control over the reins, tell of you and your divine power, reverenced by the world.

When you ruled the golden age and gave peace to the world,

O Justice untouched by evil, O Maiden most serene, (105) whether you are of the line of Astraeus, who, according to tradition, is father of the stars, or whether the true story of your origin is lost in time, it was your custom to walk proudly and joyfully in the midst of the people. You did not disdain to enter the houses of men, which were then untainted by crime. (110) You delivered judgements and taught the populace, untaught before, educating them in virtue in all the activities of their life. Men were not yet so savage as to bare their swords in rage against each other; discord among blood relations was unknown; no one sailed the seas, men's own lands being (115) satisfaction enough. Greed for wealth from far away did not cause them to build ships and entrust them to the hazards of the winds. The peaceful lands bore fruit unaided for those who dwelt in them. There were no boundary stones marking off their owners' small domains, for they were quite safe without them.

(120) However, when the age of silver, less attractive than that before, arose, Justice rarely visited the cities, tainted with crooked dealing, but came down from the high mountains only late in the day, her face veiled and her sorrow-filled eyes hidden. She accepted the hospitality of no one's hearth and home. (125) She merely chided the frightened crowds when she saw them: 'Offspring forgetful of the fathers that have gone before you, destined to have a progeny that is becoming ever more degenerate, why do you call upon me with your vows when you have ceased to follow me? I must go elsewhere; (130) I will leave this generation of yours to its own devices and to bloody crime.' When she had finished speaking, she flew away over the mountains, leaving the people thunderstruck and expecting an even worse fate than their present one.

But when the offspring of the bronze age came to the earth, the seeds of virtue were overwhelmed by vice and could no longer resist it; (135) men were delighted by the discovery of the metal iron; the ox, accustomed to the plough, defiled their tables; the most just maiden swiftly left the earth and gained a place in the sky, very close to the Ploughman who slowly follows his setting waggon.

(140) A star of outstanding brightness marks the shoulders of the gentle Maiden. No brighter star surrounds Helice: the one

that shines in her tail is no brighter, nor is the one which gleams in her shoulder, the one in her forefeet or the one in her hindfeet, nor the one that gives itself to her shaggy buttocks. (145) The other stars, which complete her at the head and neck, were unknown to the poets of old and travel on unhonoured.

You will discover the Crab lying below the middle of Helice, the Twins beneath her head. Below her hindfeet you will find the shaggy mane of the tawny Lion. (150) When the violent chariot of the sun touches this sign the heat of summer, which began in the Crab, is doubled. Then water is scanty and the earth in a wretched plight; the farmer rejoices at his luxuriant crops and carefully stores them. I would not then use oars on the azure sea, (155) but would rather loosen the sail-ropes and entrust the sails to the wind, receiving the puffs of the West Wind in the billows of the sails.

There exists also the semblance of a Charioteer; he is either Ericthonius, born in the land of Attica, who first yoked horses, or Myrtilos, sunk in the waters of the Myrtoan sea. (160) The appearance of the sign suits the latter better: you will observe that he has no chariot and, his reins broken, is sorrowful, grieving that Hippodamia has been taken away by the treachery of Pelops. This huge sign sets at an angle to and on the left of the Twins and opposite the head of the larger Bear. (165) Moreover, he carries with him divinities: one is considered to be the nurse of Jupiter (if the infant Jupiter really did suck the breast of the faithful Cretan goat); the brightness of the star is witness to the gratitude of her nursling. The Charioteer carries her over his shoulder; (170) his hand displays the Kids, which, when the sky above has lifted them from the Ocean, are a most unfavourable sign to sailors; more than once the Kids have seen a ship tossed about, the sailors trembling and bodies of the dying scattered over the cruel waves.

Near the Charioteer's feet lies the fierce Bull, (175) his brow bearing fiery horns, his threatening head illuminated. His very shape will tell anyone, however ignorant of the sky, that here is the head, flaring nostrils and horns of the Bull. The Hyades gleam on his brow; the fiery star occupying the tip of his left horn enters from below the right foot (180) of the Charioteer and binds these gods together, providing the connection between them. Myrtilos rises as far as the top of his head when the Fishes rise; all of him is visible with the Bull; the Bull sets in the Ocean in front of him, when Myrtilos' head is still shining above the earth.

Cepheus, descendant of Iasus, also climbs the sky, as does his wife (185) and his whole family, for Jupiter is the founder of his line; the kingly nature of one's father is often an advantage. He stands behind the short Cynosura, stretching out his hands, his feet apart. The line joining his right foot to the tip of Cynosura's tail (190) is the same length as the line from his left foot; the line joining his feet is shorter. Where his belt girds his flanks, you are looking towards a coil of the winding Snake. Cassiepia sits on high near her husband. She is clearly visible, even when the moon has been shining all night. (195) She is short, however, and her constellation is adorned with few stars. Their disposition resembles a key whose iron teeth are placed under the bar before a pair of doors to remove it. Her face contorted in agony, she stretches out her hands as if bewailing abandoned (200) Andromeda, unjustly atoning for the sin of her mother.

Andromeda lies not far away; you can see all of her when the night is not yet dark, so great is the brightness which shines in her face and large shoulders and surrounds her middle, where her fiery girdle gleams and her dress is tied. (205) Nevertheless, the signs of punishment remain: her arms are stretched far apart as if she were being held by the weight of a hard rock.

A flying Steed shines above Andromeda's head. The star which gleams on her crown also shines under the Horse's belly; three stars, set an equal distance apart, (210) mark his shoulders and flanks. The shape of his head is dim indeed; his neck too is marred by the feebleness of its light and remains unhonoured. However, where this animal chews the bit, his mouth foaming, a gleaming star appears, brighter than those on his head and long neck and of very much the same brightness as those on his shoulders and large flank. (215) The individual stars do not, however, represent the whole of his shape; the first group show a Horse, at the middle the image disappears and the body is broken off, thence his image is unformed. He is the offspring of the Gorgon, and stood on the summit of the Boeotian mount Helicon at a time when water did not yet flow down from it

(220) and drew out the water from the fountain of the Muses with a blow from his right foot. It was from this that the water so formed derived its name: the spring is called Hippocrene (Horse Spring). Pegasus, however, beats his swift wings in the topmost circle of the sky and rejoices in his stellification.

The Ram follows, travelling along by far (225) the longest circle, but completing his course just as quickly as the Bear. His swiftness as he hastens to touch the distant turning post with his horns compensates for the shortness of the orbit in which the Bear, daughter of Lycaon, travels, turning the sky around with her movement. His shape is not clear, nor are his stars bright enough (230) to be seen if the moon prevents it. His position should be fixed by reference to the belt of Andromeda, gleaming nearby. The Ram presses upon the line in the middle of the sky that sunders its two hemispheres, as do the Claws and the gleaming belt of Orion.

There is an even nearer constellation by which you can discover the position of this god: (235) mark the position of Deltoton (that remarkable gift of the Nile, owing its origin to its divine waters). It has three sides, two equal, one shorter, but brighter. The Ram is near this last side. Deltoton is midway (240) between the Ram's back and the sorrowing daughter of Cepheus.

Beyond the Ram lie the twin Fishes, of which one stretches towards the region of the South Wind, the other seeks the region of the North Wind, that comes from Thrace, and it hears the harsh sound of the winds blowing from snow-clad Haemus. Their movement is not free, (245) but each is held by a chain at the tail, the chains being joined at the one knot. A star lies on this knot. The stars of the Fish which looks towards the blast from Thrace may be seen at Andromeda's elbow.

Underneath both feet of the Maiden vowed to destruction lies the winged form of Perseus, pleasing to the girl he saved. (250) The size of the hero is in itself sufficient evidence of his parentage: he shines so huge in all his parts, so much of the sky does the son of Jove occupy. His right hand resembles a hand lifted up; it shines on high near Cassiepia; his legs seem to be hastening and he seems to be desirous of cleaving the clear sky with his wing-bearing feet.

(255) Under his left knee lie the Pleiads, a most reliable sign of the Bull. A small space contains them all, nor would they be easily visible, except for the fact that they lie together and present to the eye the combined radiance of them all. Tradition has it that there are seven; one, however, has been taken away from this number (260) because the eye cannot separate such small bodies. Despite this, antiquity has faithfully preserved all their names: Electra, Alcyone, Celaeno, Merope, Asterope, Taygete, and Maia, all begotten by a father who carries the heavens (that is, if Atlas really carries (265) the gods and the kingdom of Jove and rejoices in this weight). The Pleiads do not rival many stars in brightness; it is, however, their special honour to mark two periods, the time when the warmth of spring first reminds the farmer of his fields and that when winter arises: the experienced know that it should be avoided in the safety of harbour.

(270) There is also the Lyre, the delight of Mercury, most welcome at the banquets of the gods. It shines in the sky before the figure worn out with toil, whose left foot presses on the temple of the winding Serpent and whose right hand is held aloft.

(275) On the other side, the Lyre looks on the Bird which was either formerly Phoebus' Cycnus or the winged adulterer who came down to Leda's bedroom, concealing Jupiter's deceit under a false appearance. The Lyre of Mercury has its abode between the failing sign and the gleaming Swan. You will observe that much (280) of the Swan is without stars, much, on the other hand, bright, much in-between. Both his wings are bright, his right wing, which lies near the elbow of King Cepheus, and his left, which flees Pegasus, who presses upon it.

The flank of the Horse shines between the Fishes; the Water-Carrier's (285) right hand, with which he pours out water, stretches out beside the Horse's head. Capricorn is submerged in the Ocean before him and his fiery stars always seem to be hastening to their hidden place of rest. When the sun is travelling around the turning point in chill Capricorn, only a short time intervenes between its rising and setting. (290) The brief period of daylight does not allow you to travel the distance you had hoped to, and when black night increases the terrors of the

deep and you loudly invoke the dawn, your watch for it will be
in vain. Then comes numbness, the swift South Wind seethes
over the sea, the sailors are slow at their tasks and trembling
locks their limbs together. (295) Nevertheless, rash men show
no proper regard for the time of year. No day dawns that sees
the sea at last free from ships; there is always a ship floating on
the swelling waves. When on land, the thought of daring the
waves is pleasant, but when the ship is caught with the bitter
briny foam leaping up at its sides, (300) some men look at the
curved harbours on the shore and talk of the lands they have
found by the keenness of their gaze as if they have received a gift;
others, however, are tossed on the deep far from the land; some-
times they are scared out of their wits by the mountain of water
towering over them. Only a thin wooden plank protects them
and wards off the fate threatening them, (305) for in their ship
death is as near to them as the waves.

The sea is already closed to those who are wise even when the
sun has touched the war-waging Bow and the Beast who is
pulling back the arrow in his curved bowstring. The sailor
escapes the hostile night and the long period of darkness in
harbour. (310) The Scorpion is the sign that we then mark as
rising at the end of night; he then shines above the azure sea as
far as his tail; the heavy Bow follows close on him, and, unlike
him, comes forth when it is light. Then the Little Bear returns
aloft; all Orion is immersed in the waves, Cepheus as far as his
head and shoulders.

(315) There is also an Arrow, guarded by Jupiter's Bird. It
is uncertain what bow it was sent from. It should be no source
of wonder that Jupiter's weapon-bearer has come into the sky,
for he it was that snatched away Trojan Ganymede (although
he was burning with eagerness, his talons did not harm him)
and was made guardian of the weapon that was the cause of
Jupiter's passion (320) for the boy. Troy paid for Jupiter's
madness by its destruction.

Then there shines the short Dolphin, which has few stars and
lies close to Capricorn; it carried the nymph, the daughter of
Atlas, to Neptune's marriage bed, taking pity on a lover.

We have told of the constellations which turn through the
ether in the upper part of the sky (325) and look upon the

north and are accustomed to gentle breezes. Now another order of signs is arrayed. It lies near the horizon and feels the hidden blast of the raging South Wind.

The first is Orion, who is whirled along beneath and at an angle to the breast of the Bull. No other constellation more accurately represents (330) the figure of a man than the stars scattered throughout his body. His head, mighty shoulders, fiery belt, scabbard and swift, lucent foot, and the Dog which guards him with its fearsome mouth are very bright. It belches forth fire from its mouth; its body is not as bright. (335) The Greeks have given the star in its mouth its own name, Sirius. When it lies near the sun's rays, summer blazes; when it rises, it affects crops in two very different ways: the healthy it strengthens, but that with shrivelled foliage or feeble roots, it kills. There is no star the farmer likes more or hates more. (340) He starts to observe it from its first appearance.

The Dog pursues the long-eared Hare, and it flees. Both constellations rise and set in the sea in this way. You will find the small Hare under Orion.

Where the Dog's tail, whose light is feeble, ends, (345) the stern of the Argo gleams with stars. It does not travel freely forwards, but is dragged by its stern, as happens when sailors approaching land hold their ship stationary by pulling on their oars and, now bound to fulfil their vows, tie the ship's stern to the shore, in their eagerness to touch the longed-for dry land. (350) The Argo shines in the sky because part of it was smashed when Jason escaped the clashing rocks through the divine power of Juno. Where the mast rises, there is no great bulk in the side; its form is cut away where the bow should be and there is nothing there. (355) Only the stern, with its rudder lowered, gleams.

From afar off the Sea Monster sent by the daughters of Nereus pursues Andromeda, exposed on the rocks. The path of the sun lies between them. Despite this, she is terrified by the monster of the sea. She rejoices, however, in her position in the other hemisphere near the stiff North Wind. (360) It is the South Wind that drives on the Sea Monster. This one constellation stretches alongside two, for the Ram and the Fishes are carried along above it. It does not extend much beyond the

River which wept over Phaethon, who, having lost control of his father's horses, had fallen into its waters, (365) Jupiter's flames issuing from his wound. His sisters, forming a new forest, and sorrowing over their arms, unknown to them before, also mourned him.

Eridanus flows in the middle of the gleaming stars. Part of this river flows along and strikes Orion's left foot. (370) The knot which alone connects the Fish, which lie far apart, shines above the crest of the Sea Monster. There are also free stars in the sky which do not, by their appearance, represent any shape. Some lie under the flank of the Hare, in other words behind the ship that travels stern foremost, and are situated between the coils of Eridanus and the helm of the Ship. (375) You can see that they form no figure. There are, furthermore, stars which form no part of the named constellations scattered throughout the sky between them. Although they lack their own constellation, they can be found by reference to the stars of one nearby.

There is also a Fish that swims alone, apart from the twin Fishes. (380) It shuns the north and travels entirely in the south; it lies under the belly of Capricorn and looks towards the lowest part of the Sea Monster. There are other stars, at the lowest point of the Water-Pourer, where his feet lie. The group of stars lying between the place where the Sea Monster's tail and that where the head of the Southern Fish turns (385) has no name, nor any reason for having one, so slight is the brightness of all of them that it is all but lost. Not far from here the Water-Carrier pours out water with his right hand and stars resembling splashing water fall from his pitcher. One, under the tail of the scaly Monster, shines brighter than the rest, (390) another lies under the feet of the sign pouring forth water. There is an unremarkable Garland a short distance in front of the Archer's swift legs.

Where the Scorpion turns the sting in his erect tail, you can see, near the South point and opposite Arcturus, the Altar with its sacred fire. (395) Arcturus' slowness to touch the Ocean in his setting compensates for the closeness of the incense-bearing Altar's turning posts to each other. The Altar has scarcely appeared in the sky before it is cast headlong in steep descent into the immense, seething Ocean. Nature has given man many sure signs to protect him (400) and has persuaded him by means of them to avoid disaster that is pressing upon him. The Altar can be numbered among the sure signs of trouble at night. If the other constellations of the sky are dimmed by a covering of clouds, but the Altar is gleaming, you should then be afraid of a violent South Wind destroying the calmness of the sea. (405) Then the yard-arm should be thickened by wrapping the sail around it, so as to allow the taut ropes to let the wind through the void left where the sails were. If, however, the wind catches the ship's slack sail and flaps it about, either the ship will tilt forwards and sink, sucking in the hostile sea at its bows, (410) or if Jupiter the saviour looks favourably upon them, the men who have been tossed about on the sea will just manage to fulfil their last vows for safety. Their fear will not leave them until the part of the sky is visible which shows men gazing upon it that a North Wind has sprung up.

There exists also the huge body of a Centaur, which lies next to fire. (415) His head, shaggy breast, and belly are those of a man and lie under the gleaming Claws. Beneath the Virgin there rises the huge sides, legs and shoulders of a Horse. In his right hand he either carries game from the woods or, (420) being a worshipper of Jupiter, is bringing to the nearby Altar gifts to appease the gods. This is that famous Chiron the pious, the most just of all those born from a cloud and the teacher of great Achilles. If a thin cloud accompanies him when his shoulder lies at the midpoint of his journey in the sky above and hides his human parts, (425) all his equine parts being visible, he announces the arrival of the East Wind.

Not far from here the Snake is drawn along. Its tail grazes the Centaur from above, its body lies under the Lion, its head extends towards the Crab. It adjoins three signs. The Mixing Bowl weighs down its first coils, (430) the Crow pecks at its further coils with its squawking beak. All of these constellations shine, the Crow with its feathers, the Mixing Bowl with its light weight and the Snake, extended over the space of three signs.

The Forerunner of the Dog rises with his gleaming light under the Twins.

These adornments of the sky are carried in it night and day. (435) Each constellation is allotted its place; all keep their positions once allotted and they do not change over a long period of time.

There are five other celestial bodies, which travel under a different law: they have their own movements and in their courses they sweep around in a circle in the opposite direction to the sphere of the fixed stars; they wander from the constellations they are in and change their positions. (440) You cannot find any other constellation where these gods have a permanent abode. They are often seen, rising and setting in continually changing places. Their paths are long; travelling slowly, they complete their journeys, measured in years, with difficulty. (445) Time, and the amount of effort involved, will show whether, fate permitting, I can afterwards direct this work into those erudite studies.

Four circles which, between them, indicate the divisions of a year, cut the zodiac, whose nature has been revealed. One, lying at an angle to the others and running between them, binds them together. They are not of the same length. Two of them are (450) equal to each other, and larger; there is another pair ... equal to each other, but smaller than the aforementioned. The latter pair always lie apart, the former are joined by constellations they have in common. These wheels bisect each other, just as if someone were cutting off two bows from each of them. (455) A fifth circle is seen in the clear night. It is unlike the others. While the stars, being apart from each other, emit a pure light, this circle is the colour of milk and shines as a road in the middle of the darkness. This milky way which revolves around in the sky is exceeded in length by none of these circles.

The circle which faces the north (460) and travels through regions high up near the neighbouring Bears, runs through the middle of the Twins, touches the feet of the Charioteer and crosses Perseus' left foot. Its passage cuts through both the flanks of Andromeda, who lies at a slant across it, and cuts off the whole of her right arm from the shoulder. The tip of the hoof of the spirited Horse strikes this road in the sky. (465) The gleaming white Swan's head lies near it. The part of the kneeling figure from the elbow shines above it, as do the Snake's first stars. The Maiden, however, escapes it. The Crab and the Lion lie entirely on it. It cuts the Lion's body right through from the loins, which face it as it approaches, (470) and comes out at the mane on his shaggy breast. The Crab's gleaming eyes are divided from each other as if a ruler ran between them and each belongs to a separate side. If a man were to divide this circle into eight parts, he would note that at any one time five would be shining above the earth, (475) three be hidden in the waves and concealed briefly by the shadows. When the sun touches the Crab on this circle, fear a devouring summer and diseases that weaken the body. At that time the sun reaches the topmost point of his everlasting journey. At no time does he drive his gleaming chariot closer to the zenith. (480) He struggles against the sky's hostility while he is attempting to reach his goal; from then on he is swept swiftly downwards. Capricorn holds the turning point of the sun's journey in winter within his icy stars, the Crab that of summer within his blazing sign.

The latter is nearer the North Wind, the other feels the blast of that of the South. (485) The circle that lies down in the south divides Capricorn in the middle and joins the knees of the Water-Pourer; the Sea Monster holds it fast in the coils of its tail; it touches the swift feet of the Hare and cuts the lowest part of the Dog's belly. It also cuts the ornamented stern of the sacred Ship, (490) the Centaur's shoulders and the Scorpion at the point where the tip of its tail, containing its sting, writhes. The large Bow gleams on it. There, the sun has left the north and is nearer the south. With his feeble light he brings cold winter. You will perceive three parts of this circle stretching in an arc across the sky; (495) five are hidden in the waves and carried in the long night.

Between and in the middle of these circles there travels a circle second to none in size. When the sun carries his gleaming fires on it, he apportions an equal period to night and day. This arrangement, which makes the sky's signs evenly balanced, occurs twice a year, (500) at the beginning of fertile spring and when summer is failing. Both the constellation of the Ram and that of the Bull are touched by this even circle, but all of the Ram, the leader of the signs, shines on it; only the Bull's shoulder and two stars of its bent leg lie on it. It cuts Orion through the middle, the first part of the (505) Snake's coils, the light Mixing Bowl and the end of the pecking Crow, where its stars fail in its black tail. You will find the Claws there, their stars forming a figure extending across it. You will also see there the middle of the lofty Snake and . . . in the middle, the Snake-Bearer, and not far from it, the Eagle. The whole head of burning (510) Pegasus lies on it and the circle adheres to its long neck. The axis runs straight along in the middle of and at right angles to these circles, whose course and constellations we are noting. Three of them revolve forever equidistant from each other. They can neither change their courses nor join their furrows. (515) The fourth lies at an angle to them and by itself binds together these three circles. It ties together the two opposite ones at its extremities; it bisects and is bisected in turn by the one between them. Not even if a man skilled in the arts of Pallas had fashioned these circles would the separate circles have been better joined by the one circle. (520) Three of them always rise in the same places; there are always the same fixed points where they set.

The fourth varies its place of rising from the Ocean (travelling at an angle to the others) by as much as Capricorn is distant from the Crab, bringer of heat. The variation (525) in its place of rising into the etherial breezes is as wide as that of its place of setting in the sacred waters. (530) [This last circle does not, however, escape mortal sight.] This circle is the sun's path, illuminated by the twelve signs.

The well-known Ram with the golden fleece is here. He it was who once carried Phrixus into the land of the Tauri and betrayed Helle. It was because of him that the ship Argo was fashioned. The treacherous Colchian Medea, (535) putting its guardian to sleep, gave his fleece to the object of her illicit passion. Here too is the horned Bull. Deceived by his appearance, Europa was bereft of her home and her virginity. Carried through the sea on his back, she realized his deception. She bore him offspring on the shore of Crete. (540) Here too are the Twins, who never went down to the underworld, but will always remain, a most favourable sign for sailors, in the sky, where the father of the gods himself put these young sons of Leda. The Crab too has been made a constellation, by Juno, daughter of Saturn, because it dared to bite Hercules, descended from

Alceus, when he was cutting down the prolific Hydra in close combat. (545) Juno's character never changed; she was ever a jealous mother-in-law towards him. Then, next to the Crab, comes the Lion of Nemea, then the dutiful Maiden. The next sign is the Scorpion, which occupies twice as much of the zodiac as the other signs; with the addition of its Claws, it gleams with a doubled radiance. (550) The goddess will sing to me of the Scorpion after Orion has first been mentioned. Coming after it, bent in an arc, lies the pliant Bow of the Arrow-Bearer, whose custom it was to entreat the Muses' favour by clapping; received into heaven, he carries the same gleaming weapons that Phoebus carries. There follows the discoverer of the conch; (555) the happier age of the gods, accompanied by its blast, followed warring Jupiter into battle against the giants. It received the reward of its support of the just cause in stellification, with the same double form it had on earth. In the midst of an awe-struck, quaking throng of foreigners and your own people, Augustus, you were carried into the sky on the body of this sign, under which you were born, (560) and returned to your mother stars. The next sign, Deucalion, pours forth water, that hostile element he once fled, and in so doing draws attention to his small pitcher. The Fishes, twin gods of Syria, complete the year. Then the order I have already given begins again. (565) [The Wool-Bearer, the Bull, the Twins, then the Crab, the Lion, the Maiden, the Scorpion, the Bow-Bearer, cold Capricorn, the Water-Carrier and the two Fishes] (526) If one were to divide the zodiac into six equal parts, the length of each straight line so formed would be found to be less than that of the arc encompassing two signs and equal to the distance between the circumference and the earth. As much of the zodiac shines in the clear air above as lies sunk in the deep waters of Ocean below. (570) Every night six signs, never fewer, are being drawn through the sky at any one time; no night is longer than the time taken for a bow cut off from the complete circle of the zodiac to travel into the air above.

You must often wish to know how much of the night remains and console yourself with the thought of the coming light. (575) The first indication of the sun's position is the sign it is travelling in, because Phoebus always shines in only one sign.

Look then at the other signs, noting what stars belong to each and which of them are rising, setting or culminating and how long each takes to rise when it leaves the azure sea (580) (some leap forth swiftly, others are carried up more sluggishly and leave the Ocean at a slow pace). If the zodiac, the path of the sun, happens to be hidden by an engulfing cloud, or the sign in its ascent into the sky is concealed by the peak of lofty Athos, of Cyllene, snow-white Haemus, (585) by the Gargaron of Ida, or Olympus, abode of the gods, then, if you know the constellations that are rising with it, on the right and the left, you will always know what time of night it is and when dawn will come.

When it is beginning to allow the Crab out into the air, (590) the Ocean receives the plaited Cretan Garland; the Southern Fish sets, tail first, as far as its back; all of the Serpent-Bearer's shoulders are submerged; only the tip of Snake's tail shines; the sea holds its fearsome coils. The Guardian of the Bears does not remain here much longer than these constellations. (595) His feet are submerged when the Scorpion's stars are just beginning to sink beneath the waves; nevertheless, his head stays aloft while the Goat, stiff with cold, brings terror to the clear sea. Even then, the Ploughman, sated with the light of the stars, scarcely manages to set and ⟨tarrying⟩ more than ⟨half⟩ the night ⟨at length⟩ leaves ⟨the sky.⟩ (600) The whole of Orion, lacking none of his stars and with glittering shoulders, lies in the opposite part of the sky; the god has a large scabbard and a belt engraved with brilliant light. There too Eridanus lifts both his horns into the clear heavens.

When the first star on the Lion's mane shines, (605) all those constellations which were partly visible when the Crab was rising, entirely set beneath the waves and flee the jaws of the rising beast. Jupiter's Bird, with its star-studded wings, sets completely, but the kneeling figure worn out with toil is immersed in the waters only as far as his shank; the head of the monstrous Snake, (610) the Swift Hare, the Forerunner of the Dog, Sirius himself and, of the whole of the swift Dog, the fore-feet, return to the sky.

Learn now the constellations which shun the Maiden as she rises; the Dolphin will then have already sunk into the waters it knows so well, likewise the sweet-sounding Lyre and the Arrow, girt with flames. (615) The snow-white Swan will have hastened to touch the waves; scarcely even the part of its flying wings near the tail is illuminated. The river Po grows black, for it is very near the earth. Then the Steed hides its head and all its neck; in the opposite quarter, the Snake is carried higher, (620) to where the Mixing Bowl is placed. The stern of the ship the Argo and the whole of the Dog arise; when the dutiful Maiden has risen as far as her feet, that famous ship shines, mainmast and all.

The rising of the Claws will also be marked by its own signs. Then the Ploughman, with all his hairlike rays, leaps forth from the Ocean; (625) Arcturus, by the brilliance of his countenance, announces his coming; the Ship occupies the regions above the horizon, as does the Snake, though minus its tail. The kneeling figure returns aloft as far as his bent shank. The rest of him has not yet struggled forth from the borders of invisibility and he keeps the upper part of his knee inverted alongside the Lyre. He shows himself in the heavens twice in the one night. (630) He follows the sun's chariot as it sets, while the long night is beginning and flees from the Ocean as it rises. His shank is visible when the Claws begin to shine; when the Scorpion comes forth, (635) this bent form is brought forth into the heavens as far as his back. When the son of Philyra is rising from his grandfather's waters, then the whole of this wretched sign gleams. Part only of the twisted Garland then returns to the sky and the tip of the tail of noble Chiron can be recognized. Pegasus hides his wings and all the rest of his body. The Swan's tail no longer shines, but follows its breast, which has already set. The maiden (640) Andromeda hides her face; the huge Sea Monster sets, fiercely pursuing it. His crest still shines in the sky. King Cepheus hides his head, but is otherwise untouched by the waves.

The Scorpion does not begin to rise before the famous River has disappeared; (645) it puts Orion to flight and he fears its pursuit. Look favourably upon a poet, I beseech you, Diana. I am not the first to write of this; poets of old have done so before me. They have told how a man once dared to touch the undefiled garments of the maiden goddess and so defiled her sacred virginity. (650) This impious man was then doomed to punishment and tried to kill off all the wild creatures in the sacred woods with a tree trunk and hand over Chios, thus tamed, as a gift to Oenopion. But the sister of Phoebus could not endure this, and caused the earth to split open suddenly and bring forth an avenger of her injured deity, (655) a scorpion, which she set against the huge Orion as an even more formidable foe.

Desist, mortals, the anger of the gods is never mild. Wretched Orion still fears being wounded by the poisonous sting of the Scorpion and, as if part of his punishment were still to come, flees its weapon; nevertheless, he is already setting (660) when the Scorpion is touching the eastern horizon with his burning breast. None of Andromeda is left, nor does any of the Sea Monster enjoy the light. The mass of the ever revolving sky draws Cassiepia down and drags the rest of her after her head and shoulders, and she falls into the sea, her beauty spoiled. With it she once vied (665) with the daughters of the old man of the sea, when, in her folly, she had looked upon the ritual performances of Doris and Panope from the Canchlian shore. She sets in the Ocean. The whole Garland returns to the sky and all the Snake frees itself from the darkness. Chiron's feet are still obscured and await the rising of the Bow; (670) his whole head and body are already visible. Then the Beast which the Centaur carries in his right hand comes forth into the sky, the Snake is revealed and his coils are clearly visible and all of the kneeling figure, except for his left hand, leaves the sea.

When the Bow begins to return from beneath the waves (675) Chiron has already lifted his swift feet, now dry, from the Ocean and the Snake-Bearer is gleaming among the stars above. None of the slithering Snake is invisible and, recovering his hand, the misshapen figure lacks none of his parts. Already the Lyre and the Swan's right wing are with the stars above the horizon. (680) Then Cepheus just scrapes the earth with his sign in his return. The Dog conceals all its stars, Orion is hidden and the Hare, ever safe, lies in the waves. But the rear part of the ship the Argo, where the sign is fashioned into a curved stern, still shines. (685) Perseus and the well-known Goat star set.

All the Charioteer sets when Capricorn begins to rise; so too all the ornamented stern of the Ship, which holds the tutelary deity for which it is reverenced. Then the Forerunner of the Dog departs into darkness; the Bird with curved claws, that carries weapons and is more pleasing to Jupiter than all the others, returns. (690) All the Swan's stars, the light Arrow, the little Dolphin and the Altar equipped for sacred rites, return; the Garland less renowned than the Cretan one also rises.

The Water-Pourer, in his ascent into the sky, summons Pegasus, who trusts in his wings, to rise up with him as far as his mouth and his neck. (695) Chiron is drawn backwards beneath the waves into the black region of invisibility; his tail is dipped into the Ocean, which has not yet received his head, monstrous shoulders or breast marred by bristles. It hides more than half the Water Snake; a third of it still shines.

The rising of the Fishes hides all the Water Snake and the twy-formed Centaur. (700) When the South Wind summons the twin Fishes, the Fish which looks upon the gloomy South also rises. It rises with the Fishes, completing its rising when the swift Ram lifts his horns into the sky. The Fishes bring forth Cepheus' daughter. Joyfully she (705) escapes the sea and the daughters of Nereus and is carried into the sky.

The Wool-Bearer at his rising hastens to hide the sacred Incense-Bearer; Perseus shines in his native element, the air . . .

When his wings are restoring Perseus to the air, the Pleiades escape from the waves and can be recognized in the Bull's right shoulder. (710) Myrtilos is carried along stuck on the Bull's horn and without any chariot. You cannot see all of him; the whole of him has not yet returned to the sky; his right side is still immersed in the waves. His head shines; his left hand carries the tiny Kids; Jove's nurse shines at his shoulder; (715) his left foot rises nearest the earth; the rest of him appears with the Twins, completing his constellation.

The Sea Monster's crest and tail alike gleam when the Bull rises; then you can see the Ploughman near the earth.

The setting of the Snake Bearer as far as his knees (720) will be a sign that the Twins have left the Ocean and returned. All the Sea Monster's scaly body then gleams; let the sailor then perceive the source of the river Eridanus as he gazes at the sky, while Orion lifts himself from the clear horizon. He gives an indication of the time of night (725) and whether the winds will be fierce or there will be a calm one can trust.

Fragment ii

The sun has but one path, lit by the twelve signs. Along it the moon too is hurried; Venus is carried along the same path, as are Mars with his plumed helmet, swift Mercury, (5) Jupiter, to be reverenced because of his rule over the sky and slow Saturn, whose light is dismal. Two forces affect all of them: one is innate and shows the planets' own proper motions in a sign (under its influence they travel around the heavens at a slow pace); the other force seizes upon them against their will—it carries around the sky. (10) The sun, which is in the middle of them, defines the length of the year, the moon that of a month. You can see that the sun takes a year to return to the place from which he began his journey through the signs in his flying chariot. The moon travels this distance more quickly and the period of a complete revolution is shorter for her; she is content to add day to day to make a month. (15) The period Venus takes to complete her journey is a year. Mercury is no slower than her. Mars completes one revolution every two years. While the father of the gods above is travelling though the twelve signs, the sun will have already completed twelve annual journeys . . . All change their velocity: at one time you would think they were hastening and had speeded up, at another that they had become sluggish . . .

Fragments iii and iv

The Ram scatters dreary rain mixed with hail and falling snow over the nearby ridges. The Bull carries water and arouses violent winds. Under him Jupiter often casts his thunderbolts, (5) the sky is violent, fires are sent from it, and it thunders. Under the Twins winds gently caress the azure sky and moisture seldom travels down from sky to earth. Everything grows mild under the peaceful sign of the Crab. The Lion is dry, seeing that his breast is particularly hot. (10) The Maiden returns water and stirs the air into activity with winds. The Balance is a gentle sign; scarcely even dew falls under it. The Scorpion continually threatens the sky with fire and fierce winds; they are often stiff from the dense snow. (15) Under the Bow-Bearer breezes seldom descend to earth; he is milder as regards rain and finds the earth quieter. Capricorn spares in other respects, but hardens the cold, permitting men's feet to become unsteady and slip on the ice. The being who pours forth water also excites rain in heaven. Under the Fishes everything is mixed together: (20) the sea, churned up by the wind, rolls its seething waves towards the stars; the sky is heavy with showers and hides the sun, the earth is smitten by hail and covered by hard snow.

The god who occupies a particular sign at a particular time adds his own influences: everything seems to be torpid under Saturn. (25) He seldom draws lightning from the clouds, but makes the winters dry throughout, covering the waters with ice. Rain congeals into hail; from the presence of snow, hail is dissolved and the winds become harsher. He is the most sluggish of the gods. (iv 1) Jupiter is more propitious than he is. When he has escaped the sun's flames and his own countenance is visible . . . you will see the crops that were entrusted to Ceres springing up and the fruit beginning to form its brightly coloured flower; (5) your cattle will not disappoint you in their breeding; suddenly there will be a great many calves lowing in their enclosures and lambs bleating in the high-fenced fold.

When he touches the horns of the savage Bull, Jupiter will grant rain, so that the earth does not become too dry and deprive the crops of moisture. When he leaves the Pleiads (10) and enters the Twins, he draws up the moisture he has given. In the Crab he is very mild; his influence is moderating and tempers the consuming heat. Under the father of the gods the terrible Lion himself wards off imminent diseases and closes the gates of the underworld. When in the Maiden, Jupiter lets the farmers pay their vows. (15) Then the crops are already ripe and a garland made of ears of wheat hangs at the front of the house, when the harvest has been completed. The Balance ripens well the clusters of grapes, swelling with juice. Entering the Scorpion, Jupiter stores the gifts of Bacchus; while climbing the Archer, he gives his cold (20) to winter, making it perpetually gloomy; in Capricorn, however, he is more moderate. He is very harsh when exercising sway over the Water-Pourer and the Fishes. If he halts his chariot, wearied, in one of the signs—if in the Wool-Bearer or the African Lion, he thunders—to all the signs he gives months of wintry weather.

(25) When Mars has escaped the sun's fires, whether it be the Ram, Twins, the fierce Lion, the Claws with their level balance, the being skilled with the bow or the Pourer of Water who contains the god, the air will be covered in a thick blinding mantle of dense clouds (30) and there will be no headlong winds to churn up the sea. When the War-Bearer brings his fiery orb to a standstill and holds his chariot locked in immobility in one of these signs, then the expanse of the sky will be shattered by frequent thunderclaps; clouds will burst and discharge rain and hail. (35) But on the other hand, when he has come to a halt in one of the signs of the wintry part of the zodiac, he will pour forth all the powers that his violent godhead can command. Nevertheless, he will not be harsh, but will pour forth from the gleaming sky only a moderate amount of rain, when he touches the horns of the Bull with head held low, the wheat-bearing Goddess or wintry Capricorn. (40) Carried into the Crab, he will moderate the baneful influence of Sirius' heat when Sirius at his rising breathes his deadly influence over the earth. When he is placed in the Scorpion, which lifts up the sting in its tail in its search for victims, or in the Fishes, which conclude the cold signs of winter, he does not disturb them, (45) nor does he hide the sunlight of the sparkling days with showers or any obscuring medium. If, however, the prevailing atmosphere is overcome and changes the day's weather, and pours winds onto the water, the sea will then be bitingly cold and the North Wind will dominate the whole world.

(50) Nurturing Venus, shining in the sign with the gleaming fleece and rising before dawn, binds the soil, normally easy to work, into clods, under the influence of the cold of spring. Rising at the same time and climbing onto the Bull of the sky, she hides the earth with black rain, thunder and frequent hail. She makes the weather more moderate when she is in the Twins. (55) Neither clear skies nor clouds will last long when she gleams in the sign of the burning Crab: nothing is certain at that time. Shining mildly, she moderates the burning heat when she takes up her abode within the borders of the Nemean

sign. In the case of the Maiden and the Balance there are (60) clouds which tend to stay more in the one unchanging place, always merely threatening. The sky is also unreliable when Venus lies above the fierce Scorpion, for nothing then follows a fixed law. With what violent rain does Jupiter then overwhelm all the lands! The pitiless hail then comes down through the atmosphere in a dense, continuous stream (65) and it thunders frequently.

When Venus enters the territory of the sign which threatens to shoot its arrows, rain falls on the earth and winds agitate the sea. The sounds of the heavens terrify the hearts of men when Venus touches the abode of the being with goat's horns. (70) The watery sign of Aquarius presages cold showers; wintry rains and hard hail fall down from the twin Fishes while she is travelling back to the first sign of the zodiac. Nurturing Venus gives these effects when, as morning star, she rises when dawn ⟨reddens the sky,⟩ but when, as the evening star, (75) she summons the fires of the sky and begins to bring night upon the earth, she will, in her appearance, give you the monitions that follow. In spring you must beware of rain and jagged flashes of lightning. When she shines in the golden sign of Phrixus' Ram, there will be clouds and thunder mixed with rain and (80) winds battering the world with their never-ending blasts and an attack of pitiless hail from the sky above. When Venus shines in the Bull at a time that spring is more attractive . . . The same unsettled weather persists in the Twins: after giving periods of sunshine, she brings clouds into the sky: (85) when clouds have gone, you will look in wonder on the sudden appearance of the sun. Now it will be windy, now there will be cold showers and immediately afterwards it will be fine. Venus will vary fine with overcast weather. If the goddess, fickle though she is, enters the extensive territory of the Crab, the world will be peaceful; the sun will not (90) burn men with its pestilential heat, nor will signs densely packed with stars shrivel their weakened frames; the atmosphere will be mild at a time when it shouldn't be and will temper everything under the influence of this tranquil sign. Venus prevents the world from being parched by the burning sun when she is visible in the sign of the mighty Lion.

(95) Under the Maiden there will be rain and the mighty

sound of thunder in the clouds, emitted from these hollow bodies due to the wind locked in them. Venus will deprive autumn of rain but fill it with unbroken clouds, when the Claws are overcoming the last of autumn's mildness with its first icy cold. (100) The Scorpion, however, is seldom marred by rain— thus the earth, which holds rain, is not then weighed down by it. But Venus overwhelms everything with hard and incessant rain when she is carried across the curved horns of the Centaur's bow, which is fitted with a swift arrow. The being with goat's horns brings rain and forces out a sound from clouds burst by frequent thunderbolts (105) and overwhelms men's vision with the shimmering brilliance of Jupiter's burning weapon. Aquarius, who pours forth showers of water, predicts the same. When Venus marks its position, the last constellation, the Fishes, shows a sea swelling from its buffeting by cruel winds.

(110) Since you now know the exact effects Venus produces, learn now what effects Mercury, the god of Mount Cyllene, produces in the world, when he has just escaped the flames of the sun's chariot and is travelling in his accustomed path through the constellations of the morning. When he shines in the sign of the Ram with the golden fleece, (115) there arise violent and angry winds and merciless hail, that must be endured without a break. You will notice that there is also rain coming in some region or other; it does not fall then on every field. His journey to the curved horns of the Bull is indicated by hail. (120) In the Twins he promises fine weather for the sower and a tranquil sea and sky for the sailor. ⟨In the Crab⟩ . . . clouds and showers; he mingles heat and cold. But it will be consistently hot, despite the cooling effect of the West Wind, when he shines in the fiery abode of the monstrous Lion. (125) But when he occupies the sacred dwelling place of fiery Astraea, he brings all kinds of weather mixed together; in the Balance, however, rain only. The Scorpion threatens rain; everywhere there is wind and hail; thunder bursts from the clouds. When the god of Mount Cyllene has touched the Bow of the Centaur (130) or climbed into the abode of twy-formed Capricorn, he will either bring sudden and frequent showers down from the sky or burst the mighty heavens by hurling a thunderbolt. The Phrygian youth who pours forth water brings no clouds into the

serene heavens. (135) There is no other sign under which you can be more sure of cool winds and sounds in the sky, although one can recognize the same phenomena under the Fishes.

Since I have told you what the fire of the god of Mount Cyllene effects when it rises with the first light of the sun, it is time to learn also what it effects at the setting of the sun. (140) There will be a spring entirely cursed with winter rains and frequent thunder; this will overcome the flourishing countryside and the hope of a new harvest will be flattened by the force of the hail and blighted by frost, when, while entering the realm of the mighty thunderer, he climbs onto the back of the Ram. (145) Following on this, if you diligently enquire what the star-studded horns of the Agenorean Bull, the Twins, or the Crab with his raging sign, effects, you will perceive that the Bull rages with hail and that Mercury proceeds in the Crab and the Twins in the same discreditable manner. (150) But he will burn with cruel heat when he lies where the fiery Lion has planted his feet. The just goddess with an ear of wheat in her hand mingles tranquil calm with cold winds. The Balance does not dissent from the goddess who carries it, but, like her, announces that calm will return and the sea and the sky are free from the effect of wind. (155) The Scorpion seldom brings showers, but when Mercury touches the bright stars of the Bow-Bearer, he often brings rain down from the black clouds and carries cruel thunder. Under the being with goat's horns, gentle showers fall continually from the sky. Cold Aquarius shivers from the effects of the raging East Wind; (160) he causes winter rain to fall and clouds to be smitten with a rending sound and perpetual fire. If my labours do not deceive my enquiring mind, but are leading me along a reliable path, the Fish will certainly exhibit the same signs.

Fragment v

Mighty Atlas, skilled in calculation, made the stars and the celestial spheres known to all peoples and calculated exactly all the movements of the planets. Men from Egypt and Tyre, using his discoveries, ⟨ventured onto⟩ the sea at the beginning of spring . . . (5) Aeolus divided the world into parts, allotting all the winds and breezes their own. ⟨He showed⟩ in what direction

Boreas drives down the rain clouds, from what direction Notus drives them up, from what abodes Eurus and Zephyrus proceed against the waves. He arrayed these brothers in a ring against the sea.

Fragment vi

I do not see why I should not pass you over, Greece, with your rich language, and call them *triangula* instead.

COMMENTARY

1–16 The author has romanized Aratus' invocation of Zeus (1–18) into an invocation of the *princeps*. See section 6 of the Introduction (Identity of the author and date of the poem).

6 Sol . . . rapidissimus There is no need to emend to *rabidissimus*. *Rapidus* is used as an epithet of *sol* in Verg. *G*. 1.92, 1.424 and 2.321.

9 I have preferred *parta* to *tanta* as it is the reading of both μ and *Z̧*. If *tanta* is right, *parta* is a variant which has found its way into both μ and *Z̧*, *tanta* disappearing without a trace. But *tanta* is much more probably a corruption of *parta*, perhaps from reminiscence of Verg. *G*. 2.344, which begins *si non tanta quies*.

11 I have preferred *Z̧*'s *ad* to *O*'s *in*, for *tollere ad caelum (aethera) . . . uultus (ora, oculos)* is the regular expression. At Ou. *Fast*. 4.315 (*ter tollit ad (in) aethera palmas*) the manuscripts are divided between *in* and *ad*. In favour of *in*, it could be argued that *in* is sometimes used as the equivalent of *ad* (cf. the large number of examples from all periods quoted by *TLL* 7.1.738.50ff) and that *in* could have fallen out after *is* and the gap been filled in with *ad* in *Z̧*.

12 While *Z̧*'s *agnoscere* may be possible here (cf. the *Oxford Latin Dictionary* on the use of the word), *cognoscere* is clearly suitable, and is the reading of *O*, which is more often right than *Z̧*, where they can be compared with each other (cf. section 3 of the Introduction). I have always printed *O*'s reading in preference to *Z̧*'s where I can see nothing to choose between them. As *O* is more often right than *Z̧*, it is reasonable to expect that one will be more often right than wrong if one follows it where there is no other criterion than *O*'s authority available.

15 *Z̧*'s *cogor* is unsuitable, as nothing is forcing the author to write in Latin rather than Greek. If the author is Tiberius, he would not have made such a complaint (cf. section 6 of the Introduction), if Germanicus, in view of Tiberius' liking for others to use Latin, it would be a most impolitic thing to say. *Conor* is entirely suitable, and agrees with preludes in other didactic poems: Lucr. 1.25 *conor*, Ou. *Fast*. 1.15 *conanti*, Manil. 3.4 *conor*, Gratt. 22 *nisus*, *Aetna* 24 *molimur* (all quoted by Housman, p. 29/499).

16 numenque secundes This = *fac ut numen tuum secundum sit* (Goodyear). I can find no exact parallel for this usage. Cf. however Verg. *Aen*. 7.259–60 *di nostra incepta secundent/auguriumque suum*, Ou. *Her*. 13.136 *blandaque compositas aura secundet aquas*, Verg. *G*. 3.296–7 *ut omnem/expediat morbi causam euentusque secundet* (*euentus* is acc.pl.).

26 *Plaustra* is an alternative to *Vrsae*, hence *ue*, not *que*, is required.

26 quae facies stellarum proxima uerae. *Est* must be understood, and also *faciei* with *uerae*, from *facies* earlier in the line. *Stellarum* goes with *uerae faciei*, not with *facies*, for ploughs are not 'a shape, consisting of stars'.

Z's *uero* must be rejected as, with it, *stellarum* has to be construed with *facies*. *O*'s *uera* is an assimilation to the case of the previous word, *proxima*. I suggest *Z*'s *uero* is a conjecture of a man who had *uera* in his text.

26–7 *Plaustraue* is based on Aratus' Ἅμαξαι (line 27), but the rest of 26–7 and *si melius dixisse feras* in 28 are additions to him. The contents of 26 are similar to *Arat. Schol.* p. 345.11–12, ed. Maass: 'They look like carts, but according to the legend they are bears.' Compare the contents of 27 with *Arat. Schol.* p. 345.15–16: 'There being four stars representing the wheels, three the pole.' Cf. also *Souda* ρ 295: 'A pole: . . . also the three stars in the Bear's tail, according to Heraclitus'). The pole (*temo*) is defined by Varro *L.L.* 7.75 as the thing that holds together the yoke and the cart.

30 *Orbis* and *axis* are both suitable. *Axis* often means 'the sky' (cf. e.g. Verg. *Aen.* 4.481–2 *maximus Atlas/axem umero torquet stellis ardentibus aptum*), but here it could also mean 'the axis', as this turns the sky.

31 The dative case *ueteri . . . famae* seems to me better than the transmitted genitive *ueteris . . . famae*. *Veteris si gratia famae* (= 'if the charm pertaining to the old tale really exists') puts the emphasis on *gratia* and seems to imply that this charm can have some sort of objective existence outside the mind of the hearer. *Veteri si gratia famae* (= 'if there is charm in the old tale' i.e. 'if you are prepared to accept the old tale') gives the right emphasis. *Est* is understood with the clause. *Veteri* became *ueteris* by the addition of an *s*, under the influence of the following word, *si*.

35 The transmitted *fouerunt* (3rd person) refers to *uos* in line 32 (2nd person); the persons should be the same, hence either *fouerunt* should be emended to *fouistis* (Housman) or *uos* to *eas*, referring to *feras* in 28, as Schmidt, in his edition of 1728 (*teste* Breysig). Housman's conjecture is much better as (1) *istis* could easily have fallen out before *iouis*, and the gap been filled with *erunt*, (2) the change of *eas* to *uos*, whether accidental or deliberate, is not very likely, (3) masculine and feminine plurals of *is* are rare in poetry of our author's period. The only form to be found in his poem is *eos* (at 304). After *fouistis*, as Housman remarks, the 3rd person is regained by means of the proper names *Helice Cynosuraque* in line 39.

36–7 are an addition to Aratus. Callimachus *Hymn.* 1.51–4 gives the same story as our author, but mentions shields, not *cymbala*.

38 There is no reason to suspect *Corybantes* because the word Arat. 35 uses is Κούρητες (Curetes). Our author has taken these two to be synonymns (cf. Strabo 10.3.7 'Some say the Curetes and the Corybantes are the same').

Dictaeae texere deae could be got from the readings of μ and ν, line 38 then meaning 'the Corybantes, servants of the goddess of Dicte, hid him'. The goddess of Dicte would be Rhea, or Cybele, the mother of Jupiter. The Corybantes were her *famuli* (cf. Serv. *in Aen.* 3.111 *Corybantes* δαίμονες *sunt, ministri matris deum*). Cybele is nowhere else, as far as I know, called *Dictaea*, although she is called *Idaea parens* in Ou. *Fast.* 4.182, *Idaea mater* in Lucr. 2.611 and Verg. *Aen.* 9.619–20. Ovid, however, insists on her Phrygian connections (i.e. associates her with the Ida near Troy, not the one in Crete) with *Berecyntia* in 181, Lucretius with *Phrygiasque cateruas* and Vergil with

Phrygiae in 617. But such a mention of Cybele corresponds with nothing in Aratus and the corruption of *deae* or *dei* to *Z*'s *datis* is less likely than the reverse.

Far more likely that the author wrote *Dictaeis texere adytis*, corresponding closely with Arat. 35–6 Δίκτῃ ἐν εὐώδει/. . . ἄντρῳ ἐγκατέθεντο ('They placed him in a cave on fragrant Mt Dicte'). Cf. also Verg. *G.* 4.152 *Dictaeo caeli regem pauere sub antro*. The rare word *adytis* is liable to corruption, first to *datis* (preserved in *Z*) and then further in *O*. *Deae* probably arose from *dei* under the influence of *dictaeae* before it.

48 abrupti fluminis instar This renders οἵη ποταμοῖο ἀπορρώξ (Arat. 45). Both phrases mean 'like a portion of a river'. Aratus has taken ἀπορρώξ from Homer (cf. *Od.* 10.514). All he means is that the Snake's course is like a river's. The noun ἀπορρώξ is connected with the verb ἀπορρήγνυμι (= 'break off'), hence our author uses *abrupti* from the Latin *abrumpo*, with the same meaning as the Greek verb. Our author's phrase results from a close adherence to his original, and is only comprehensible by referring to it.

49 I can see nothing, except *O*'s authority, to choose between *torquet* and *uersat*. *Versat* could have been written in imitation of Verg. *Aen.* 5.407–8 *magnanimusque Anchisiades et pondus et ipsa/. . . uolumina uersat* or *Aen.* 11.753 *saucius at serpens sinuosa uolumina uersat* or it could have been interpolated from a memory of these lines. *Torquet* is used of a snake's coils by Ou. *Met.* 3.41–2 *ille uolubilibus squamosos nexibus orbes/torquet*. *Volumina uersat* introduces alliteration, a device used frequently by our author (cf. e.g. *mirabile monstrum* at the end of the next line and *et Coruus pennis et paruo pondere Crater* in 431), but this does not seem sufficient reason for preferring it to *O*'s *torquet*.

50 mirabile monstrum is used parenthetically of the situation as μέγα θαῦμα is in the corresponding passage of Aratus (line 46). Cf. also Verg. *Aen.* 9.120–2 *hinc uirgineae (mirabile monstrum)/reddunt se totidem facies pontoque feruntur* (line 121 is spurious).

51 cauda could be either nominative or ablative, the sense being the same. The elision of the long *a* of the ablative before a short syllable can be defended from that of *ae* in iv 20.

Redit was omitted in *O* because of the similarity of its letters to the preceding *tendit*. After its omission *tendit* was taken with *ad Cynosuran* and *superat* fashioned out of *supra* to provide a verb for *cauda Helicen*. *Supra* also occurs in the line above, but this is no objection to it here. Cf. my note on the *instantis/instantia* repetition in 302 and 304 (two consecutive lines).

53 flexu . . . alto The coil of the Serpent, which encompasses the Little Bear, seems to be lifted high into the air, like his head; whereas the portion between the head and this coil, and also the tail, seem to touch the ground.

58–60 The corresponding passage of Aratus (58–60) states that 'His head is tilted, very much as if he were nodding to the tip of Helice's tail; his mouth and right temple are in line with the tip of Helice's tail'. The transmitted text of our author mentions the stars of the Serpent and Great Bear mentioned by Aratus, but not that the Serpent's stars seem to point to the Bear. As the sense is incomplete without this, I have followed Courtney in printing a lacuna between *mento* and *lucetque*.

60–2 Arat. 61–2 states that 'Its head travels where the most extreme points of rising and setting blend'. The further north a star is, the nearer to the north, and the nearer to each other, are the points at which it rises and sets. When a star is x° from the north pole, it never sets for an observer at latitude x° north, but just touches the horizon. Its points of rising and setting have become one.

Hac . . . qua can be restored from Aratus' τῇ . . . ἤχι (61). L's *utque* in 61 arose from a dittography of the preceding *ut* in *caput*. The *quae* of *OE* is an alteration of *qua* to agree with the following *proxima signa. Proxima signa/ occasus ortusque* = 'the nearby points of rising and setting' (cf. 521 *atque eadem occasus remanent certissima signa:* 'there are always the same fixed points where they set', where *occasus* is also a genitive dependent on *signa*). The whole sentence means 'Where the head of the setting Snake shines, the nearby points of rising and setting are touched by the one head' i.e. part of the Snake's head never sets, but just touches the horizon where the other part of the head rises and sets. This statement was only true for a latitude about 36° north. Aratus does not mention the setting of any part of the Snake, but Cicero's text (Fr. X ed. Buescu *hoc caput hic paulum sese subitoque recondit/ortus ubi atque obitus parte admiscentur in una:* 'a little bit of this head unexpectedly sets, in the region where rising and setting are mingled together') is similar to our author's, his statement being probably a reworking of Cicero's. Probably Cicero's statement goes back to the astronomer Attalus (quoted by Hipparch. p. 34.17–21).

63–4 These lines are an expansion of Arat. 48. *Sunt* is understood, as Breysig remarks (*apparatus*, ed. 2).

66 This constellation is not distinguished from the others by a lack of a *numen*, but of a *nomen*, hence Morel's *nomen* is required. But the text *non illi nomen, non magni causa laboris* is still not satisfactory. Housman (p. 31/502) remarks 'This is a bold and strange assertion, that the labour of Engonasin has no cause. Aratus says nothing of the kind; he says that its cause is unknown: 64 sq.' Housman accordingly conjectured *cognita* for *magni*. After *ta* was lost before *ca*, the non-word *cogni* was corrected to *magni*. This word has also been introduced by conjecture or accident at 206 (duri *OZ* magni τ) and 389 (flamma μZ magna ν). Housman commends a further conjecture, communicated to him by Postgate, as follows: 'But this change [*magni* to *cognita*] though necessary in itself, renders *illi* ambiguous, so Dr Postgate corrects *ulli*'. The ambiguity is that *cognitum* may or may not be understood with *nomen* from *cognita*. If it is understood, *illi* must be understood with *cognita*. The sense is thus either 'It has no name and why it toils is unknown' or 'It does not know its own name or why it toils'. But the second alternative is unsatisfactory. It either states that the constellation is suffering from amnesia or that its labour has in fact no cause (the very statement that Housman rightly objects to above). With *ulli*, ambiguity is removed. *Cognitum* must be understood with the first statement, *ulli* with the second, the meaning being 'No one knows its name or the cause of its toil', *non ulli* corresponding to Aratus' οὔτις, the sense being the same as in Aratus.

67 dextro . . . genu nixus Aratus (66–7) says that he is crouching on his knees (pl), Cicero (Fr. XI ed. Buescu) agreeing with him. Hipparchus has no note on Aratus here, nor does the scholia. Ptolemy's star catalogue, however, agrees with our author. It describes a figure kneeling on his right knee and standing on his left foot. See also my note on 274.

68 Our author's *passis ad numina palmis* (an addition to Aratus) is probably in imitation of Verg. *Aen.* 3.263–4 *pater Anchises passis de litore palmis/numina magna uocat.* The details are found in Hygin. *Astron.* p. 41.18–21 ed. Bunte *Araethus autem, ut ante diximus, hunc Cetea Lycaonis filium, Megistus patrem, dicit; qui uidetur, ut lamentans filiam in ursae figuram conuersam, genu nixus palmas diuersas tendere ad caelum, ut eam sibi dii restituant.*

69 Aratus (70) states that his right foot treads the Serpent. Our author agrees with the correction by Hipparch. 1.2.6. Either could be right, depending on whether Engonasin is facing towards, or away from, the observer.

69 *Laeua* Grotius, *scaeua* Buhle, but poets of our author's time avoided short vowels before initial consonant collocations such as *sc*, nor is *scaeuus* found in our poem (*laeuus* occurs 14 times).

70 *Super* does not scan. *Subter* agrees with Arat. 71–3.

71 clara This translates Aratus' ἀγαυὸν(71). But the Garland is not very bright. The magnitudes of the eight stars included in it by Ptolemy are 2.23, 3.66, 3.84, 4.15, 4.22, 4.64, 5.02 and 5.43. Hipparchus' commentary actually mentions six stars, not mentioning the two faintest.

73 The transmitted *terga nitent stellis* ('his back gleams with stars') fails to render Arat. 74 ('The Garland is near his back'), although the following renders Aratus' statement about the position of Ophiuchus relative to Engonasin. Hence Breysig (ed. 2) conjectured *Sertis* for *stellis*. The plural *Serta* is used of the constellation in line 85. Dahms conjectured *Serta nitent tergis* (misreported by Breysig). The plural *terga* is used of Engonasin in line 70. But Dahms' conjecture involves altering two words; I have preferred Breysig's, which alters only one.

74 *O*'s *lapsum* indicates that the figure has already sunk to its knees, which have given way (*succiduis*) under the weight it is carrying (cf. Arat. 66–7). *Z*'s *lassum* is supported by 65 *effigies . . . defecta labore.*

75–9 Aratus (77–81) states that the Snake-Carrier's shoulders are bright, his hands not as bright, but not faint. Our author adds that his head is bright, repeats from Aratus that his shoulders are bright, states that his hands are faint (Arat. 81 states that they are not faint) and adds that the remainder of the Snake-Carrier is faint. Cicero is missing in this section.

78 Our author has retained Aratus' reference to the full moon at the middle of the month (line 78). This was true for Greek months, which were based on the phases of the moon, but not for Roman of the author's own time.

81–2 Aratus (84–5) states that Ophiuchus treads the Scorpion with both his feet and stands on its eyes and breast. The catalogue preserved at

Hygin. *Astron.* p. 87.18–23 ed. Bunte concludes the list of stars of Ophiuchus *in dextro crure I, in utroque pede singulas sed clariorem in dextro.* The stars ω Ophiuchi and ν and σ Scorpii respectively fit this description and agree with Aratus' statement. Our author agrees with the 'correction' by Hipparch. 1.4.15, who probably assigned the feet the same stars as are assigned to them in Ptolemy's catalogue.

83 μ's *nam* explains the preceding *impar est manibus pondus;* ν's *iam* has no point.

85 quantum etc. This includes in the Serpent the star π Serpentis (as in the catalogue mentioned in the note on verses 81–2). Ptolemy places this star north of the head.

87 Elsewhere *stella crinita/sidus, astrum, crinitum* = 'a comet' (cf. *TLL* 4.1205.66–75). But *toto crine* (= 'with all his stars') is transmitted at 624 (cf. my note on this verse). *Crine* and *crinita* seem to support each other. From the variant *crinata* Maass (quoted in *TLL l.c.*77) conjectured *clinata*, a word found in Cic. 53 and 86 (*clinata est*) and 259 (*clinato corpore*). A star, a point of light, cannot lean, but I think *clinata* may be defended on the grounds that the author is thinking of the inclination to the Garland of the area of the Snake represented by this star. Cicero uses the word of the inclination of the Horse's hoof to the Swan in 53–4: *iam uero clinata est ungula uemens/fortis Equi propter pinnati corporis alam.*

89 I have printed *Z*'s *insigni.* 'Germanicus uses *lumine* twelve times, never without an epithet, except at 266, where it means "in respect of brilliancy" and to add an epithet would be impossible' Housman p. 28/498. Arat. 90 (and also 607) says the Claws are faint. Here our author calls them bright (and at 416 he gives them the epithet *candentis*). He omits an epithet at 623 (which corresponds to Arat. 607, which calls them faint). Perhaps in making the Claws bright (falsely) our author is following Cic. 323: *claro cum lumine Chelae.* *Claro* is purely Cicero's fill-up, for at 393 he correctly renders Arat. 607 with *obscuro corpore Chelae.*

90 *Inde* and *ipsam* seem to me equally good (for the connective used by Arat. 91 (δὲ) favours neither). A similar elision to *ipsam Helicen* is found at the beginning of 5: *quantum etenim.*

sequitur … baculoque minatur Cf. Col. 7.3.26 *tum qui sequitur gregem … baculo minetur*, Apul. *Met.* 3.28 (Oud. p. 230) *duos asinos … minantes baculis exigunt.* Ptolemy's star catalogue (7.5) also represents the constellation as carrying a stick.

91–2 are additions to Aratus. The story of the stellification of Arctophylax (or Arcas) is given in Hygin. *Astron.* 2.4; Eratosth. *Catast.* 8 and Ou. *Fast.* 2.153–90 and elsewhere, that of the stellification of Icarus in Hygin. *Astron.* 2.4; *Fab.* 130 and in the schol. Iliad 22.29 (Vol. 2 p. 232.24ff ed. Dindorf).

92 The use of *penso* here is the same as in Vell. 2.88.3: *praematuram mortem immortali nominis sui pensauit memoria.* The construction of compensating for a disadvantage (acc. case) with an advantage (abl. case) is found also in Tac. *Agric.* 22.3 ⟨*hostes*⟩ *soliti plerumque damna aestatis hibernis euentibus pensare.*

ν's *munera* comes from *munera* in the same place in the line above. μ's *munere* is a correction to restore the construction. O's *ripam* probably came from *uitam* by (1) substitution of r (from the *re* of *sidere*) for u, (2) substitution of *ripam* for the meaningless *ritam*.

96–7 The ear of wheat is represented by one star, α (magn. 0.96), by far the brightest in the constellation. Its rays presumably represent the *maturae aristae*.

98–102 are an addition to Aratus.

101 flexis laetus habenis This = 'rejoicing in my control of the reins'. *Flectere habenis* = 'control the reins', as in Verg. *Aen.* 12.471–2; Stat. *Silu.* 5.1.37–8: *notat ista deus, qui flectit habenas/orbis et humanos propior Ioue digerit actus.* The control consists in halting, as in *Aetna* 345 *cum rexit uires et praeceps flexit habenas.* The author halts his horses (i.e. has a break in his description of the constellations) in order to relate the story of *Iustitia*, which occupies lines 103–39.

103 & 105 *Regeres* and *es* are needed to agree with *te* (98).

103–9 Aratus (98–101) says that either she was (whether a descendant of Astraeus or of someone else) always in the sky, or she was once on earth as Δίκη (Justice). Our author says she was either the daughter of Astraeus or of someone else, but in either case dwelt on earth as *Iustitia*.

105 siue illa Astraei genus es is an unusually close rendering of Aratus, who has in 98 εἴτ' οὖν 'Αστραίου κείνη γένος.

109 penatis A Roman addition.

114 If *priuata* is sound, our author here contrasts *mare*, which is *publicum* (Lachmann on Lucr. 1.360 quotes Marcianus 1.2 & 4 pr. D. de diuis. rer. 1.8 *naturali iure omnium communia sunt illa, aer, aqua profluens et mare* and Hor. *Od.* 3.24.3–4 *caementis licet occupes/terrenum omne tuis et mare publicum*) with *tellus*, which is divided among private owners (*priuata*). Schwartz's *proauita* is thus unnecessary.

119 The transmitted *signo* is corrupt, for a *terminus* is a *signum*, hence *signo* cannot be contrasted with it. Housman p. 30/501 quotes in evidence that *terminus* is a *signum* Ou. *Fast.* 2.640 describing *Terminus* as *separat indicio qui deus arua suo* and 2.663, addressing *Terminus: si tu signasses olim Thyreatida terram.* In defence of *sine eo tutissima* (Lachmann proposed *sine eo* without any supporting argument) he quotes Ou. *Fast.* 2.660 *omnis erit sine te litigiosus ager* (addressing *Terminus*) and *Met.* 1.93 (of men in the golden age) *errant sine uindice tuti.*

Terminus is a Roman touch. The whole passage 108–19 is Roman and adapts Aratus freely. In particular, a Greek custom of giving judgement is omitted (Arat. 105–7). Lines 117–19 contain a reference to private ownership of land in the golden age, of which Aratus makes no mention.

122–4 The words from *ore* (end of 122) to the end of 124 are additions to Aratus. Cf. in particular the Roman words *rica* (123) and *larem* and *penatis* (124).

genas The adjective *tristis* shows that here, as sometimes in other poets (cf. *TLL* 6.1767.63ff), *genas* means 'eyes'.

rica That this was a Roman item of dress is shown by Varro *L.L.* 5.130, contrasting *rica* with *mitra et reliqua fere in capite postea addita cum uocabulis Graecis.* Cf. also Forcellini-Corradini on the word. Gellius 7.10.4, talking of

Euclid, a disciple of Socrates, and a Megarian, hence only able to visit him in disguise, says: *sub nocte, cum aduesperasceret, tunica longa muliebri indutus et pallio uersicolore amictus et caput rica uelatus, e domo sua Megaris Athenas ad Socraten commeabat.* Like our author, he uses *rica* of the dress of a non-Roman woman.

124 With the transmitted *descendens* '*que* in 124 connects nothing with nothing' (Courtney p. 139), hence I have written *descendit.* Courtney posited a lacuna before 124, but the *descendens* phrase would then be dependent on the missing clause, a clause coordinated to 124 by the *que* of *nulliusque,* and Iustitia would be said to be omitting to enter men's houses while flying down from the mountains. A scribe accidently wrote *descendens* for *descendit* and neither he, nor anyone else before Courtney, realized the defective construction he had created.

128 In *abit* the last syllable is lengthened in imitation of Greek practice. Cf. Verg. *Ecl.* 3.97 *ipse, ubi tempus erit, omnes in fonte lauabo* and Luc. 7.75 *quo tibi feruor abit aut quo fiducia fati.* There is no mention of vows in Aratus. *Z*'s *precatis* probably arose from a reminiscence of Verg. *Aen.* 9.624, which ends *per uota precatus.*

130 At 111 *sinceris artibus* means 'virtuous practices'. Similarly here, *indomitis artibus* means 'unrestrained practices'. Iustitia is leaving them; they will loose their *sinceris artibus* and become *indomiti,* this resulting in *scelus cruentum.* There is no need to emend the text. *Artibus* has nothing to do with the arts of civilization, which do not come into our author's account at all.

135 Arat. 129ff mentions only the bronze age. But Cic. Fr. XVII ed. Buescu talks of the *ferrea . . . proles.*

138 On the absence of *est* with *sortita* cf. 318–19 and my note on iii 17.

138–9 Arat. 136 says 'near the much-seen Ploughman'. Our author's picture in 139 probably comes from Arat. 581–5, which call his setting his approach to the place where he unyokes his oxen, a process taking more than half the night.

140 *Placidae* corresponds with nothing in Aratus or Cicero's rendering (Fr. XIX ed. Buescu).

140–1 Aratus (138) states that the star lies above the Maiden's shoulders (so Cic. Fr. XIX ed. Buescu). Our author says that it marks both her shoulders. His position corresponds to no bright star. Aratus refers to β Leonis, or Denebola, the star at the tip of the Lion's tail. Denebola is of magnitude 2.14, not much fainter than η Ursae Maioris, or Alkaid, the star at the tip of the Great Bear's tail, which is of magnitude 1.86. Like *placidae,* *praestanti lumine* corresponds with nothing in Aratus or Cicero.

146 *Sine honore feruntur* means that the stars are faint. It was inspired by Aratus' ἀνωνυμίη φορέονται (146), which means that the stars mentioned in 138–45 do not have individual names.

145 The subject is *ignes,* understood from *ignis* in 141. *Ignis* is masculine, hence Grotius' *alii* is required in place of the transmitted *aliae.*

150–6 adapt Aratus freely.

150 The sun entered Cancer in ancient times around 22 June, Leo about 22 July (assigning the solstices to the beginning of the signs, as Hipparchus).

152 *O*'s *tunc* is required to balance the following *tunc*.

155 *Excutio* is also used in this way in Verg. *Aen.* 3.682–3 *rudentes/excutere et uentis intendere uela secundis.* There is a verbal resemblance to our author in *Laus Pis.* 229 *ab excusso dimittere uela rudente.* The *rudentes* are the sheets (ropes attached to the lower corners of the sails, regulating their angles).

157–62 These myths are an addition to Aratus. The one about Ericthonius is given in a similar form in Eratosth. 13 (Robert p. 98). The one about Myrtilos is mentioned in Hygin. *Astron.* 2.13 (p. 48.4–6 ed. Bunte) and *Fab.* 224 (briefly) and in Eratosth. 13 (at end).

158 Ericthonius That this, not *Erichthonius*, which is transmitted here, is the form used by classical writers, is shown by the many examples from old manuscripts collected by W. Schulze, *Orthographica* (p. 78 of the 1958 reprint).

165 numina Stars and constellations are called deities here and at 180, 234, 265 and 601. These are additions to Aratus, who, however, at 188 calls Cassiepia δαιμονίη.

The *illa* of Lactantius' codices probably comes from Lactantius himself. While misquotation is possible, Lactantius probably deliberately altered the text in order to make a sense unit of his quotation.

165–8 *Capra* or *Capella* is represented by the star α (magnitude 0.05, making it the sixth brightest of all the stars). Hipparch. p. 162.28–164.1 puts it in the Charioteer's left shoulder (as does Arat. 162).

165–73 expand Aratus somewhat. 165–8 correspond to Arat. 163 'There is a story that Zeus sucked at her breast'. The details added by our author resemble Manil. 5.132–3 *officio magni mater Iouis. illa Tonanti/fida alimenta dedit.*

169 With *totam* the author signifies that the Goat is slung over the Charioteer's shoulder; he does not use his hands to support it (one of them carries the Kids). Arat. 162 (σκαιῷ δ' ἐπελήλαται ὤμῳ 'It is pushed up against his left shoulder') states the same. *Z*'s *portans in manibus* is unmetrical (the metre requiring a long *a* in *manibus*, whereas in *manus* the *a* is short). I suggest it is an interpolation based on *O*'s text and came into being in a way, if not exactly like, at least something like those given below. *Portans* probably began as *portat*. This was either a gloss on *gerit*, which it displaced, *totam* then being lost before *portat*, and *at* after it, this leaving *hanc Auriga umero portat manus Haedos*, which an amateur metrician altered into *Z*'s text, or *portat* was written for *totam* under the influence of the following *gerit*, which was then omitted as unnecessary, the unmetrical *hanc Auriga umero portat at manus Haedos* being then altered by an amateur metrician to *Z*'s text. Cf. also my note on 550, where *O* and *Z* differ even more.

169–73 Hipparch. 162.28–164.1 puts the Kids in his left hand. They are put in the left wrist by Aratus (166) and Ptolemy; according to the latter there are two Kids, represented by the stars η (magn. 3.17) and ζ (3.80). Aratus says in 166 that they gleam faintly, a detail omitted by our author.

Aratus (158–9) says that the Goat and the Kids have seen men storm-tossed. Our author makes only the Kids a *nautis inimicum sidus.* The meaning is that the time of the year when the Kids (*Haedi*) and, in Aratus' case, the

Goat (*Capella*) as well, are first visible on the eastern horizon after sunset is one liable to storms. α Aurigae (Capella) and ζ Aurigae were first visible at latitude 36° north in 130 B.C. about 13 September, the day when sunset was around 6.05 p.m., twilight ended around 7.35, Capella rose around 6.46 and ζ Aurigae around 7.11 (η is very near ζ and rises at almost the same time; they are only visible later than Capella as they are much fainter). In the times of Aratus and our author and latitudes near 36° north, the times of first appearance were similar.

176 '*Sua*, standing in agreement with the subject of the verb, refers to the verb's objects *caput* and *naris* and *cornua* . . . Ou. *Fast.* 6.413 *aquas sua ripa coercet*' Housman p. 31/502–3. Cf. also the passages cited in Housman's note on Manil. 2.72 (*nec sua dispositos seruarent sidera cursus*, which is explained by him on p. 31/503 of his Germanicus article as = 'dispositi cursus sua sidera desiderarent, acciperent aliena'). Cf. also 623 *surgentes etiam Chelas sua signa notabunt.*

181 On the Charioteer's identification with Myrtilos cf. 157–62, with my note.

186 *Maiestas* is a Roman notion introduced by the author. The statement *prodest maiestas saepe parentis* is appropriate to the author himself, whether he is Tiberius or Germanicus.

187 patulis manibus Aratus says in the corresponding passage (183) that Cepheus resembles a man stretching out both his hands. In 630–1 he says that with his bright hand Cepheus warns Andromeda of the Sea Monster's presence.

188–91 Here our author is not following Arat. 184–5, who states that the distance from either of Cepheus' feet to the tip of the Little Bear's tail is the same as the distance between his feet, but agrees with the correction by Hipparch. 1.2.12. The distance between the feet is about nine-tenths of their distance from the Bear's tail. Thus Aratus is nearly correct.

188 latus This is used to signify a mathematical line, as in 529. That this is the sense intended is made clear by the *regula* used in line 191.

188–90 Quantum latus a pede dextro/Cepheos extremam tangit Cynosurida caudam/tantundem ab laeuo distat = 'How long a line from Cepheus' right foot touches the tip of the Little Bear's tail, so far is it distant from the left.' Understand *Cynosuris cauda* as the subject of *distat* from the *Cynosurida caudam* at the end of the previous line. The lines mean that the distance from the tip of the Little Bear's tail to either of Cepheus' feet is the same. *Quantum latus* = *quantum est latus quod*, similar ellipses being found in Verg. *Aen.* 3.641–4; 7.222–3; 9.667–9.

192 *Respicit* is unsatisfactory. Cepheus cannot be the subject, for he cannot look at the Snake from his belt; *balteus* cannot be the subject, as it has no eyes. Arat. 186 has μεταβλέψειας. Emend therefore to *respicis*.

194 *Refulsit* is a gnomic aorist, i.e. indicates something which has been happening in the past and continues to happen now. Ζ's *cum stellas* probably arose after omission of *caelo* (most probably *caelo cum* became *cum caelo* and *caelo* was lost after *cum* and before *lu*). Adopting Ζ's *cum stellas*, Baehrens conjectured *retundit* for *refulsit*. Housman p. 28/498 quotes in support Auien.

1753 *sidera luna retundit;* 513–14 *astra/ . . . aciem quibus aurea luna retundit* and Cic. 247 *pleno stellas superat cum lumine luna.*

194 Arat. 188–9 says that Cassiepia is not bright on a night of the full moon. This is accurate. Hipparch. 1.5.21 says the statement is misleading. Our author's statement in 194 seems to be based on Hipparchus. It is accurate, if it means that the main stars are visible on a night of the full moon, not if it means they are bright. Our author and Hipparchus are misleading, not Aratus.

195 Our author's *breuis* does not represent anything in Aratus. He has omitted Aratus' statement that Cassiepia is formed into rows (191).

196–8 *Talis* (like the preceding *qualis*) is used adverbially. *Talis disposita est stellis* = 'She is arranged in this way by means of her stars'. With *O*'s *dispositis, talis* is left hanging on its own and *sic* needs to be supplied with *dispositis stellis* (its omission is odd).

Conceivably the author wrote *talis dispositus stellis, dispositus* being a noun used *metri gratia* for *dispositio* (it is found in the poets Ausonius and Corippus). Tac. *Hist.* 2.5 (*disposita prouisuque ciuilium rerum peritus*) uses it to match *prouisu.*

200 meritae non iusta piacula matris This is an addition by our author. Cf. Ou. *Met.* 4.670–1 *illic immeritam maternae pendere linguae/ Andromedan poenas iniustus iusserat Ammon.*

201 The *a* ending of *Andromeda* is long in the original Greek.

Nondum goes with the following verse. It is a little ambiguous. Our author does, however, have sense pauses near the ends of lines. Cf. in particular 418.

Arat. 198–9 states that Andromeda is easily recognizable at night. Our author states that she is entirely visible even before night has fully fallen; this statement is dubious.

202–4 Arat. 200–1 catalogues the parts of Andromeda which are easily recognizable (τοίη . . . τοῖαι implies they are bright). Our author's catalogue is the same, except that he has omitted the tips of the feet. He also states specifically that all the parts mentioned are bright. The head is formed from α, which lies below the Horse's belly (208–9: cf. my note). It is of magnitude 2.02 and so is bright. The stars at or near her shoulders (δ, magn. 3.21, ε 4.37, π 4.43, ρ 5.10, σ 4.53, θ 4.61) are not at all bright. Her girdle, formed from β (2.03), μ (3.93), and ν (4.53) is not bright, except for β.

203 *Sic* governs the *ambit* as well as the *candet* clause, hence *O*'s *ac* is required, not *Z*'z *hanc. TLL* quotes no use of *media* to mean 'the middle regions of the body'. Hence I accept the easy change to *mediam.*

208–10 The star which occupies Andromeda's head and lies below the Horse's belly is α Andromedae (magn. 2.02). The three stars on the shoulders and flanks are α and β Pegasi (on the shoulders) and γ (on the flanks). With α Andromedae they form what is now known as the great square of Pegasus. Arat. 209 says they form a square. In 209 *stellae* must be understood with *tres* from the *stella* of 208.

210 capiti tristissima forma Hipparchus, quoted by Ptolemy 7.1 (in the section on stars in line with those of the Water-Pourer), assigns θ (magn. 3.52) and ν (4.84) to the head.

211 Hipparchus, quoted by Ptolemy 7.1, assigns ζ (magn. 3.47) and ξ (4.19) to the throat.

212–14 The star is ε, magnitude 2.42, making it, as our author, following Aratus, states, a rival of the stars in the shoulders and flanks.

213 exit The star is represented as so close to the Horse's mouth that one can say of it that it is actually 'coming out'. *Exit* is an addition of our author.

218–22 contract Aratus somewhat. The only detail not in Aratus that our author gives is that Pegasus struck the ground with his right foot (220). Aratus says (220) προτέρου ποδός (i.e. with his forefoot).

222 aethere summo On the circles of the sky, of which that of the fixed stars is the highest, see my note on ii 10.

224 The word *longe* is an addition to Aratus (225–7).

224–8 The Ram travels round the celestial equator (*terit medii diuortia mundi* 232), the Little Bear turns around in a small circle near the pole. But, since the Ram travels much more quickly, both take the same time to make one complete revolution.

228–30 Aratus does not mention the Ram's horn or horns. But Cicero does (Fr. XXXII ed. Buescu *exin contortis Aries cum cornibus haeret*). The Ram is, as Aratus and our author rightly remark, not bright. Its brightest stars are α (magn. 2.00), β (2.65), 41 (3.65) and μ Ceti (which Hipparchus assigns to the Ram), whose magnitude is 4.25. α and β should, however, be clearly visible even on a night of the full moon. Hipparchus assigns α, β and γ to the head (in his commentary, p. 58.21–3), assigning α to the muzzle. Ptolemy in his star catalogue tells us that Hipparchus assigned it to the muzzle in his star catalogue. Ptolemy assigns β and γ to the horn. It is not clear whether Hipparchus did so or not. The Ram's head rises before its body, hence our author's statement in 228 is appropriate.

232 medii diuortia mundi = 'the equator'. *Z*'s *summi mundi* refers to the zenith. There is no *summi diuortia mundi*, except perhaps the meridian (if a line can be said to divide a point) and the stars of the Ram, in common with the other stars, lie on it only once every 24 hours.

Summi seems to have been interpolated from the *me* left when the *dii* of *medii* was omitted before the *di* of *diuortia*.

234 *Z*'s *motu* is an interpolation, presumably after the loss of *signo* (perhaps lost from its similarity with the *scere* ending *cognoscere*, the preceding word).

234–8 The triangle is formed from α (magn. 3.53), β (3.00) and γ (4.08). The line joining β and γ forms the short side.

235–6 The scholia in the 1st ed. of Breysig's Germanicus (p. 81.8–10) say of Deltoton: *alii dicunt Aegypti esse effigiem stellis figuratam in tribus angulis id est in trigono et Nilum inundationem facientem.* In other words the constellation (called Deltoton as it is shaped like the letter δ, whose capital form is Δ) represents the Nile delta—the fertile area of Egypt shaped like the letter delta (the fertile area being small in the south, large in the north, the Nile having several mouths). **donum hoc spectabile Nili** The delta is fertile because of inundation by the Nile. It is the gift of the Nile, as Herodotus 2.51.1 also states.

236 in sede These words are perhaps used to make it clear that the words from *donum* to *undis* form a parenthesis, and it is the triangle in the sky that the author is talking about observing. An alternative explanation is that *in sede* is metrical fillup.

237–8 In 237 *tres* agrees with *ductus*, hence *ductuum* must be understood with *duorum* and *ductus* with *unius* in 238. It follows that the transmitted *breuior* cannot be correct, for *ductus* cannot be understood with both it and *unius*. Write therefore *breuius*; the noun understood with it is *spatium*, from *spatia*. *Breuius* probably became *breuior* to correspond with *clarior*.

238 The shorter side is more distinguished than the others as the stars forming its ends are much closer together and it also contains δ (magn. 4.87).

239 hunc Aries iuxta This detail is not found in Aratus, who merely says (in 238) 'The stars of the Ram lie a little to the south of those in the Triangle', nor is it correct, as in fact one of the longer sides of the triangle (that formed by α and γ) is the nearest to the Ram.

240 Cepheida Andromeda.

241 *Austrum* and *austros* are equally good. Horace, Ovid and Vergil use singular and plural indifferently. (Cicero in his *Aratus*, however, has the singular eleven times, the plural not at all).

241–2 alter in Austrum/tendit is an addition to Aratus, made to balance the following statement, and is inaccurate.

243 niueus quas procreat Haemus is an addition to Aratus.

246 nodum stella premit The star is α Piscium, magnitude 3.94. Aratus (244) calls it beautiful and bright (which it is not). Our author has omitted this statement.

247 astra (dextram OZ) As Housman remarks (p. 31/503) Arat. 246–7, Eudoxus apud Hipparch. 1.2.13, Cic. 18 and Auien. 557 say (correctly) the *left* shoulder. Hence Maybaum (p. 39) emended *dextram* to *laeuam*. But Housman, with far more probability, emended it to *astra*, remarking '*Piscis* is genitive; -*as as* shrank to -*as*, and *tra* suggested dextr*am*. I do not even write *cernuntur*: compare 722 "Eridani et primos *deprendat* nauita fontes", σκέψαιτό κε Arat. 729. For *ulnam* alone = ὦμος ἀριστερός compare 282 *iuxta ulnam* = κατὰ δεξιὰ χειρός [279], 169 *umero* = σκαιῷ ὤμῳ [162]. There is no more need to say of the Fish on which side of Andromeda he lies than to say it of the Ram, 231 "zonae regione ... Andromedae", Arat. 229'.

250–1 Perseus is neither particularly large (Engonasin and Ophiuchus are a good deal larger) nor particularly bright. Its brightest stars are α (magn. 1.79), β (varies between 2.2 and 3.5), ζ (2.83), ε (2.88), γ (2.90), δ (2.99) and ρ (3.3 to 4.1).

251 ab Ioue = 'the son of Jupiter'. For this use of a phrase as the equivalent of a noun cf. the examples collected by Housman on Manil. 2.552–3.

252–3 Our author calls the *dextera sublimis* and also *sublatae similis*, i.e. both 'raised up' and 'similar to a hand raised up'. There is a similar passage in Aratus (66–7: τὸ δ'αὖτ' ἐν γούνασι κάμνον/ὀκλάζοντι ἔοικεν), which virtually means 'the being on his knees is like one on his knees'.

254 As Perseus is already touching the sky, *O*'s *tangere* is unsuitable. As *Z*'s *findere* makes good sense, I have adopted it.

256 breuis has locus occupat omnis closely renders Arat. 255–6 ὁ δ'οὐ μάλα πολλὸς ἀπάσας/χῶρος ἔχει ('a not over-large space holds them all'). The statement is accurate, as they are contained within a rectangle of about 1° by 1½°.

The transmitted *est* introduces a verb too many. *Et*, conjectured by C², is a suitable substitute, so too *sed*, contrasting the fact that the Pleiades are a clear sign of the Bull with the fact that they occupy a small space, so too the connective *at* or *ast*. But I prefer *has*, suggested to me as a possibility by Kenney (*has omnis* referring back to the Pleiades as *hos omnes* in Ou. *Fast.* 3.97 *Romulus hos omnes ut uinceret ordine saltem* refers back to *Sabinis* in 95) because of Auien. 569 *locus has habet artior omnis*, which seems to be based on our author. Note that Cicero begins his second statement about the Pleiades (29) with *hae*.

257–8 nec faciles cerni etc. The magnitudes of the six brightest are 2.86 (η), 3.62 (27), 3.69 (17), 3.86 (20), 4.16 (23) and 4.29 (19). The seventh Pleiad is either 16 (magn. 5.45) or 21 and 22 (seen as one star of magnitude 5.28 by the unaided eye). Other stars have sometimes been seen by unaided observers. No extant ancient author identifies individual stars with individual Pleiades.

259 carpitur A metaphorical use, as in Plin. *Ep.* 3.9.11: *erat in consilio Sertorianum illud exemplum, qui robustissimum et infirmissimum militem iussit caudam equi—reliqua nosti. Nam nos quoque tam numerosum agmen reorum ita demum uidebamus posse superare, si per singulos carperetur.*

262 The *que* at the end of *Celaeno* is lengthened in imitation of the Greek practice with τε. Cf. Housman *CQ* 21 (1927), 12; *Classical Papers* vol. 3 pp. 1125–6.

262–3 Aratus (262–3), Cicero (35–6), our author and Avienius (580–1), all list the Pleiades in different orders, although Cicero's is close to Aratus', Avienius' to our author's, suggesting imitation. The prose writer Hyginus (*Fab.* 192) has the same order as our author, probably indicating his catalogue was copied from him.

264 I have preferred *O*'s *si uere* to *Z*'s *si uero* as (1) the reading of *O* (2) it is paralleled by the *si uere* transmitted by both familes at 166, where precisely the same scepticism is expressed (3) *uero* being commoner, the corruption of *uere* to *uero* is more likely than the reverse.

264–5 The caveat beginning with *si uere* is an addition to Aratus.

sustinet Atlas ... superos cf. my note on 165 and also Iuu. 13.46–9: *nec turba deorum/talis ut est hodie, contentaque sidera paucis/numinibus miserum urguebant Atlanta minori/pondere.*

267–9 Our author has omitted Aratus' reference to sowing (267) and in 269 added from Hesiod 619–22.

In 268 neither *O*'s *uentus super immouet atri* nor *Z*'s *uentus super imminent agri* makes sense. From the above it is clear that a reference to the beginning of the summer half of the year, preferably specifically to spring, is required. Grotius conjectured *ueniens super imminet aestas*, but *super imminet aestas*, implying the full blaze of summer, does not fit *ueniens . . . aestas*, which implies the weather is still mild. Haupt's *uernus tepor admonet agri* gives just the sense required.

270–1 is an addition to Aratus, whose statement in 268–9 'when still near his cradle he pierced it' (i.e. to fit strings to it) is omitted.

270–1 Haupt defends *deorum/multum accepta epulis* with Hor. *Carm.* 1.32. 13–14 *o decus Phoebi et dapibus supremi/grata testudo Iouis*. The transmitted text began with the false word division *acceptae pulis*. The meaningless *pulis* was corrupted to *prohs*. A marginal correction of *pulis* to *pluris* adhered to *multum* and became corrupted to *plurimulum*. Winterfeld (in *De tribus Germanici locis*) proposed *accepta est proli* for *plurimulum accepte prohs* but (1) this necessitates deleting *plurimulum*; why would anyone want to add it? (2) It makes the author give the mythology in the first sentence, the position of the constellation only in the second, whereas elsewhere the position is given in the first. (3) If *deorum proli* means 'the gods' it is an odd way of referring to them; if it refers to Mercury it is even odder. He was the offspring of only one god, Jupiter. Schwartz's *accepta toris* ('welcome to the gods' couches') only makes sense if we take it as the equivalent of 'welcome to the gods reclining on couches'. It too leaves *plurimulum* unexplained.

272–3 as transmitted are obvious nonsense. Our author has already rendered Arat. 66–70 in 67–9, but replaces Aratus' 'right foot' with 'left foot' (from Hipparchus). It seems then that what we require here is a statement that Engonasin treads the Snake with his left foot. This is given, and sense is restored, by writing *torti subiecta Draconis/tempora laeua premit cui planta erectaque dextra* (*cui* added by Baehrens, the second halves of 272 and 273 transposed by Housman). This means 'whose left foot presses on the temple of the coiling Snake, which lies below it, and whose right hand is lifted up'. The order is *cui planta laeua subiecta tempora torti Draconis premit* ⟨*cui*⟩ *que dextra erecta* ⟨*est*⟩. Engonasin's right hand and upper arm is raised according to Ptolemy's configuration. There is no ambiguity in *laeua* in Housman's text, for *dextra* shows that it goes with *planta*, not *tempora*.

I suggest that the eye of the scribe copying the verses slipped from the *em t* of *effigiem torti* to the *emit* of *premit* in the verse below and he thus wrote *torti subiecta Draconis* as the second half of 272. He then wrote out the line below correctly and, noticing that he had made a mistake, wrote the omitted half line in the margin. The next scribe put the half line back into the text, but to replace the first, not the second, *torti subiecta Draconis*, so giving the transmitted text. *Cui* may well have been lost in the process, although it could, of course, have been lost earlier or later.

Housman's text exhibits a postponement of *cui* and a coordination of *premit* and *erecta*. *Cui* is 7th word in its clause. It is 6th in Hor. *Epod.* 12.21–2 (where, however, it is an interrogative, not relative, pronoun) and *Culex* 221–2 ⟨*Cerberus*⟩ *anguibus hinc atque hinc horrent cui colla reflexis/sanguineique micant ardorem luminis orbes*. It is 5th in Cat. 68b. 131–2 *aut nihil aut paulo cui tum concedere digna/lux mea se nostrum contulit in gremium*, Ou. *Ibis* 566 *per facinus soror est cui sua facta parens* and Sil. 3.95–6 *tua iustior aetas/ultra me improperae ducant cui fila sorores*. *Premit* and *erecta* are coordinated. Two clauses, introduced by *cui*, one of which has a verb to be understood (or a past participle as a finite verb) are found in Verg. *Aen.* 5.87–8 *caeruleae cui terga notae, maculosus et auro/squamam incendebat fulgor* (note also the postponement of *cui*) and *Aen.* 7.485–6 *cui regia parent/armenta, et late custodia credita campi* (*credita* = *credita est.* cf. our author's *erecta*). There is an example in Silius (4.193–4) and four in Statius (*Theb.* 2.716–7; 4.475–6; 8.639–40; 11.95–6).

Housman p. 32/504 says 'With the coordination "premit . . . erectaque" compare 137 sq. "deseruit . . . et sortita", 318 sq. "rapuit . . . et appositus": a very similar verse in Manil. v 551 "astrinxere pedes scopulis, iniectaque uincla" '. As in our author, *cui* is postponed and introduces two clauses with different subjects in Manil. 1.390–1: *singula fulgentis umeros cui lumina signant/et tribus obliquis demissus ducitur ensis.* Our author postpones the relative pronoun to 3rd place in its clause in 208 *uertice et Andromedae radiat quae stella.*

Although there is no hyperbaton in the passage as emended by Housman, support may be derived for his transposition from considering examples of hyperbaton in our author collected in my note on iv 137–9. Cf. also Housman's note in *JPh* 18 (1890), 6–7 (*Collected Papers*, vol. 1 pp. 139–40).

274 I comment on this line together with lines 627–8.

275 *O*'s *quae* and *Z*'s *qui* (assimilated to the gender of the following *Cycnus*: cf. Lewis & Short *s.u. qui* II A3) are both possible.

275–7 The mythological details are an addition to Aratus. The first story, of Cycnus, son of Phoebus, is given by Antoninus Liberalis 12 (with the information that the story is told by Nicander in the 3rd book of his *Metamorphoses* and by Areus the Spartan in his poem *Cycnus*). The second is very common. Cf. e.g. Manil. 1.337–40.

276 The sense requires *thalamis* to be dative, meaning 'into her bedroom', not ablative 'from her bedroom'. But I know of no passage where such a dative is used after *labor*, whereas the ablative is common. The dative is found after *illabor* in Verg. *Aen.* 3.89 *da, pater, augurium atque animis illabere nostris* and Hor. *Carm.* 2.17.27–8 *me truncus illapsus cerebro/sustulerat.* The loss of *il* between *qui* and *lapsus* is very easy, especially as it results in a change into a commoner word.

277 I do not think that *uolucer* is an *epitheton ornans*, but that its position between *falsa* and *sub imagine* in effect states what the false appearance was. Goodyear suggests the author may have written *uolucris*.

279–81 Arat. 276–7 read: 'The main part of the constellation is wreathed in mist; the parts around it are rough with stars which are not very large, but not dim'. The catalogue preserved in Robert pp. 144–5 assigns one star to the body, 13 to the other parts of the Swan, Ptolemy one to the body, 16 to other parts (Hipparchus mentions 12 stars, and assigns all of them to the same parts as Ptolemy). Thus Aratus' first statement is accurate; the second is also, if it means that the stars forming the other parts are *on average* neither very bright nor very faint. Hipparchus (p. 62.21) objects to Aratus' statements on the grounds that the Swan has many stars and bright stars. But Aratus does not say that its stars are either many or few, and the Swan

contains only three stars of first or second magnitude, α (1.26), γ (2.24) and
ε (2.45). Our author's statement in 279–81 (*multa . . . erunt*) is reasonably
accurate and seems to represent what Aratus means in 277. His statement
penna utraque laeta (281) probably derives from Robert's catalogue, men-
tioned above, which assigns 10 of the 14 stars to the wings. The two brightest,
α and γ are, however, not in them.

283 ala is nominative and a synonym of *penna*, not ablative, as Pegasus'
wings are on the opposite side of his body from the Swan.

284–5 Hipparch. 204.17–18 forms the pitcher held in the Water-Pourer's
right hand from ζ, η and π Aquarii, he forms the Horse's head from θ and
ν Pegasi (cf. my note on 210). These groups are near each other.

288–9 are additions to Aratus.

288–305 treat Aratus freely.

292 The transmitted *spectaueris* gives the sense 'you will have seen the
dawn in vain', i.e. dawn will be of no use to you. But line 290 states that the
period of daylight is of some use, if not sufficient. The meaning of the line
should be 'dawn will come after you expect it', for the lines of Aratus cor-
responding to our author 290–2 state 'you will not travel far by day, since
the day is very short, nor will day be near you when you are terrified of
night, however much you call upon it' (lines 288–91). Hence Grotius con-
jectured *expectaueris*, which gives the right sense (so too would *speraueris*), but
Baehrens' *speculaberis* is preferable to either, for our author is imitating Verg.
G. 1.257 *nec frustra signorum obitus speculamur et ortus*. *Speculor* has the sense
'look out for' in *G.* 4.166 *inque uicem speculantur aquas et nubila caeli.*

293 *Aut* is unsuitable, as *rigor* is conceived of as continuous. ā (= aut) was
written for ē (= est). This was expanded suprascript to *aut*, and replaced ā
in *O*, ā still surviving in λ as the *a* at the end of *rigora*. In 303 λ has a, *O* e.
Dahms also suggested, calling it inferior, *et*. It impairs the *tunc, tunc* structure.

rapidus Baehrens wrote *rabidus*, comparing 327 *sentit et insanos obscuris
flatibus austros.*

294 I can see nothing except *O*'s authority to choose between *alligat* and
occupat. *Occupat* could be the work either of the author or of someone else,
from a reminiscence of *tremor occupat artus* found in Verg. *Aen.* 7.446; 11.424
and Ou. *Met.* 3.40 (the clausula *occupat artus* also occurs in Ou. *Met.* 1.548
(where ζ² has *alligat*) and 14.757 and Verg. *G* 4.190). *Alligat* can be defended
from Sil. 3.124 *tremor implicat artus.*

295 corresponds with nothing in Aratus. Cf., however, Hesiod *Op.* 684–5
(of spring sailing): 'Yet men, in their ignorance of mind, even do this'.

sed is better than *O*'s *et* as (1) 295 is contrasted with the preceding and
(2) *Sed* to *et* is a likelier change than the converse.

299 assultat This is the earliest recorded use of the word *assulto.*

300 '*Litore* is ambiguous, as it could very naturally be taken with *pros-
pectant*, with the meaning "from the shore". The author may have written
this verse in the way he did under the influence of Cat. 64.52 *namque
fluentisono prospectans litore Diae*' Goodyear.

301 Of the text with *alii* Housman p. 32/504 remarks 'This is a foolish
distribution, to say that some of the sailors look out for the land and others

(who are not looking out) descry it. "aliis narrant" would be reasonable but not elegant: I hardly doubt that he wrote "inuentasque acie terras" '.

302 & 304 The *instantis/instantia* repetition is not objectionable. Cf. *supra/ supra* at 51–2, *labore/laboris* at 65–6.

302 The clausula *instantis aquae mons* is imitated from Verg. *Aen.* 1.105 *praeruptus aquae mons.*

307 This line expands Aratus' ῥύτορα τόξου ('the drawer of the bow') in 301. *Duco* is not used elsewhere with *spicula* as its object as far as I know. But *tendo* is (Verg. *Aen.* 9.606 *ludus ... spicula tendere cornu*: 'it is their sport to aim arrows from their bows') and it is also combined with *duco, cornu* being the object of both verbs, in *Aen.* 11.859–61 *cornu ... tetendit/et duxit longe donec curuata coirent/inter se capita.* In our author *ducentem* is used of the action of drawing back the arrow together with the bowstring, so curving the bowstring (*sinuato neruo*) and bringing the ends of the bow (*capita* in Verg. *Aen.* 11.861 quoted above) towards each other. Sagittarius is also represented as threatening to shoot arrows by Manilius (1.269–70 and 4.347).

308 cf. 295.

311 As the Scorpion's tail is the last part of him to rise (Arat. 305–7), the line means that all the Scorpion has risen.

312 grauis arcus corresponds to Aratus' μέγα τόξον ('large bow') in 305.

in lucem magis exit i.e. the Scorpion rises at the end of night (310), the Archer, however (*magis* contrasts what the Archer does with what the Scorpion does) comes forth when it is light (*in lucem*).

313 *Z*'s *regit* makes no sense, *O*'s *repit* does not scan. Winterfeld (p. 560) proposed writing *tunc repit Cynosura alte*, but it is easier to write *redit* with Grotius. *Alte redit = in altum redit*, as in Cic. 77 *emergit Scorpios alte* and 403 *hic genus et suram cum Chelis erigit alte.*

Aratus says in the corresponding passage (308–9) 'Then at the end of night Cynosura's head is very high up'. This statement is not very accurate. When the Scorpion was rising the Little Bear's head was about half way to the zenith. Hipparchus takes Aratus to mean by 'very high up' that it is culminating, and has no difficulty in proving this wrong (p. 68.20–70.7). If our author's *alte redit* means the head is returning towards the zenith, it is correct; if it means it is near its lowest point (the head and the rest of the Bear did not set in Mediterranean latitudes) it is not very accurate. Our author's statement is probably based on Hipparchus.

314 umeris et uertice Arat. 310 says from hand to waist. Our author is following Hipparch. 1.7.20.

316–20 are additions to Aratus. The story of Aquila is given in the sources quoted by Robert pp. 156–7. Cf. e.g. Hygin. *Astron.* 2.16 *Haec est quae dicitur Ganymedem rapuisse et amanti Ioui tradidisse.*

Housman p. 32/504 quotes to illustrate *quo (telo)* in 319 Hor. *Carm.* 1.27.12 *qua pereat sagitta* and continues 'Germanicus identifies the Arrow as one of Cupid's, and the Eagle, who carried Ganymede off, is appropriately set to guard it. 315 "incertum quo cornu missa Sagitta" is only a translation of Aratus' ἄτερ τόξου ("missore uacans" Cicero) and signifies that this arrow, unlike that of Sagittarius, has no bow belonging to it in the starry heavens'.

317 There is no word *ardum*. I suggest *ardens*: 'burning with eagerness'. Although burning with eagerness to do Jupiter's bidding (the same word is used of Aquila's zeal to provide Jupiter with weapons in Stat. *Theb.* 3.506–7 *non fulminis ardens/uector adest*), Aquila does not harm Ganymede when he snatches him away (*unguibus innocuis . . . rapuit*). *Tamen ardens/unguibus innocuis . . . rapuit = quamuis ardens tamen innocuis unguibus rapuit.* This use of *tamen* is illustrated with a large number of examples by Housman on Manil. 4.413 (examples where *tamen* follows the word it governs) and on Luc. 1.333 (examples where, as here, it precedes). From Housman's note on Lucan I select the passages from poets before or contemporary with our's where *tamen* immediately precedes an adjective. They are Prop. 3.24.30 (3.25.10) *nec tamen irata ianua fracta manu* (= *nec quamuis irata tamen fracta*) and Ou. *Met.* 2.337 *ossa tamen peregrina condita ripa* (= *quamuis peregrina tamen condita*) and *Trist.* 1.1.96 (I quote 95–6) *si quis erit qui te dubitantem et adire timentem/tradat, et ante tamen pauca loquatur, adi* (= *quamuis pauca, tamen loquatur*). Ellis conjectured *aptum*. The natural meaning of *aptum/unguibus innocuis*, 'equipped with harmless talons', being absurd applied to Ganymede, it must be taken as 'suited to unharming talons', the contrast being 'although suited to unharming talons, nevertheless he was carried off', i.e. he was not hurt, but he was still carried off. The meaning is by no means easy to see, and the corruption of *aptum* to the meaningless *ardum* is not as likely as that of *ardens* to *ardum* by anticipation of the ending of *Phrygium*. Moreover, the Statius extract quoted above may well be in imitation of our author. Orelli conjectured *Catamitum* for *tamen ardum*. This is not very close, and *Catamitum* is usually used as a synonymn of *Ganymedes* (it comes from the Etruscan form of *Ganymedes*). I do not think the author would have put alternative spellings of the same proper name in apposition.

318–9 rapuit . . . et appositus On this coordination see Housman's note on 272–3 (quoted in my commentary).

322–3 tulit etc. is an addition to Aratus.

Atlantida nymphen Amphitrite. cf. Robert pp. 158–9.

324–7 are much more picturesque than Arat. 319–21.

328–35 treat Aratus freely, expanding him.

328 in obliquum = the adverb *oblique*. This use of the phrase is also found in Verg. *G.* 1.98, Ou. *Met.* 2.130, Liu. 28.14.17 and Manil. 5.80 (quoted by *TLL* 7.1.746.78ff.) *In obliquo*, which is offered by *Z*, only occurs in Chiron, who wrote in the 4th cent., when both ablative and accusative were tending to be used indifferently. (cf. *TLL* 7.1.785.84)

329 non ulla etc. The author states (correctly), that Orion is the brightest of the constellations representing a man (no other being nearer, hence brighter). The author implies in 526–9 that the stars are all the same distance from us.

331 I can think of no better explanation of *Z*'s *exit* than that *ard* was lost and *et* expanded to *exit*. The *s* at the end of *humeris* in *OZ* comes from the following *sic*.

335 Of Breysig's *hanc* for *hunc* Housman (p. 27/497) says 'perspicuity requires the alteration though grammar does not' (i.e. the reference must not be back to *Canis*. But *hunc* could refer to either *Canis* or *ignis*. Hence *hanc* is required, for it refers unambiguously to *flammam*. It is this *flammam* which is called Sirius).

336–40 When Sirius *tetigit Solis radios*, i.e. was first visible on the eastern horizon just before sunrise, the hottest part of summer began. In Aratus' time the date was about 20th July, in latitude 36° north. There the twilight began about 3.10, Sirius rose about 4.15, the sun about 4.56. In our author's time the date was similar. Eudoxus (Fr. 147a ed. Lasserre: Geminus p. 212 ed. Manitius) gives the date as 22 July.

336 *O*'s *accenditur aestas* can be defended from Gratt. 58–9 *ante . . . quam maturis accenderit annum/ignibus . . . Plias* (of the onset of summer), *Z*'s *accenditur aestus* from Verg. *G.* 4.401 *medios cum Sol accenderit aestus* ('when the Sun has fired the heat of midday').

338 *Languida* makes it plain that a word indicating blight is needed in place of the *adstete/adsuetas* transmitted. *Z*'s *adsuetas* looks like an attempt to make sense out of *adstete* and the *as* acc. ending an attempt to provide an object for the interpolation *cernis* which arose after *radix* had been omitted after *languida*. Conjecture should be based on *adstete*. There is no need to look further than Baehrens' *adstrictae* (= 'shrivelled up'). Cf. Plin. *N.H.* 17.251 *macie corticis ex aegritudine astringente se* ('the bark becoming meagre and shrivelling up due to disease'). Burman's *adfectae* introduces a word which no more describes a harmful than a favourable effect. Ellis' *adflatae* (= 'burned up') is too strong for the conditions before Sirius, which are described here. It is suited to those after his arrival, when *frondes . . . exanimat* (cf. iv 40–1 *terras cum letifer ortu/Sirius afflauit*). Better than either is *adflictae* (cf. Col. 2.16.2 *quod ⟨pratum⟩ nec tempestatibus adfligeretur ut aliae partes ruris*). But Baehrens' *adstrictae* is closer to *adstete*.

343 paruum He occupies about 10° square.

344 languenti Not very accurate. Ptolemy assigns η (magn. 2.40) to the tail (as does Hipparch. 270.19–20, for he states that the star at the end of the tail has a right ascension of 90°. In 130 B.C. that of η was 90°5′).

347 The process is that described in the corresponding passage of Aratus (346–7) 'Everyone rows the boat astern and, travelling backwards, it bites into the shore'. The process is described by Cic. *ad Att.* 13.21.3 (letter 351 in Shackleton Bailey's edition) *inhibere . . . est . . . uerbum totum nauticum. . . . arbitrabar sustineri remos cum inhibere essent remiges iussi. id non esse eius modi didici heri . . . non enim sustinent, sed alio modo remigant. inhibitio autem remigum motum habet et uehementiorem quidem remigationis nauem conuertentis ad puppem.* If the transmitted *remos* is right, our author believed what Cicero believed until August 45, that when near the shore the sailors rested on their oars (the meaning of *inhibet remos* in Quint. 12 *prooem.* 4). If Gronouius' *remis* is right (*remos* could easily have arisen to supply an object for *inhibet*), the author knew the truth. *Remis* suits Aratus better, for Aratus represents the sailors as doing something, not merely resting on their oars.

348 uotis damnatus can be defended from Verg. *Ecl.* 5.80 *damnabis tu quoque uotis.* Pareus (mentioned by Breysig) conjectured *uoti damnatus*, as this is the commoner expression. (cf. *TLL* 5.20.31–4). *Votis damnatus* is an addition to Aratus.

348–9 ab ora/praeligat Neither *ore* nor *perlegit* makes any sense here. A reference to tying up a boat is entirely appropriate. Grotius conjectured *perligat*, but the verb does not occur elsewhere. The use *praeligo ab* can be compared with Luc. 7.860 *nullus ab Emathio religasset litore funem.*

350–2 Only the rear half of Argo gleams in the sky (353–5). This can be gathered from Arat. 342–4; 349–50 and 605.

coeuntia saxa/numine Iunonis tutus cum fugit Iason comes from Homer *Od.* 12.69–72.

pars uiolata fuit According to Apollon.Rhod.2.601–2, on the outward journey (Homer refers to the return journey in the passage quoted above) the tip of the ornament with which the stern ended after curving upwards and outwards (ἀφλάστοιο . . . ἄκρα κόρυμβα) was shorn off when the Argo was passing through the Symplegades. Our author seems to be thinking of this incident here.

Z's *quae* in 350 makes the author state that the whole rear half of the Argo was smashed in the rocks. This would have killed half the Argonauts and sunk the ship. *O*'s *quia* is satisfactory, if we take the contents of the *cum* clause as more important than those of the main clause. The sense is then 'Because it carried the Argonauts to safety through the Symplegades, losing the tip of its stern in the process, Argo has been placed in the sky'. Cf. Manil. 1.414–15 *emeritum magnis mundum tenet ante periclis/seruando dea facta deos.* The greatest of these dangers was the passage through the Symplegades.

352–3 Arat. 605 'The Argo, divided at the mast' shows that *O*'s *malus*, not *Z*'s *maius*, is correct (*maius* probably deriving from the *amplius* found in *Z* in the previous line). The *Oxford Latin Dictionary* gives *O*'s text *lateri non amplior actus/quam surgit malus*, and quotes this passage by itself in *actus* section 3c. The meanings given in section 3 are (a) A linear land measure, 120 ft; (b) *actus quadratus*, an area 120 ft square; (c) (apparently) measurement, dimension; (d) a square, block. But section c does not fit in with the rest, hence it must be considered doubtful if *actus* can have this meaning. If it can, then *O*'s text should be translated 'The measurement (or 'dimension') of the sides is not larger than the mast arises'. If this means anything, it means 'the sides are the same size as the mast'. But Arat. 605 quoted above and lines 353–5 of our author show that the author must be saying that the ship is cut off at the mast. *Z*'s text *lateri non amplius aucta/quam surgit malus* (substituting *malus* for *maius*) leaves the dative *lateri* with no connection with the rest. One could remedy this by writing *latere est non amplius aucta/qua surgit malus* ('Where the mast rises, the ship is not very generously equipped with a side'). *Augeo* + abl. = 'equip with' in several passages (cf. *OLD augeo* 6a). Cf. in particular Tac. *Ann.* 15.9.1 *naues magnitudine praestantes et conexas trabibus ac turribus auctas agit per amnem.*

Orelli conjectured *auctus*, and wrote *lateri non amplior auctus/qua surgit malus* (= 'where the mast rises, there is no very great bulk in the side'). This contrasts with 353–4: = 'In the front half there is no bulk at all in the sides'. *Auctus* is used of physical bulk in Lucr. 2.481–2 *semina quaedam/esse infinito debebunt corporis auctu*; 6. 167–8 *caedere si quem/ancipiti uideas ferro procul arboris auctum*, 5.1170–1 *egregias . . . facies . . . uidebant/ . . . mirando corporis auctu* (in 1174 Lucretius mentions *uiribus amplis* in connection with the same gods. Cf. our author's *amplior*). All these passages have, however, a noun in the genitive dependent on *auctus*. Cf. also Sen. *Ep.* 38.2 ⟨*semen*⟩ *ex minimo in maximos auctus diffunditur* and the somewhat different passage Tac. *Ann.* 1.56.2 *imbresque et fluminum auctus* (= swollen rivers; the result of increase in rivers) *regredienti metuebantur*. Orelli's conjecture seems more probable, for if *amplior auctus* were the original, then *O*'s *actus* is an easy change and *Z*'s *amplius aucta* is explained as an interpolation (of which there is much in *Z*) to accommodate the words to *haec*. But if *latere est non amplius aucta* is the original, then (1) *est* was lost; (2) *latere* became *lateri*; (3) either *O* changed *amplius aucta* to *amplior auctus* (but there is not much evidence of interpolation in *O*) or *amplius* was confused with *amplior* and this led to *auctus*; (4) *auctus* became *actus*.

The transmitted *quam* in 353 can easily be explained as arising from *qua* under the influence of *amplior*.

355 *O*'s *lucida* makes good sense. *Z*'s *roscida* is just conceivable. Only the rear half is moistened, for only the rear half exists. *Roscida* = 'moistened' in Verg. *Aen.* 7.683–4 *roscida riuis/Hernica saxa*.

357 cum tamen = 'nevertheless', *cum* being simply a connective, as in Liu. 27.20.12 *de imperio abrogando eius agebat, cum tamen necessarii Claudii obtinuerunt ut . . .*

359 No sense of *lego* is appropriate. Housman p. 32/505 defends *rigenti* from Manil. 1.314 *proxima frigentis Arctos boreanque rigentem*.

360 praelegit is supported by the *praeterit* of 362.

363–6 are an addition to Aratus, who refers to the legend only with the epithet πολυκλαύτου ('of many tears') he applies to Eridanus (360). Cic. 146–8 had already mentioned the legend our author recounts.

365 uulnere reddentem flammas Iouis = 'e uulnere suo etiam tunc fumante quasi reddentem, efflantem flammas Iouis' Orelli. Our author is imitating Apoll. Rhod. 4.599–600 'this lake still gives off heavy clouds of steam from his ⟨Phaethon's⟩ smouldering wound'. Cf. also Carmen Pap. Herc. (Anth. Lat. Riese 1.49–50) *laqueis pars cogitur artis/intersaeptam animam pressis effundere uenis*, Verg. *Aen.* 2.532 *multo uitam cum sanguine fudit*.

366 *Ignotis* = 'of a type unknown before', as *ignotas* in Ou. *Met.* 1.87–8 *sic, modo quae fuerat rudis et sine imagine, tellus/induit ignotas hominum conuersa figuras*. The sisters were turned into trees, their arms into boughs. The whole process is minutely described in Ou. *Met.* 2.346–66, including 352 *illa dolet fieri longos sua bracchia ramos*. They bewail with outstretched arms, like Cassiepia (198–200).

368 laeuum ferit Orionis corresponds to Arat. 361 'It stretches beneath Orion's left foot'. *Z*'s *medium tenet* was interpolated after the loss of the *lae* of *laeuum* after the *dae* of *undae*. The left foot of Orion is represented by β (Rigel). It is of magnitude 0.08. Ptolemy calls it the bright star in the left foot in common with the Water (= Eridanus).

369–71 procul amotis This is an addition to Aratus. The Fishes are joined by chains (*uincula* 370) and a considerable distance from each other. Pegasus' flank lies between them (284).

unus . . . nodus can be defended from the *uno . . . nodo* of 245. The transmitted *usus . . . nodus* has no sense.

372 *Z*'s *caelo* is a repetition of the *caelo* in 371.

371–8 Of these lines, 371–5 correspond with Arat. 367–85. Aratus, as pointed out by D. A. Kidd (*Antichthon* 1 (1967), 12–15) has arranged his lines in an a,b,c,d,c,b,a form. Of this, our author renders only the first a and part of the b (Aratus 367–71), in lines 371–5. He then adds 376–8, which contradict Aratus, who says that only the stars beneath the Hare's flanks form no part of any constellation.

373–5 sub Leporis latus etc. Most unfigured stars are faint, but in the position indicated by our author lie stars brighter than most unfigured ones, formed in modern times into the constellation of *Columba* (the Dove). Its brightest stars are α (2.63), β (3.11), δ (3.84), ε (3.87) and η (3.95). Hipparchus 1.8.2–3 states that Aratus 367–70 is wrong in talking of unnamed stars between Eridanus and Argo and under Lepus; he should talk of unnamed stars between Eridanus and Argo. Our author 374 agrees with Hipparchus.

375 *O*'s *nota si* does not scan. With *Z*'s *nota est* the line means 'and this itself is an indication that they form no figure'. But there is nothing in the preceding that is an indication that they form no figure. Hence I have written *notes*. Cf. the use of *licet numeres* in 401 and *putes* in ii 20. If *notes* were spelled *notaes* this could easily have been corrected to *notaest* in *Z* and *notasi* in *O*. Line 375 is tacked on to the preceding with *atque*, which is used similarly in 86 and (if Courtney's transposition is correct) iii 14. Goodyear suggested *notas*, but the present indicative is only used in an address to the reader in 192 (where there is a *qua* clause with the same tense added). Addresses to the reader other than those listed above are given in my note on 494. All have the future. The present indicative by itself seems a little odd, implying 'as you read this you are looking at the stars and seeing that they form no figure'.

378 per appositi etc. Cf. Ptolemy's catalogue, which lists unfigured stars about certain constellations.

379–81 Our author omits the detail that 'men call it the Southern Fish' (Arat. 388).

380 totus derectus in Austros In Aratus' and our author's times it was about 40° south of the equator.

388–91 Aratus says of the *imitata . . . errantis signa liquoris* that they call them collectively 'the Water', (399), a detail our author omits.

391–2 est et etc. Aratus (401) states that these stars are 'lying in a circle' and does not form them into any constellation. Geminus, chapter 3 (Arat. schol. p. XXVIII, 2–3 ed. Maass) calls the constellation the Southern Garland, by some called the Canopy, by Hipparchus the Herald's Wand. The constellation is now known as *Corona Austrina*. Our author calls it *sine honore* as Aratus does not form its stars into a constellation and they are faint. The brightest are α (magn. 4.10) and β (also 4.10).

393 erecta torquet qua spicula cauda The tail, starting from θ, bends back as if it were being raised to sting.

393–8 The Altar was so far south that it only just rose in Mediterranean latitudes. Arcturus was about 32° north in Aratus' time and so set for only a short time in these latitudes.

395–7 sed quanto . . . tanto Arat. 406–7 states 'The path of Arcturus is high up in the sky, but the Altar travels swiftly to the western brine'. *Quanto . . . tanto* represents Aratus' μὲν . . . δὲ. Cf. our author's use of them in 226–8. The *et* transmitted before *magis* in 396 is unsuitable, for it can only mean 'even', the lines then meaning 'The slower Arcturus sets, the quicker the Altar does', this describing the situation as you go further north. I can see no reason why the author should desert Aratus to provide this information, hence accept Grotius' deletion of *et*.

398 The transmitted *dimittitur undis* = 'It is sent out of the waves'. With *demittitur*, *undis* can be dative (= 'into') as in Ou. *Fast.* 1.653 ⟨*sol*⟩ *cum se demiserit undis*.

399–402 Aratus 408–10 talks of night giving the Altar to men as the sign of a storm, our author of *natura* giving signs to men, the Altar being a sign of trouble at night.

403 λ's *splendenti metuendum* arose when the *te* of *splendente* was omitted before *timeto*. *Splendentimeto* was expanded to *splendentimetuendum* to restore the metre and a semblance of sense.

405 *Siccentur* is unsuitable. Drying the yard-arms is the last thing the sailors should be doing when a storm is about to burst, and impossible to do with the sails tied around them. Hence Grotius conjectured *spissentur*. 'Then I tell you, the yard-arm should be thickened by the sail bound around it' = the sails should be furled. Cf. Ou. *Met.* 11.480–3 *coepit/ . . . spirare ualentius Eurus./ 'ardua iamdudum demittite cornua' rector/clamat 'et antemnis totum subnectite uelum'*. (*antemnae = cornua*).

Both *O*'s *abstricto* and λ's *substricto* are suitable (cf. Manil. 5.551 *astrinxere pedes scopulis* and Sil. 1.689 *summo iamdudum substringit lintea malo*), but *abstricto* does not scan in its transmitted position, and if it is transposed with *spissentur*, the *ur* must be lengthened. This is best avoided. Moreover, the corruption of *sub* to *ab* is likelier than the converse.

Grotius' *spissentur* after *mihi* is unsatisfactory, as poets of our author's period avoid short open vowels before initial consonant clusters such as *sp*. Hence Lucian Mueller (*De re metrica* ed. 2 p. 387) suggested *mi* for *mihi*. This form occurs (as the metre shows) in Verg. *Aen.* 6.104 *o uirgo, noua mi facies inopinaue surgit* and 6.123 *quid memorem Alciden? et mi genus ab Ioue summo* and Ou. *Met.* 13.503 *nunc quoque mi metuendus erat; cinis ipse sepulti*. But I prefer Housman's solution (p. 32–3/505) to transpose *spissentur* and *substricto* as (1) *mihi* is very common in Vergil and Ovid's *Metamorphoses*, *mi* only occurs in the passages quoted above; (2) *mihi* commonly forms the second half of the first foot (15 times in Manilius, who uses the word 20 times). The word occurs in three other passages in our author (100,154,550), in two of them in this position.

408 laxo is an addition to Aratus.

410 respexit This verb is often used of the gods looking favourably on one. Cf. Forcellini-Corradini *s.u. respicio* 2 (a).

411 as *iactatae . . . salutis* (= 'boasted safety') does not suit the context, I accept *iactati*, referring to the sailors.

ultima . . . uota is used of vows made in their extremity, as in Ou. *ex Pont.* 4.14.5–6 (of his state of mind in exile) *ipsa quoque est inuisa salus suntque ultima uota/quolibet ex istis scilicet ire locis.*

412 *Perfulserit* can be rejected as (1) *perfulgeo* does not occur elsewhere; (2) it is only the reading of λ.

413 λ's *orbem* seems to come from the *orbis* in 412.

414–18 Aratus (437–8) says that the human parts of the Centaur lie beneath the Scorpion, the equine beneath the Claws. Our author agrees with the correction by Hipparchus (1.8.21–2).

414 flammis commissa He lies next to the fires coming from the Altar. This renders Arat. 439–40.

418 dextra makes no sense with the preceding words of 418, but good sense with what follows, and agrees with Aratus' δεξιτερὴν in 439.

421–2 are additions to Aratus.

iustissimus is defended by Ou. *Fast.* 5.413 *iustissime Chiron,* Hygin. *Astron.* 2.38 (p. 75.9–11 ed. Bunte) *Chiron . . . qui non modo ceteros Centauros, sed homines quoque iustitia superasse . . . existimatur* and school. Arat. ed. Maass p. 424.12–13.

422 nubigenas cf. Pind. *Pyth.* 2.25–48.

magni doctor Achillis cf. Pind. *Nem.* 3.43–52.

423–5 The corresponding passage of Aratus (431–5) states 'If the Centaur's shoulder is equidistant from the seas on the west and the east and a slight mist covers it (μιν . . . αὐτὸν) whereas from behind night produces similar signs ⟨of a storm⟩ on the all-bright Altar, you must then expect, not a south, but an east wind'. μιν . . . αὐτὸν refers to the whole of the Centaur, not merely to the shoulder, as the passage Aratus is imitating shows (Hom. *Il.* 21.318–19 κὰδ δέ μιν αὐτὸν/εἰλύσω ψαμάθοισιν, 'I will cover the man himself with sand'. μιν . . . αὐτὸν contrasts the man himself with the fate of his armour, already discussed). This passage of Aratus is contrasted with 413–17 (to which he refers back in 435). The scholiast (ed. Maass p. 423.4–5) says that μιν αὐτόν refers either to the shoulder or to the Centaur. Courtney (p. 139) maintains, correctly, I think, that the author 'has followed those who referred μιν αὐτόν to the shoulder, not to the whole constellation, and has tried to make the meaning plain by adding *toto clarus equo,* by which he wishes to convey that the mist covers only the human part of the Centaur, i.e. the upper half comprising the shoulders, not the lower equine half'.

427 Of the text with the transmitted *lucet* Housman (p. 33/505) remarks 'As if either *lucet* or *superne* could govern the accusative!'. He quotes in support of *mulcet* the corresponding line of Cicero (218 *Centaurum leui contingit lubrica cauda*) and Cic. 56 *huic ceruix dextra mulcetur Aquari* and 88 *igniferum mulcens tremebundis aethera pennis.*

It can hardly be said that the Snake's *tractus peruenit ad Cancrum capite.* Hence I have adopted *tractu. Ille* refers to *Hydros*; the author uses it to make it clear that *Hydros*, not *cauda*, is the subject. Courtney (p. 139) conjectures *inde*, comparing its use in 217 and 417.

429 primos is clearly correct. It contrasts with *ulterioris* at the end of the line.

431 pennis et paruo pondere Arat. 448–9 has no epithets for these signs. *Paruo pondere* is based on Aratus' ἐλαφρὸς at 519. 'The author has obviously been influenced here by a desire for alliteration' Goodyear.

432 spatio triplicis . . . sideris = 'the space of three signs'. On the use of *triplex* cf. Verg. *Aen.* 10.202 where *gens illi triplex* = *gentes illi tres*. The three signs are Virgo, Leo and Cancer.

436 nec longo mutantur in aeuo is an addition to Aratus.

437 quinque aliae stellae: the planets: Mercury, Venus, Mars, Jupiter and Saturn.

438–9 et proprio motu mundo contraria uoluunt/curricula is an addition to Aratus. Cf. Manil. 1.805 *sunt alia aduerso pugnantia sidera mundo*.

440–1 A scribe seems to have changed *possis* (corresponding to Aratus' ἐπιτεκμήραιο in 456) to *possim* because *equidem* is usually followed by the 1st person singular.

The corresponding passage of Aratus (456–7) states 'You will not discover where they (i.e. the planets) lie by reference to the others (ἄλλους) (i.e. the constellations)'. *Alio . . . signo* was suggested by Aratus' ἄλλους but is not used in the same way. It refers back to 439. The planets slip out of the signs they are in (*exceduntque loco*). It will be no use looking for them in another sign (*alio . . . signo*) and expecting them to stay in that, the author says, as they are changing their positions in the zodiac all the time (441–2).

441 diuis is used of the planets, contrasted with the signs of the zodiac (*signo* 440). *Deus* is used similarly in iii 23 *haec ut quisque deus possedit numine signa*.

444–5 Here our author changes Aratus' statement that he will not discuss the planets any further (460–1) to a promise to do so, if he can. This treatment is contained in the second part of his poem, of which fragments ii to vi are all that remain.

444 arcanis Musis = poetry about *arcana* (astronomy/astrology). Cf. Manetho 5.1 ff. ('From holy books not to be opened and from occult records which he acquired, Hermes the all-wise described the foreknowledge to be gained from individual stars of the sky'). Cf. also 15 *Latiis Musis* (= poetry in the Latin language).

446 signorum partes = 'the region where the signs lie', i.e. the zodiac. Cf. Cic. 97 *partes gelidas Aquilonis*, 142 *in partibus Austri*.

Est *O*'s and *E*'s positions seem equally good. I have preferred *O*'s on *O*'s authority.

447–54 treat Arat. 462–8 freely. The circles mentioned in 449–50 are the equator and the ecliptic, in 451 the tropics of Capricorn and Cancer.

448 The ecliptic at its southernmost point touches the tropic of Capricorn, at its northernmost the tropic of Cancer. It crosses the equator at two points, called the first point of Aries and the first point of Libra.

450 *O*'s *et* has no function (it seems to have been added *metri gratia*), the

line as presented by EL does not scan. C's *extat* is satisfactory, as it some-
times = *est* (cf. Cic. *de lege agr.* 2.88 *extant litterae, Quirites, publicae, sunt
senatus consulta complura*). But from the agreement of E and L in *est*, it seems
that *extat* is merely a conjecture. *Stat* is also possible, as it too sometimes =
est. Cf. Hor. *Carm.* 1.16.17-19 *irae . . . / . . . altis urbibus ultimae/stetere causae
cur perirent*, Lucr. 5.199 *tanta stat praedita culpa*. But closer than either is
Scaliger's *duo quorum est* (as *duo* could have easily fallen out before *quorum*).
But the repetition of *duo* seems to me heavy and pointless. Hence I have
written *est quorum*. Interchange of two words is very common. Perhaps here
est was omitted after *aequales* and reinserted in the wrong place.

451 As the line is transmitted, it is hard not to take *inter se* with *minores*,
with which it is redundant, to say the least. Moreover, the repetition of *inter
se* within such a small space is highly suspect. It seems then that (1) either
inter se is a corruption of a word similar to it, or a repetition of *inter se* in the
previous verse or comes from *inter se aequales* written above the line to
explain the construction (1 and 2 are not mutually exclusive) or (2) there
is a lacuna in which the equivalent of *aequales feruntur* has been omitted
(Courtney in a letter to me suggested there is a lacuna after *inter se*. One
could also, with more probability, posit one before it, as *inter se* would then
be further removed from the previous *inter se*). But a lacuna seems unlikely,
as the passage would then have two synonymous clauses, both containing
inter se.

If not expressed, *aequales feruntur* must be understood from the clause
above.

My first suggestion is to replace *inter se* with *pariter*. A scribe could have
accidently written *parinterse* from the verse above, the *par* being later dis-
carded. Or *par* could have been first omitted then *iter* expanded to *inter se*
from the previous verse. Or *pariter* could have fallen out before *praedictis* and
the gap been filled with *inter se*. *Pariter* here = 'likewise', i.e. *pariter inter se
aequales feruntur*. Cf. Manil. 3.472ff. *sic ultima primis/respondent, pariterque, illis
quae proxima fulgent/et media aequatis censentur uiribus astra*, 2.731 and 4.338,
also Ou. *Met.* 2.445 and Sall. *Iug.* 60.1. Baehrens suggested *aequales*, but this
is very clumsy after the same word in the previous verse. Grotius suggested
rursus (= 'on the other hand'. cf. e.g. Verg. *G.* 4.185), but there seems no
particular reason why this should have fallen out or been altered. Other
possibilities are *paulo* or *paulum* (Courtney used the latter in supplementing
his lacuna). They could (although less probably than *pariter*) have fallen
out before *praedictis*. If the author wrote either of them, he is probably
following Hipparchus, who (1.9.14-15) says that Arat. 479 is wrong in
saying that the tropics are much smaller than the equator and the ecliptic,
as they are only one-eleventh smaller. Another possibility is *multo*. If the
author wrote this, he is following Aratus.

452 signa 'Grotius understands *signa* to mean *puncta*, mathematical
points. This is not necessary: Germanicus means that the equator and the
ecliptic intersect one another at the constellations of Aries and Libra, both
which zodiacal signs, as he has said at 232 sq. and will say again at 502 and
507, are also equatorial' Housman p. 33/505.

453–4 qua se tangunt etc. refers to the former pair, the ecliptic and the equator.

454 si quis is found in both *O* and *Z* at 235, 473 and 526. *Si quis* is common, *si qui* (sing.) rare. According to Merguet's index *si quis* occurs ten times in Vergil and the *Appendix Vergiliana*, *si qui* not at all. According to Packard's index *si quis* (without a noun) occurs 47 times in Livy, *si qui* (sing.) three times. Hence I have preferred *si quis*.

455 The fifth circle is called the Milky Way.

456–8 Our author contracts Arat. 469–79.

457 *Z*'s *est* seems to me rather inferior to *O*'s *et* ,as it makes 457–8 consist of three sentences with no connective.

458 Hipparchus 1.9.14 criticizes Arat. 477–9. Our author is not open to his objection, either because he has taken account of it, or because he is severely compressing Aratus in any case.

459–72 give the information required to discover the approximate position of the tropic of Cancer. Our author's account differs from Aratus' in many respects; Aratus' account occupies lines 480–96.

460 This line is an addition to Aratus. The statement is very inaccurate.

462 terit is used in the opposite way in 232 ⟨*Aries*⟩ *terit . . . medii diuortia mundi* (the equator). *Z*'s *tegit* is not suitable, as the tropic, a line, could hardly be said to cover all Perseus' left foot.

463 *Z*'s *secat utraque latera tactu* does not scan, and the 'touch' of the tropic can hardly be said to cut Andromeda's flanks. *Z*'s reading is an unsuccessful attempt to mend the metre after the omission of *per* from *persecat*.

464 et totam ex umero dextram The corresponding passage of Aratus (484–6) states 'It crosses the middle part of Andromeda's right arm (δεξιτερὴν) above the elbow. Her palm lies higher, nearer the north, her elbow is inclined to the south'; i.e. it crosses her right arm between elbow and palm. Our author's *dextram* (= 'right arm') is a direct translation of Aratus' δεξιτερὴν (485).

The transmitted *ab* does not scan. Hence Schwartz proposed *abs*, but this form is not found before vowels. Baehrens proposed *aque umero totam dextram*, but this involves considerable rearrangement and *que* added to *a*. This is not found at all in what survives of Cicero's *Aratus*, Lucretius, Catullus, Propertius, Tibullus or the *Corpus Tibullianum*, Horace, Grattius or Manilius, nor is it transmitted in our author. It is found only once in Vergil (*G.* 4.437). Ovid probably used it in *Met.* 3.631, *Trist.* 4.4.85, *ex Pont.* 1.8.33 and 1.9.48 and perhaps in *ex Pont.* 2.9.60, *Am.* 2.14.30, *Trist.* 4.2.69; 5.2.74 and 5.13.34 and *Fast.* 3.363 (on the second list see Platnauer *Latin Elegiac Verse* pp. 80–1, discussing the non-elision of *atque*). Pseudo-Ovid probably used it in *Epist.* 21.180. Maybaum proposed (p. 39) *a cubito* for the transmitted *ab humero*, but it is not close, weakens *totam*, for the arm from the elbow is no longer the whole arm, and although closer to Aratus (if this is any merit: our author differs from him often in 459–72) it is not the same. I have accepted *ex umero*. *Ab* was perhaps a gloss on *ex*.

464 pulsu As the *ungula* is not travelling *Z*'s *cursu* is unsuitable. I think it was interpolated by the author of 464A and 472A & B (which I have printed in the *apparatus criticus*). The interpolator took *ungula* as an acc. pl. (which it is meant to be in 472A) and wrote *diuidit* to govern it and altered the beginning of 465 to fit in with the rest of 464A.

464A Cf. also my note on the previous verse. The mention of the southern *Sagittarius* in a description of the stars on or near the tropic of Cancer is ridiculous. The verse seems to be modelled on 392 *ante Sagittiferi paulum pernicia crura*.

465 I discuss the interpolation *hinc alius rapit* in my note on 464.

470 Everywhere else, as far as I know, *iuba* refers to the mane on the back of a lion, which sometimes falls over its neck and shoulders (cf. Plin. *N.H.* 8.42 *Leoni . . . colla armosque uestiunt iubae*). But the author of *Amores* 3.5 (who was not Ovid: cf. p.x of Kenney's introduction to the O.C.T) in lines 23–4 ⟨*cornix*⟩ *terque bouis niueae petulanti pectora rostro/fodit et albentes abstulit ore iubas* uses *iubae* of hairs on an ox's breast (I owe this reference to Kenney). Plin. *N.H.* 9.64 says of a variety of the fish *mulli* that *barba gemina insigniuntur inferiore labro* and Juvenal's *mullorum iubis* (6.40) seems to be a reference to this, for the bearded variety tasted better than others (Athenaeus p. 325d).

Perhaps the author wrote, not *iubam*, but *imum*. Cf. the corresponding passage of Avienius (965–7 *at circulus ima calentis/pectora perque aluum procul in postrema Leonis/succedit*). *Ima* is used with the genitive in 81 *Scorpios ima pedum tangit*. The sing. *imum* is found in Cels. 8.23 *mediam plantam imumque eius*, Sen. *N.Q.*7.17.2 *in imum cursus sui uenit* ⟨*cometa*⟩, Plin. *N.H.* 2.51 *ut sit imum eius* (*sc. umbrae*) *angustissimum*.

472A & B These spurious verses found (only in *Z*) after 472 are printed in the *apparatus criticus*. The first will only scan with hiatus between *tauri* and *ungula*. The second contains the false quantity *ophŷuci*. *Vngula dextra* was perhaps suggested by *dextram . . . ungula* in 464 (see also my note on 464). *Ophyuci humeros uastos* comes from 75–6 (*Ophiuchus/ . . . uastos umeros*), *fulgere notabis* from the ending of 474 (reinforced perhaps by the *notabis* of 75).

473 is similar to 526–7 *in sex signiferum si quis diuiserit orbem/aequales partes*.

476–82 are additions to Aratus.

479 propius The transmitted *breuius* ('for a shorter time') is absurd. I suggest *prop* was omitted from the sequence *polopropius* and the gap filled with *breu*.

482–4 Housman's transposition is necessary, for with the transmitted order *hic* and *contrarius*, which refer to *Cancer* and *Aegoceros* in 484 and 483, have no antecedents. A scribe's eye slipped from *austris* (the transmitted text in 483) to *austros* (in 482) and he wrote 482 first. Realizing he had omitted verses 483–4, he added them. His transposition marks for 482 were ignored by the next scribe, and verse 482 remained in the wrong place. *Aestatis* in 484, like *hiemis* in 483, depends on *metas*. Housman, who did not know S's reading, conjectured *astris* independently.

485–91 gives the information required to establish the approximate position of the tropic of Capricorn. Our author's account differs from Aratus' in several respects.

494 cernes In addresses to the reader our author often uses the future (the same word *cernes* (711), *noris* (587), *notabis* (75, iv 117), *quaeres* (507) *uidebis* (iv 147), *spectabis* (iv 3) and *speculaberis* (292, by Baehrens'conjecture) the present indicative only in 192 *respicis*, where there is a dependent *qua* clause with its verb in the present indicative. Hence I have preferred *Z*'s *cernes* to *O*'s *cernis*.

497 *O*'s *radios intulit* seems to have arisen after the omission of *tosex* before *tulit* in the sequence *radiatosextulit*.

499 *O*'s *libato sidera* is meaningless, *Z*'s *librato sidere mundi* = 'the sign of the world being balanced' makes no sense either. The 'sign of the world (or sky)' could be the sun, but it could also be another heavenly body. The author wrote *librat quae sidera mundi*. LIBRATQUESIDERA became LIBRATQ.SIDERA, and this was corrupted to LIBRATOSIDERA, whence *O*'s and *Z*'s corruptions. When the sun is on the equator the zodiacal signs are balanced evenly about it, half being north, half south.

501 aequo The equator is so called as it is not oblique, like the ecliptic (*obliquo currens spatio* 523).

501–9 give the information required to establish the approximate position of the equator. Our author's account differs from Aratus' in several respects.

505 tum Cratera leuem The corresponding passage of Aratus (519) has ελαφρὸς ('light') as an epithet of *Crater*, our author (431) has *paruo pondere Crater*. Hence *lĕuem*, not *lēuem*, is required here. Hence I have accepted Courtney's *tum* in place of *et*, and *O*'s *cratera*. *Secat* should be understood with *Cratera leuem Coruique forantis/ultima* from the *secat* in the line above.

forantis Frey's conjecture is supported by 429–30 *tortus . . . ulterioris/ uocali rostro Coruus forat*. *Foro* is used intransitively in Cels. 7.14 *tum acus admouenda est acuta ut foret* and 8.3.2 *estque quidam premendi modus, ut et foret* ⟨*modiolus*⟩ *et circumagatur*. If *forantis* is right, a scribe accidentally wrote *ferentis* because it is a much commoner word. Ellis (p. 239) conjectured *terentis*. But where does this mean 'peck'? Baehrens conjectured *sedentis*, which is supported by Hygin. *Astron.* 2.40 (p. 76.3–4 ed. Bunte) *Hydra: in qua Coruus insidere . . . existimatur*, but the corruption of this to *ferentis* seems less likely than the corruption of *forantis*. Aratus (520) has no epithet and so supports neither.

508 medio Ophiuchum will not scan unless there is a hiatus. I can quote no precise parallel, although Vergil's *Aeneid* exhibits similar hiatus of *o* at other caesurae, e.g.

si pereo/ hominum manibus periise iuuabit	(3.606)
inclusum buxo/ aut Oricia terebintho	(10.136)
promissam eripui genero/ arma impia sumpsi	(12.31)
concilia Elysiumque colo/ huc casta Sibylla	(5.735)
Maeonia generose domo/ ubi pinguia culta	(10.141)

Our author has a long *o* in hiatus before a noun of the form ∪ ∪ — — at the end of the line, as here, in 23 (*horrifero Aquilone*) and 218 (*Pierio Helicone*), but there there is an adjective agreeing with a noun (a common hiatus in Greek, imitated in Latin, usually with a Greek noun, although in 23 before the Latin *Aquilo*). *A medio* is, I think, also defensible. Cf. Liu. 8.24.14 *ibi foeda laceratio corporis facta. namque praeciso medio* . . . and Plin. *N.H.* 8.78 (of the basilisk) *nec flexu multiplici ut reliquae corpus impellit sed celsus et erectus in medio incedens.* Here *medio* refers to the middle of the body, although it is possible to understand *corpore* with *medio* from the preceding *corporis* or *corpus*, as it is not in our author. *A* = 'at' or 'in' is illustrated by *TLL* 1.21. 5ff (cf. in particular 63ff, of parts of the body).

But 508 will still not do, as it has a foot too many. Hence Schwartz deleted *mediam*, but *partem Anguis* is not specific enough. The tropic of Cancer also runs through *partem Anguis* (467). If it is answered that *a medio Ophiuchum* shows that it must be the middle of the Snake, as Ophiuchus holds the middle of the Snake at his middle, I reply that it is not likely the author would have left it to the reader to infer the part intended from what follows. One could also delete *celsi* (but what motive would there be for interpolating it?) but the *mediam/medio* repetition within the one line does not seem probable.

If a line has a foot too many, there is another remedy: add five feet and so form two lines. I suggest the missing feet contained the words *qua* . . . *tenet*, *tenet* being the word immediately before *a*. A scribe's eye slipped from the *et* to the *et* of *tenet* below it, and he omitted five feet. I have translated my supplement *qua . . . tenet*. For *tenet a medio* compare Plaut. *Men.* 1011 *eripe oculum isti ab umero qui tenet, ere, te obsecro.*

509 nec = *et non.* Cf. Housman on Manil. 1.656; 2.41 and other passages listed in his index.

511 *Z*'s *docemus* can be defended by *docebit* in 176–7, *O*'s *notamus* by *notabis* in 75, *notantur* in 85. But *notamus* seems to be the original: *nota* was omitted from the sequence *nanotamus* and *mus* expanded to *docemus*.

514 sulcos The metaphor is an addition to Aratus.

515 in obliquum = the adverb *oblique.* Cf. my note on 328.

522 Quartus: the ecliptic. **ab Oceano:** the point at which the ecliptic touches the eastern horizon shifts from the declination of the tropic of Cancer to that of the tropic of Capricorn, the two extremes of the zodiac. Our author is rendering Arat. 537–9. *Ab Oceano uestigia mutat* by itself could most naturally be taken to mean 'the circle travels away from the Ocean'. However, *quam latus* etc (525–6) makes the author's meaning clear. A similar ambiguity is found in Manil. 5.37 ⟨*Argo*⟩ *a dextri lateris ducit regione per astra*, but the context makes it clear that here too *a* = 'at'.

525 tam *Latus* is understood from 524.

sacris Hesiod (*Theog.* 788) calls *Oceanus* ἱερὸς ποταμός ('sacred river').

526–9 are discussed after 567.

530 This verse makes no sense after 525, 529 or any other extant line of the poem. But I can see no motive for interpolating it; I suspect it refers to the sphere of the fixed stars, which can appropriately be called *ultimus orbis* (i.e. the furthest away from the earth of the celestial spheres), and belongs to a lost description of the celestial spheres (the *astrorum globos* mentioned in v.1). For a partial explanation of the transposition see my note on 526–9.

531–64 expand Arat. 545–9, which simply list the zodiacal signs. Cicero (320–331) had already expanded Aratus somewhat. Aratus, followed by

Cicero, begins his list from Cancer, our author from Aries, the first sign.

531 On this verse cf. my note on 526–9.

535 amori = *uiro amato.* Cf. *OLD s.u. amor* 3d.

539 marito here = 'mate', not 'husband'. Cf. Hor. *Carm.* 2.5. 15–16 *proterua/fronte petet Lalage maritum.* The verse is similar to Col. 10.202–3 *caeruleo partus enixa marito/utraque.* **cretaeo** is governed by *litore,* but can also be understood with *marito,* for Jupiter was born in Crete (cf. 32–8) and so was taking her to his homeland.

I suggest *O*'s *litoreacretae* originated from *litorecretae.* A suprascript *a* between the *r* and *e* of *litore* (correcting *e* to *ae* so that the ending would agree with that of *cretae*) was inserted in the text in the wrong place.

540 This verse is imitated from Verg. *Aen.* 11.397 *et quos mille die uictor sub Tartara misi.*

544 *Z*'s *morsu . . . bello* is unsatisfactory, as it is very doubtful whether our author would have used the adjective *bellus* at all (it does not occur in Cicero's *Aratus,* Vergil, Horace (except once in his *Satires*), Grattius or Manilius). Even granted he could have used it, it would have to be ironic ('fine', 'pretty'), and irony is quite out of place, whether it goes with *morsu* or *sidere.* *O*'s *morsus . . . bello* ('a war of biting') deserves more consideration, but I think that it too is impossible. Goodyear advanced the objection to it that it is suitable of a fight in which both belligerents are biting (such as a fight between two crabs), but not when only Cancer, not Hercules, is biting. I have accepted Housman's *ausum morsu contingere uelle. Velle* is superfluous, but that is what it is in Ou. *Met.* 10.132 *uelle mori statuit* (quoted by Housman). Another possibility is *ausum morsu coniungere bellum* (*coniungere* became *contingere,* and as *contingere bellum* makes no sense, *bellum* was altered to agree with *morsu*), but I have preferred Housman's conjecture, which only alters one word.

The story is also mentioned by Hygin. *Astron.* 2.23 and Apollod. 2.79.

548 duplex = 'altero tanto maius' (used like a substantive). It is used this way frequently in Livy (cf. *TLL* 5.1.2271.6–9).

orbe = *in orbe.* Cf. Housman on Manil. 5.708.

550 *Z*'s unmetrical text gives the pseudo-sense 'What words would the great sign of Orion sing to me'. It is an interpolation from *O*'s text (for other interpolations in *Z* cf. my notes on 464A and 472A & B). Probably *diua* became *dicta* because a scribe's eye wandered to the following *dicto. Dicta . . . dicto* was thought intolerable and the word *magnus* (a favourite with interpolators. On its introduction into our author see my note on 66) introduced (in the form *magnum*) to qualify *sidus,* which the word *prius* suggested. *Orione* then became *Orionis* to fit.

O's text can be translated 'which the goddess will sing to me when she has first spoken of Orion'. The goddess is the author's Muse (cf. *Ilias Latina* 1 *iram pande mihi Pelidae, diua, superbi,* Stat. *Achill.* 1.3 . . . /*diua, refer,* imitations of θεά in Hom. *Iliad* 1.1 and *Od.* 1.10. The author outlines the mythology of the other signs. In this line he gives a reference to a passage in which he outlines that of Scorpius. The outline is given in 653–60, *dicto prius Orione* in 648–52. *Dicto prius Orione* gives a sufficient hint of the story to make it unnecessary for those well acquainted with it to refer to the later passage for elucidation.

552 Cf. Breysig's scholia p. 90.5–13: *at is quia inter Musas saepius moratus plausu cantus earum distinguebat . . . hunc Musae beneficio Iouis astris intulere . . . Nigidius . . . eadem dicit, sed non conuersatum Musis, sed cum illae cantus chorosque celebrarent, hunc procul abditum repentino plausu ad pedem ferientem oblectasse canentes.*

554 cochlidis κοχλίς is the diminutive of κόχλος, the word used by Eur. *I.T.* 303 of a shell used to produce a sound in battle.

558–60 Capricorn was Augustus' natal star, i.e. the sign the moon was in when he was born. Cf. Suet. *Aug.* 94.12 *tantam mox fiduciam fati Augustus habuit ut thema suum uulgauerit nummumque argenteum nota sideris Capricorni, quo natus est, percusserit,* Smyly, *Hermathena* 38 (1912), 156–9 and Housman's addenda to pp. lxix–lxxii of Manilius Book 1 (cf. also Housman's article 'Manilius, Augustus, Tiberius, Capricornus, and Libra' in *CQ* 7 (1913), 109–14 and *Classical Papers* vol. 2 pp. 867–72).

562 Deucalion Hygin. *Astron.* 2.29 says of Aquarius *Hegesianax autem Deucaliona dicit esse.*

563 Syriae . . . numina. Cf. Hygin. *Astron.* 2.30.

565–7 were rightly deleted as spurious by Grotius, as *postea* does not scan. The lack of a connective between *Tauri* and *Geminorum* and the switch from *et* to *postea* to *tunc,* then *que* and *et* is suspect.

566 Chelae are omitted, as they are reckoned as part of Scorpio (cf. 548–9).

567 Capricornus is not *geminus* (as *Gemini* and *Pisces* are), for it is half fish, half goat. Manil. 2.659 calls it *caper . . . genitusque ad frigora piscis* and in 2.155ff distinguishes between the twin signs *Gemini* and *Pisces* and (170–1) *ex diuerso commissis corpore membris,/ut Capricornus.* Our author calls it *biformis* in iv 130. *Gelidus* on the other hand is a common epithet of *Capricornus* (cf. 7, 289, also 483 *glacialibus astris* and 597 *rigidum Aegoceri signum*). Hence I think the interpolator wrote *Z*'s *gelidus,* not *O*'s *geminus.*

526–9 Housman p. 33/506 says of these verses in the place they are transmitted 'That Germanicus did not place them here in his phaenomena is evident from the abruptness of "signiferum orbem" '. But they belong to the *Phaenomena,* for they correspond with Arat. 541–3. As the only place they will fit is after 564, I have placed them here. After 531–64 the fact that the *quartus orbis* is the *signifer orbis* is well established. *Signiferum . . . orbem* in 526 is taken up by *huius . . . orbis* in 568.

Probably when the spurious verses 565–7 came from the margin into the text they displaced 526–9. These were then placed (along with 530, which comes from somewhere else) after line 525, crowded into a small space. The manuscript B preserves traces of this. Elsewhere it has only one verse per line, but verses 526–31 are written two to a line (in small letters) and followed by a blank of about half a page. On 530 cf. my note on the verse. 531 makes sense with 532ff and it may just happen to have been mixed with these verses. But it too may have come from somewhere else. It is very similar to ii 1 *Vna uia est Solis bis senis lucida signis,* but this need not mean that one line was interpolated from the other. The next nearest lines to each other are 473 *hunc octo in partis si quis diuiserit orbem* and 526 *in sex signiferum si quis diuiserit orbem*. In line 531 *haec* (referring to the masculine *orbis*) has been attracted into the gender of *uia*. Cf. e.g. Verg. *Aen.* 6.129.

529 *Vna tui* and *Vna suis* being nonsensical, Housmann conjectured *lunatus*, translating *lunatus lateris* as 'the curvature of the circumference' and continuing (p. 33/506) 'The words *latus* and *regula* are used again at 188 and 191 to signify mathematical lines. The substantive *lunatus* is not in the lexicons, and many of these verbal nouns are ἅπαξ λεγόμενα, *mactatus* [Lucr. 1.99] for instance and *offectus* [Grat. 406]'. *Lunatus* is derived from the verb *luno* (= 'bend into a crescent', derived from *luna*), which is found in Ou. *Am.* 1.1.23 *lunauit* . . . *arcum* and Prop. 4.6.25. The past participle *lunatus* (used as an adjective 'crescent shaped') is found in several passages.

571 μ's *austros* is unsuitable, as the zodiac no more belongs to the south than to the north. It is a conjecture expanding *au*, which is preserved in ν. Orelli conjectured *auras*. The *ras* was omitted at the end of this long line.

572 I suggest that ℨ accidently repeated *orbis*, then changed the first *orbis* to *aeui* to remove the repetition.

573–81 Arat. 559–63 makes no mention of the fact that the signs take different times to rise. Our author's addition of this fact (579–81) agrees with Hipparchus' comments on Aratus in 2.1.2ff.

578 The antecedent is *signum,* understood from *signo* in 576. Hence the adjectival *quod* (referring to an antecedent), not the substantival *quid* (referring to no antecedent), which is transmitted, is required. On *qui* and *quis* cf. Kuehner-Stegmann 1.655–7.

579 ue is connective (= 'and'), not disjunctive (= 'or') here. Cf. Hofmann-Szantyr p. 503. The *que* of ν is an alteration to a more common particle.

582 caua = 'engulfing'. Cf. Fordyce on Cat. 17.4 *OLD s.u. cauus* 3e quotes examples of *caua* . . . *nube* and the like.

583 From this verse onwards only one family is present, from 583 to the end of fragment iii only the inferior family ℨ. Hence more emendation is required than before. I offer an explanation of why only ℨ has 583–725 and fragments ii and iii in the Introduction on the manuscripts, section v.

585 Ides C and L present no-words, E's *iden* is unsuitable, as the accusative has no construction. Hence Grotius conjectured *Ide*. But this introduces what Housman (p. 34/507) calls a 'disagreeable asyndeton' between *Gargaron* and the other names of mountains, and it also presupposes that *Gargaron* and *Ide* are two separate mountains. But Homer talks of Γάργαρον ἄκρον/῎Ιδης ὑψηλῆς ('topmost Gargaros of tall Ide') in *Iliad* 14.292–3, and Strabo says, apropos this passage 'At the present time people point out in the upper parts of Ide a place called Gargaros' (13.1.5). While another *Ide* (in Crete. cf. Martin on Arat. 33) is mentioned, when *Gargaron* and *Ide* are presented together, only the *Ide* made famous by Homer can be meant. Hence I have written *Gargaron aut Ides*. Our author seems to be imitating the passage of Homer quoted above in his use of the genitive, taking ἄκρον as an adjective with Γάργαρον (as it is in ἀνὰ Γαργάρῳ ἄκρῳ in *Iliad* 14.352

and 15. 152). Possibly, as *Ide* is very extensive, and shaped like a centipede (Strabo 13.1.5), our author could have thought of it as a region of which *Gargaros* forms a part. For this use of the genitive cf. Kuehner-Stegmann 1.414, who quote among other passages Liu. 28.6.12 *ad Cynum Locridis.* Housman's *Gargaron aut ingens* supplies an adjective which suggests *Gargaros* is likely to conceal a constellation behind it (as do *altus* and *superis habitatus*), but, while *Ide* can rightly be called *ingens*, it is less appropriate to call its topmost regions *ingens*. Moreover, *Ides* is closer to the transmitted text.

587–8 There are verbal resemblances to Verg. *G.* 1.424–6 *si* . . . */respicies, nunquam te crastina fallet/hora neque insidiis noctis capiere serenae.*

Tempora noctis is used the same way as in 724. The transmitted *uentus tithonius ortus* is corrupt. The sense required in *numquam sqq.* is 'the time of dawn will not escape you'. Grotius conjectured *ueniens Tithonius ortus* ('the coming Tithonian rising'). *Veniens* is used in a future sense, as in 425 *uenientis nuntiat Euros* and Cic. 75 *hoc signum ueniens poterunt praenoscere nautae.* But it would be odd if *Tithonius ortus* did not mean 'the rising of Tithonus', whereas the required meaning is 'the rising of the wife of Tithonus' (i.e. of Aurora, the dawn). Hence I have written *Tithonidos* (Stat. *Silu.* 5.1.34 uses *Tithonis* to mean *Aurora*. The same genitive is found in *Doridos* in 666). The two words before *ortus* have had their endings assimilated to that of *ortus.*

589–725 (= Arat. 569–732) detail the constellations which rise or set with various zodiacal constellations. Hipparch. 134.3ff states (quoting no relevant evidence, for there is no evidence) that Aratus is specifying what constellations have risen or set when each zodiacal constellation begins to rise (i.e. what constellations rose or set with the preceding sign). Our author has followed Hipparchus by adding *primum* in 589 and *prima* in 604 and 674. That the other signs are beginning to rise is left to be understood.

590 excipit Oceanus Cf. Hygin. *Astron.* 1.8 (p. 27.7–9 ed. Bunte) *Oceanus . . . prope totius orbis alluit fines; itaque et signa occidentia in eum decidere existimantur.*

Our author is rendering Arat. 572 'The Garland sets'. Aratus qualifies the statement in 573–4 'Half of it is visible; the last part ⟨of the Crab⟩ casts down the other half of the setting Garland'. Aratus does not specify when half of it is visible. It can only be just before the last part of the Crab rises. With this last part, the Garland entirely sets. Our author has not rendered 573–4.

591 dorso = 'as far as its back', as *genibus* in 719 (*at cum se genibus demisit pars Ophiuchi*) means 'as far as his knees'.

occidit et dorso Piscis renders the second half of Arat. 572 'The Fish sets as far as its backbone'. **caudaque priore** renders the 'travelling backwards' of 575–6 'But the other travels backwards; his upper parts are carried in the region of night, his other parts, down from the lowest part of his belly, are not yet carried there'. Our author has omitted the rest of 575–6, just as he has omitted 573–4.

592 at = 'whereas', a sense illustrated by *OLD s.u. at* 1b. Grotius conjectured *et.*

mergitur in totos umeros Ophiuchus Arat. 577–8 states that the

Crab carries down the part of Ophiuchus between his knees and his shoul-
ders. Our author has omitted the reference to the knees, and added *totos* to
the shoulders.

592–3 Anguis/ultima cauda micat Here our author is not following
Arat. 578 ('It carries down the Snake almost to its neck') but agrees with
the correction by Hipparch. 2.2.10, who says that only the tail is above
the earth.

593 tortus habet unda timendos By replacing the transmitted *illa*
with *unda*, Thierfelder introduces the required contrast between the tail,
above the horizon, and the rest of the Snake, which is *medium cingens
Ophiuchum* (80) with its coils, below it. Another possibility is *tortus tegit ille
timendos* (*ille* was conjectured by Grotius), the *ille* referring to the Snake in
contrast to its tail (cf. 427, if *ille* is sound there). But as *ille* would refer to
Ophiuchus, if that did not give an absurd sense, it is better absent, hence I
have adopted *unda*. **habet unda** Cf. Cic. 381–2 *mergitur unda/Delphinus* and
Auien. 1256–7 *haec habet occidui plaga gurgitis, ista sonoro/supprimit unda salo.*
Illa could have been written by someone who thought (consciously or
unconsciously) 'water has no coils, but a Snake has'.

594 The corresponding passage of Aratus states (579–80) 'No longer are
there large parts of the Guardian of the Bears on both sides of the horizon;
only the lesser part is in the region of day; already the greater part is in the
region of night'. Hipparchus (2.2.15) says that Aratus is correct in this
statement. Hence this line must originally have been equivalent or similar
in sense to these verses of Aratus. The transmitted *his . . . subiacet astris* ('It is
close to (or 'below') these constellations') is wrong, pointless in the context,
and does not correspond to Aratus. *Multo . . . longe* is meaningless, *multo*
requiring a following comparative or superlative. Hence I suggest the author
wrote, not *longe subiacet*, but *longius hic iacet*. *Iacet* is used of constellations in
the passages collected in *TLL* 7.1.21.81ff. Cf. in particular Cic. 84 *hic,
missore uacans, fulgens iacet una Sagitta. Hic* is a vague word, corresponding to
Aratus' προτέρω βεβλημένος ('cast in front'). Here I take it to mean 'at
the western horizon'. I suggest *hic* was lost from the sequence LONGIUSHI-
CIACET and the missing syllable made up by changing *longius iacet* to *longe
subiacet*.

595–7 Here our author is not following Arat. 581–2, who states that
Bootes sets with four zodiacal signs. In 2.2.14ff Hipparchus states that
Aratus is in error in this statement. Our author seems to have derived 595–7
from Hipparch. 2.6.1 or (more likely) a similar account. Hipparchus states
there that Bootes begins to set with the 5th to 6th degree of the Scorpion and
completes the process with the 18½th degree of Capricorn, and that the most
northerly star in his crook is the last to set (as his crook is raised above his
head our author's *ore* is roughly equivalent to this). In 598–9 the author
returns to Aratus (582–3).

597 freta lucida terret This he does by threatening to set.

599 noctis plus parte relinquit makes no sense. The required sense is
given by Arat. 583 βουλυτῷ ἐπέχει πλεῖον δίχα νυκτὸς ἰούσης ('He tarries
in the unyoking of his oxen (= setting) while more than half the night goes

by'). Aratus is following Homer *Iliad* 16.779 ἠέλιος μετενίσετο βουλυτόνδε ('The sun travels towards the place of unyoking—i.e. of setting'). The required sense can be obtained without changing any words by assuming there is a lacuna in which some such words as *moratus/dimidia, tandem caeli conuexa* have fallen out.

603 This line is a picturesque way of saying 'The River rises'. The river god Eridanus (mentioned in 363 *Amnem qui Phaethonta suas defleuit ad undas*) has two horns on his head, as the river god Achelous (Ou. *Ep.* 9.139 *cornua flens legit ripis Achelous in udis*). Our author's *cornua* was suggested by the word κέραος in the corresponding passage of Aratus (588–9 'Ωρίων . . ./ πάντα φέρων Ποταμόν, κέραος παρατείνεται ἄλλου 'Orion . . . bringing after him the whole of the River, is stretched out at the sky's other flank') although in Aratus κέραος = 'horizon' (or 'flank of the sky').

604–5 correspond with Arat. 590–1 'When the Lion is coming, the constellations which were setting with the Crab are carried down completely'. The transmitted *caelo nascente* is absurd, and a mention of Cancer is missing. Hence Schaubach emended *caelo* to *Cancro*.

610 Sirius ipse is an addition to Aratus.

611 totius contrasts the Dog itself with Sirius, a part of the Dog, and is taken up with *totusque Canis* in line 621.

Both L's *rabidi* and CE's *rapidi* are good (on *rapidi/rabidi* applied to *Canis* cf. Housman on Manil. 1.396).

612 Exorsae can hardly be used by itself, with no indication of what the Maiden has begun to do. Hence I have accepted *exortae*, which means 'while rising', as in Manil. 5.631–3 *Piscibus exortis cum pars uicesima prima/signabit terrae limen fulgebit et orbi,/aerius nascetur Ecus* and 5.102.

613 The sense required is 'The Dolphin sets' (cf. Arat. 598). The transmitted *motis* is nonsensical (as if the constellation made a splash when going in!). Sense is restored with *notis*. '*Notis*, quia Delphinus est ἔνυδρος' Grotius, quoting Manil. 5.394 *at cum se patrio producens aequore Piscis. Deflexerit* (= 'turn side from') is also wrong, and *defluxerit* should be restored. Cf. Auien. 754–5 *Sirius alto/defluit ab caelo. Notis undis* is dative.

616 This line corresponds with Arat. 599–600 'Ορνιθος πρῶτα πτερὰ μέσφα παρ'αὐτὴν/οὐρὴν . . . σκιόωνται ('The first part of the Swan's wings, up to the part of them alongside the tail, is obscured'). πρῶτα = 'first part', as in 747 πρώτης . . . νυκτός = 'in the first part of the night' and in 660 Στεφανοιό τε δεύτερα κύκλα = 'the second part of the Garland'. Our author uses *uolans* of the wings as they are stretched out in flight (*nunc quoque diductas uolitat stellatus in alas* Manil. 1.341).

617 Eridanus is near the western horizon, hence its stars are fainter than when they are higher up in the heavens, for more of their light is absorbed by the atmosphere. The corresponding passage of Aratus (600 Ποταμοῖο παρηορίαι σκιόωνται) means that the edge of the River has set. *Nigrescit* was suggested by σκιόωνται, but does not correspond to it. Cf. my note on *cornua* (603).

620 Creterra tenus ἄχρι παρ' αὐτὸν/κρητῆρα (Arat. 602–3). **aplustria** corresponds with πρύμναν (604).

621 'uehementer displicet "*sed* cum pia Virgo *nascitur*". nam quae antecedunt ipsa referuntur ad ortum incipientem Virginis (612 accipe quae uitent exorsae Virginis *ora*). necessarie flagitatur aliquid, quod *totam* Virginem ortam esse significet' *Maybaum* p. 47. Hence Housman conjectured *pede*, stating: '. . . For 'pede nascitur' compare 596 'occulitur pedibus', Auien. 1138 'pede proferat ortum'. I had also thought of this:

> sed, cum pia Virgo
> nascitur ipsa, Ratis media plus arbore lucet.

For *ipsa* signifying the main body of a constellation as opposed to a part of it see Cic. 403 sq. 'hic *genus* et *suram* cum Chelis erigit alte,/*ipse* autem praeceps obscura nocte tenetur'. But *ipsa* next to *ratis* is a trifle ambiguous, and so would *ima* be'.

623 sua Cf. my note on 176.

624 tum Perhaps the transmitted *nunc* arose under the influence of the *no* at the end of the preceding word.

crine is used of the rays of a constellation's stars, as in Auien. 81 and 253. Cf. also our author 87 *stella . . . crinita*, with my note.

626 The transmitted *celsaque Puppis habet* = 'the Ship occupies the regions above the horizon' (*habet = occupat* in 478 *tunc habet . . . fastigia summa* and 239 *medium Deltoton habebit*, and our author uses *celsa astra* of the stars above the horizon in 676 *celsis Ophiuchus fulget in astris*). But the noun *celsa* does not occur elsewhere until late Latin (cf. e.g. Claud. 28.30 *caelicolae cum celsa tenent* and *TLL* 4.774.63ff). Hence both Courtney and I have thought of emending *habet* to *adest*, so making *celsa* agree with *Puppis*. Dahms (p. 273). suggested that there is a lacuna after *Puppis*, and he supplied the word *adest* in it.

cauda minus = 'minus his tail'. Cf. 673 and the use of *plus* in 622 **Hydra** corresponds to Aratus' Ὕδρη (611).

628 noctem = 'the region of invisibility', the part of the sky below the horizon, as in 695. An unknown hand has altered *supremā* in L to *suprema* (probably to agree with *fluctuata*). Hence Grotius conjectured *nocte . . . suprema* together with *eluctata*. But *TLL s.u. eluctor* quotes no uses with the ablative. It is often followed by the accusative. Cf. e.g. Sil. 13.741–2 ⟨*Hannibal*⟩ *Alpes/eluctatus adest*.

274 summa genus subuersa tenet qua se Lyra uoluit = 'he keeps the upper part of his knee upside down alongside the Lyre'. *Summa genus* = 'the upper part of the knee', i.e. the part of the leg just above the knee joint. Cf. Val. Flacc. 3.525 *summo palla genu*. Our author uses a neuter pl. with the genitive of a part of the body in 81 *ima pedum*. Both *O*'s *uoluit* and *Z*'s *uersat* are suitable. Cf. Cic. *Rep.* 6.17 ⟨*orbis summus*⟩ *in quo sunt infixi illi qui uoluuntur stellarum cursus sempiterni. huic subiecti sunt septem qui uersantur retro contrario motu atque caelum*.

The verse is unsatisfactory in its transmitted place, because the relative positions of Lyra and Engonasin have already been given in 271–2 ⟨*Lyra*⟩ *caelo nitet ante labore/deuictam effigiem*. It does not correspond to Arat. 271–2 ('The being crouching on its legs has his left knee near it'—i.e. the Lyre). Arat. 271–4 is summarized by 278–9 *inter defectum sidus Cycnumque nitentem/*

Mercurialis habet sedem Lyra. Hence Housman transposed 274 to follow 628. Lines 627–8 and 274 render Arat. 612, 614–15 (613 being a spurious line found late in the manuscript tradition) 'Of the being ever on his knees and crouching beside the Lyre, the Claws only lift up the right leg as far as the part above the knee'. Thus *crure* in 627 means 'shank' (the part of the leg below the knee). The shank, according to Ptolemy's configuration, is the part of Engonasin between the stars τ and χ Herculis, and is bent at an angle of about 90° to the thigh, the part between τ and η. τ and χ Herculis and the stars between them rise before the rest of the constellation; the next part to rise is the upper part of the right leg (our author's *summa genus* being the first part of this). Housman is mistaken in his statement that Grotius transposed 274 to follow 627. In fact, he transposed it to follow 608, where it makes no more sense than where it is transmitted.

633–5 correspond to Arat. 620–3 'He himself . . . awaits the rising of the Scorpion and the Drawer of the Bow. These are the signs that lift him up: the Bow lifts up his head and left hand, the Scorpion his middle parts and all the rest of him'. But 633 states Engonasin has entirely risen. That is true only under Sagittarius. Hence, if the verse is to be retained in its transmitted form, it must be transposed. It must be replaced by a verse which completes *cum Scorpios exit.* A mention of Sagittarius, missing from the transmitted text, must also be introduced. Grotius proposed the following:

cum Scorpios exit,	632
haud cunctatus abit; cum Chiron surget ab undis,	634
Arcusque ipsa pio caelo referetur imago,	635
iam totis radiat membris miserabile sidus.	633

But *abit* (= 'leaves the sky') is unsuitable. Grotius would have done better to write *adest.* Even then, the objections remain. (1) It is not stated how much of Engonasin rises with Scorpius. (2) Chiron = the Southern Centaur elsewhere in our author (421, 637—a few lines below this passage—669, 675 and 695). (3) *Arcus ipsa . . . imago:* what is the force of *ipsa?* Why is there an archer, but only the *imago* of a bow? (4) *pio caelo* is very odd. But *suo caelo* is not satisfactory, as the sky above the horizon is no more Sagittarius' element than that below.

Breysig produced the following:

cum Scorpios exit	632
non totis radiat membris miserabile sidus;	
at cum tantum aberit, quantum Lyra surgit ab undis,	
Arcus ipsa suo caelo referetur imago.	635

But an assertion that Lyra and Engonasin have risen as far as each other does not tell how far each has risen, and *non totis membris* is wrong, as Engonasin does not come forth minus a bit of each of his four limbs. Ellis' and Maybaum's conjectures (which may be found in Breysig ed. 2) do not even give a semblance of sense.

Sense is restored by Housman's reconstruction, which I have printed. The statement that under Scorpius Engonasin has risen as far as his back (635) is equivalent to Aratus' statement that only his head and (upraised) left hand remain below the horizon (623). Engonasin is *obstipa,* for he is *defecta labore*

(65), μογέοντι . . . ἀνδρὶ ἐοικὸς ('like a toiling man') Arat. 63. Housman (p. 35/509) remarks '*suo* in 635 of course agrees with *tergo*. 634 must once have worn this shape: at si lyra cum tantus abitisurgit ab undis, which was reduced to metre by transposition omission and insertion: *quantum* was suggested by *tantus*. For the caesura see 23, 442.

'One point remains obscure. Some writers, as Sen. Thy. 861 and Luc. ix 536, identify Sagittarius with Chiron, who was as everyone knows the son of Philyra and the grandson of Oceanus. Germanicus however elsewhere identifies Sagittarius with Crotus and Chiron with the Southern Centaur, and he calls that Centaur by the name of Chiron in this same context, verse 637. Now Crotus, like Chiron, was a grandson of Oceanus, for the scholia (Breysig ed. 1 pp. 90 and 159) call him "Oceani nepos" on the authority of Nigidius; but his mother's name is generally given as Eupheme. Whether others held Philyra to be his mother, or whether Germanicus, having read in Nigidius' astronomical works that Crotus and Chiron were both grandsons of Oceanus, jumped to the conclusion that they were both sons of Philyra, I cannot determine. Philyra has other sons than Chiron: Hyginus mentions Dolops, Suidas makes her the mother of Aphrus king of Libya'.

633 Arat. 623 specifies the parts of Engonasin which rise with the Archer, our author simply states that he has entirely risen with it, as Arat. 620–1 implies.

636 torta *Tota* is unsuitable, as the Garland has only partly risen (*imperfecta redit*). Ellis' *torta* is defended by Prop. 3.20.18 *testis sidereae torta Corona deae*.

638 corpore All of Pegasus, not just his breast (*pectore*) and wings, sets, according to Arat. 627 ('The Horse then sets after his vanished head'). Hence I have accepted Maybaum's *corpore*. *Pectore* comes from a repetition of the same word in the same place in the following verse.

640 Andromedā Cf. my note on 201.

641 insequitur Arat. 629–30 states 'The South Wind, high in the air, carries against her the Sea Monster, a great source of terror'. *Insequitur* fits this better than *sequitur* and also explains the preceding *occasum* (*occasu insequitur* became *occasum sequitur*).

uementi The unmetrical *uentis* was corrected in two ways, the first by inserting *et* after it (simply a conjecture), the second by expanding it to *uenientis* (this may be a conjecture, perhaps based on 606 *uenientis defugit ora*, but *ien* may have fallen out after *uen* and been replaced suprascript, this not deterring someone from conjecturing *et*). E records the first correction, E^c the second, λ combines them both. *Venientis* is of course impossible, as Andromeda is setting. Housman suggested *uementi*, an epithet transferred from *Pristis* to *occasu* as *auersos* in Manil. 5.140 *Taurus in auersos praeceps cum tollitur ortus* is transferred from *Taurus* to *ortus*. Housman quotes (p. 35/510) Plaut. *Rud.* 71 '*uehemens* sum exoriens, *cum occido uehementior*'. From Aratus, quoted above, Orelli suggested *metuentis*, but this is not very close. Another possibility is *uergentis*.

642 crista super caelo fulget The crest on the Sea Monster's head still shines. His rear part has set.

642–3 caput etc. Here our author is not following Arat. 633, who states that Cepheus' head, hand and shoulders set, but agrees with the alteration by Hipparch. 2.2.50.

If Cepheus' head has set, he cannot be what the transmitted text represents him as being, *altis intactus ab undis*. He is *alias intactus ab undis*.

644 non prius 'Grotius alters *quam* to *quum* for the sake of sense; but the repetition of *Scorpios* has no point' Housman p. 35/510. **fluxerit** can be defended from Luc. 8.172–4 *fluunt labentia caelo . . . /sidera*. Cf. also our author's *Delphinus . . . defluxerit undis* (613). Grotius' *fugerit* is further from the transmitted *fulserit*.

647 The transmitted *non ego non primus* contains a *non* too many. I think *haec ego non primus* the closest substitute (HECEGO was reduced to HEGO and *non* interpolated (from the following *non*?) in place of the H). Other possibilities (further from the transmitted text) are *non ego sum primus* (Burman) or *non ego nunc primus* or *non ego nunc primum* (suggested to me as possibilities by Goodyear) or *hoc ego non primus*. Except with Burman's conjecture, *cano* should be understood from the following *cecinere*.

651 '*Angustus stipes* is a cudgel affording insufficient room for a colony of white ants which have eaten it hollow' Housman p. 36/510. Housman defends his *augustas* from Avienius' imitation of our author in 1180–3 *cum sacrata Chii nemora et frondentia late/bracchia lucorum, cum siluae colla comasque/ deuotae tibimet* (Diana) *manus impia demolita est,/audax ut facinus donum foret Oenopioni*. Orelli's *ambusto* has merit. Cf. Sil.8.549 *gestabant tela ambustas sine cuspide cornos*.

658–60 The corresponding passage of Aratus (643–6) states 'The scorpion, which killed him . . . They say it is for this reason that when the Scorpion comes forth on the other side of the sky, Orion flees at the western horizon'. The transmitted *quamquam parte relicta/caeli poene fugit tamen altis mergitur undis* = 'although he almost sets, nevertheless he sets'. Grotius' *quamquam parte retecta/teli paene fugit* (which does not remove the absurdity of the transmitted text) suggested to me *tamquam parte relicta/poenae, tela fugit* (*tamquam* became *quamquam* under the influence of the following *tamen; poenae tela* became *tela poen(a)e* by transposition (cf. 78 and 576) and *tela* became *teli* to fit the metre. It is a small step from *teli* to *celi* (*caeli*)). *Relinquo* is used with an abstract noun such as *poena* in Cic. *Rep.* 2.62 *non prouocatione . . . relicta*, and with the notion of a part being left in Cic. *Post red. in sen.* 24 *exiguum reliquae uitae tempus . . . ad commemorandam gratiam mihi relictum putarem*. The sting in the tail of the Scorpion is called *spicula* (pl.) in 393, 491 and 657, as it is called *tela* (pl.) here. *Tamen* in 659 contrasts Orion's fears (657–9) with his real safety (659–60).

661ff Our author omits Aratus' statements about Cepheus (649–52). Cf. my note on 642–3.

665 canchli A scribe has altered this unfamiliar word to *cancri*, which occurs *passim*. Plin. *N.H.* 5.65 describes *Arabia Petraea*. It appears from his description that a tribe called the *Canchlei* occupied the north east of this area. Hence *litore Canchli* refers to the shore of the Mediterranean just south of Palestine. Konon, whose *floruit* is placed by Photius *Bibl.* 186 p. 130 b25

(Jacoby *F. Gr. Hist.* 1.190) in the reign of Archelaus (36 B.C.–A.D. 17) relates (Fr. 40 Jacoby 1.204.35ff) that 'the territory of Cepheus extended from our sea [the Mediterranean] to the Arabians living on the shores of the Red Sea'. Our author is following this account of the locality of Cepheus' kingdom.

667 totius . . . Corona Arat. 659–60 νειόθεν . . . /οὐρανὸς ἀντιφέρει Στεφάνοιό τε δεύτερα κύκλα ('In the east the sky carries from below the remaining half-circle of the Garland').

670 *uastus et* is an interpolation made after the loss of a *iam toto* by haplography.

673 & 677–8 Arat. 672–3 states that Engonasin's head as well as his left hand rises with the Archer. Our author omits a mention of his head. Hipparch. 188.10–11 states that the star at the tip of his left hand is the last to rise.

675 & extulit (676) render Arat. 663–4 (τοὶ δ' *etc*).

676 extulit *Effero* is often used of the rising of stars (cf. *TLL* 5.2.146.81ff). *Expello* is not so used; it is too vigorous a word. Cf. *TLL s.u. expello.*

celsis astris Cf. my note on 626.

This line & **677** (to **serpens**) represent Arat. 665–8. Our author has omitted the detail that both Ophiuchus' hands rise with the Scorpion, declared wrong by Hipparch. 2.2.55.

677 trunca recepta & 678 'The construction in my opinion is "recepta manu desinit esse trunca membris" ' Housman p. 27/497.

679 Cycni dextera penna is an addition to Aratus (cf. Hipparch. 2.3.3). Our author seems to have used a fuller source than Hipparchus, however.

680 Our author is not following Arat. 674–5, who states that Cepheus rises as far as his breast, but agrees with Hipparchus 2.2.59 (cf. my note on 642–3).

Cepheus rediens cum sidere gives the absurd sense 'Cepheus returning with his constellation (i.e. himself)'. Nor do I think it possible to take *cum* as a conjunction, when it comes just before *sidere* and so far from the beginning of the clause. *Cum* is corrected by Grotius to *tum* at 636.

radit . . . sidere In Manil. 1.365 *Haedi cludentes sidere pontum, sidere* is equally otiose.

682 The transmitted text makes good sense, but is not close to the corresponding passage of Aratus (677–8) δίνουσιν . . ./πάντα γε μὴν ἀτέλεστα διωκομένοιο Λαγωοῦ ('All the stars of the Hare, pursued without end, set'). Hence I suggest the author may have written something like this: *et semper tutus ab illo/sed semper metuens instantem, totus in undis/est Lepus. Totus* corresponds to Aratus' πάντα ('all') and its similarity to *tutus* in the same place in the line above explains the omission. The *semper* in the supplementary line corresponds to Aratus' ἀτέλεστα ('without end').

685 Arat. 685–8 says that all Perseus save his right knee and foot set with the Archer. Our author agrees with the correction by Hipparch. 2.2.60.

687 uenerandae numine Grotius quotes Val. Flacc. 8.202–3 (of the Argo) *puppe procul summa uigilis post terga magistri/haeserat auratae genibus Medea Mineruae.*

688–9 armiger etc. Cf. 316–20.

690 omnibus et stellis The author states this because part of it has risen before. Cf. 679 with my note.

691 paruus Delphinus An addition to Aratus. The information is given by Hipparch. 2.3.10.

692 is an addition to Aratus. On the Southern Garland see my note on 391–2.

693–4 ore/et ceruice tenus As far as its head and feet, according to Aratus 694.

698 Hydram plus mediam condit = 'It hides more than half the Water Snake'. The construction is the same as in Liu. 34.1.3 *ne qua mulier plus semunciam auri haberet* and 36.40.5 *plus partem dimidiam ex quinquaginta milibus hominum caesam.* Our author is not following Arat. 697–8, who states that only its head and neck set. Hipparch. 2.3.5 states Hydra begins to set a sign earlier than Aratus states. Our author has altered Aratus from another source.

702 et liberat ortus & 703 render Arat. 703 'It does not rise completely; a small part of it awaits the rising of the next of the twelve signs' (Aries). The transmitted *et* seems to me possible (*et* introduces a contrasted statement in 341 *auritum Leporem sequitur Canis et fugit ille*, the lengthening of the *it* of *surgit* can be defended from the *abit* of 128) and so too perhaps *ortus*, which, if nominative, could be partly defended from Auien. 1283 *Phrixei postquam pecoris proruperit ortus*, if acc. pl., from 126 *eduxerit ortus*, 1032 *protulit ortum*, 1138 *proferat ortum* and 1077 *commouet ortum.* But the transmitted text is certainly suspect. Goodyear suggested *se liberat ortu* (perhaps the transmitted *ortus* (= 'having risen') would do). This is supported by the passage of Avienius corresponding to the first half of this line (1274 *haud toto tamen hic se corpore promit; se* could have been modelled on our author) and more strongly by our author 668 *totum se liberat Hydros.* Grotius suggested *sed* for *et* and, adopting this, Thierfelder *ora* for *ortus.* Although the fact is not mentioned by Aratus, the mouth rises last. Another possibility is *Orcus* for *ortus*, the sky below the horizon being regarded as the underworld, as in Manil. 2.794 (talking of the western horizon) *fugit mundus praecepsque in Tartara tendit.*

704–5 Our author is not following Arat. 704–9, who states that part of Andromeda rises with the Ram, but agrees with the alteration by Hipparch. 2.3.17.

705 Nereidas ... fugit By coming out of the sea, she escapes the sea nymphs, who had her chained to a rock.

707 If Perseus is still rising when the Pleiades appear (708–9), he can't have already risen under the Ram. Hence a line or lines must have been lost after 707, in which it was stated how far Perseus has risen under the Ram. If our author followed Arat. 711 what is lost meant 'as far as his head and shoulders', if Hipparchus' alteration (2.3.26) it meant 'except for his left knee and foot'.

709 Tauri I can see nothing to choose between this and Dahm's *Taurus* in sense (*dextro Taurus cognoscitur armo* = 'The Bull can be seen as far as his right shoulder'. Cf. my note on 591). But *Tauri* is closer to the transmitted text.

710 This line is an addition to Aratus. **sine curribus ullis:** our author also states in 161 (*sic nulli currus*) that he has no chariot. The transmitted text of the line is unsatisfactory, as, if the constellation has no chariot, he can't be *fixus in curru*. Hence Dahms suggested *fixus et in cornu*. Our author also states that the Charioteer's foot is stuck in a horn of the Bull in 178–80 (the one star representing both. This configuration is as early as Eudoxus— quoted by Hipparch. 14.4–5). Halma suggested *ut* for *et* (*fixus ut in curru* = 'stuck as if in a chariot'). *Fixus* being unsuitable (what is the Charioteer stuck to?) Goodyear suggested *flexus*, Kenney *nixus*. But there is no evidence the Charioteer is still practising his arts in a phantom form in heaven, indeed our author (161 *ruptis maestus habenis*) states he has given them up. Nor is he represented as bent in the sky, but as upright, facing the observer.

718 uicinum etc. Our author is not following Arat. 721–3. The information given by Aratus that Bootes sets with four signs is omitted. Cf. also my note on 595–7.

719 at I have changed *et* to *at* for two reasons. (1) Both the other sections into which 589–725 is divided which begin with a particle (604, 674) begin with *at*. (2) Avienius has *at* transmitted in the corresponding passage, which in other places is clearly modelled on our author (1308–10 *at cum iam pedibus repetit fluctus Ophiuchus/ut genua Oceanus uasto procul aequore condat,/ signum erit eoa Geminos procedere parte*) and the corruption of *at* to *et* is more likely than the converse.

genibus See my note on 591.

demisit The transmitted *se dimisit* means that Ophiuchus is rising (cf. my note on *liberat* in 702), but Arat. 724 says he is setting. Ovid uses *se demiserit undis* of setting in *Fast.* 1.653.

721 Pristis Κῆτος Arat. 726.

terga = 'body'. Cf. Housman on Manil. 1.340 (and his addenda to that line).

722 deprendat σκέψαιτό κε Arat. 729.

Our author concludes his rendering of Aratus at Arat. 731.

Fragment ii

I offer an explanation of why only *Z* has 583–725 and fragments ii and iii in section v of my introduction on the manuscripts.

1 This verse asserts that the sun never varies in the path it travels among the constellations. A similar sort of assertion is made about the constellations in 435–6 (= Arat. 452–3) *sors sua cuique data est, semel assignata tuentur/ immoti loca nec longo mutantur in aeuo*. Verse 1 is similar to 531, on which see my note on 526–9.

6–9 These verses are explained by Housman in his note quoted on lines 17–20 below.

The two clauses explaining the first motion (this is innate and is their proper motion) are balanced by the two explaining the second (this is not innate and is the motion of the sky).

10 Our author is referring to the nine celestial spheres (the *astrorum globos* of v 1). These are, in order, that of the fixed stars, of Saturn, Jupiter, Mars, the sun, Venus, Mercury, the moon, the earth (Cic. *Rep.* 6.17) The sun is *medius*, for it is the middle one of the whole nine, and the middle of the seven spheres of the planets.

15 On an average Mercury and Venus take a year to travel through the zodiac.

17–20 exist only in E and have never been printed before in the text (Baehrens and Breysig ed. 2 printed them in the *apparatus*). The common ancestor of C and L omitted them. Breysig declared them spurious on these grounds. (1) A mention of Saturn is missing. It has been lost in the lacuna I have marked. (2) Verses 19–20 mean the same as 8–9. As Housman (footnote on p. 37/512) points out, this is untrue. 'Verses 8 and 9 distinguish between the proper motion of the sun and moon and planets through the zodiacal signs from west to east and their diurnal motion about the earth from east to west in common with all the heaven. Verses 19 and 20 refer to the periodical acceleration and retardation of the former of these two motions'.

20 The transmitted *sumpto* could be sound if *pigro sidere sumpto* can equal *pigritia sumpta* (but I can quote no parallel for this). As the words completing the sense are lost, Baehrens' *somno* could, for all we know, be right.

Fragments iii and iv

Fragments iii, preserved only in *Z*, and iv, preserved only in *O*, are continuous, as Housman saw. Fr. iii 1–22 describes the general effects on the weather of each sign, iii 23–iv 163 the effects of each planet in each sign.

iii 1–2 are transmitted: *grandine permixtus aries niuibusque caducis/spargunt uicina tristis supra iuga piscis* (-es E). A scribe has replaced the original endings of 2 and 3 with *Pisces* and *Aries*, for the names of the zodiacal constellations were running through his mind as he copied out this passage. *Pisces* are mentioned in 19–22. The plural *spargunt* probably arose under the influence of the plural *Pisces*. As the subject is *Aries*, the verb should be singular. *Permixtus* is unmetrical, for the lengthening of the *us* cannot be defended from Vergil's practice, for, while he sometimes lengthens *us*, he has no examples where the *us* of an adjective immediately followed by its noun is lengthened (cf. the discussion by Nettleship in Conington-Nettleship's Vergil ed. 3 vol. 3 pp. 486–91), and the lengthening of the a in *uicina* is also indefensible (cf. Housman *CQ* 21 (1927), 1–12; *Classical Papers* vol. 3, 1114–26). Grotius proposed:

> grandine permixtas Aries niuibusque caducis
> spargit uicinas supra iuga tristia nubes.

But (1) *nubes* implies that clouds fall down to earth together with hail and snow. (2) The trajection of *tristia* away from the word it agrees with and into the centre of the line and its acquisition of an ending which does not agree with a nearby word does not seem very likely. Ellis proposed:

> grandine permixtos Aries niuibusque caducis
> aspargit (or dat spargens) uicina supra iuga tristibus imbres.

(Noctes Manilianae p. 241).

But more than just the word *tristibus* is required to introduce a reference to
men affected by the weather. I have printed:

grandine permixtos Aries niuibusque caducis

uicina aspergit tristis supra iuga nimbos.

Our author uses *nimbos* with *grandine* in iv 34 *tum resoluta dabit nimbos cum
grandine nubes*. The picture is of clouds lying near the ridges and rain, snow
and hail falling from them. I suggest the *a* of *aspergit* was lost after the *a* of
uicina, *spergit* changed to the Latin word *spargit*, then the words were trans-
posed (cf. my note on 658–60). *Permixtos* was changed to *permixtus* to agree
with the next word *Aries*. For the clausula of line 2 cf. 312, 370, 466, 570
and 609.

6 Against *perstridunt* (1) the word does not occur anywhere else; (2) it must
be construed as the equivalent of *stridunt per*, but there are no similar uses
elsewhere in our author; (3) *stridunt*, implying a harsh or loud sound, does
not suit *leuiter*. Hence I have accepted Housman's *perstringunt*. *Praestringunt*
is also possible.

9 The weather will be hot under the Lion, as his breast burns with rage.
Cf. Auien. 395 *assiduis ardet Leo uiscera flammis*.

12 caelo minitabitur ignis (= 'threaten the sky with fire': the con-
struction is illustrated with this, and other passages by *TLL* 8.1025.51–67) is
strictly illogical, since lightning is actually flashing in the sky, not merely
threatening. But the author perhaps means that lightning is flashing all the
time and there is a continual threat of more. One would perhaps expect the
sense 'it is continually threatening fire from the sky', but I find it hard to
believe the author would have expressed this with the simple ablative *caelo*
when the natural way to take *caelo* is dative. If he meant this, I think he
probably wrote *caeli*. This use of *minitor* can be illustrated from Sen. *N.Q*
2.12.1 *fulguratio . . . comminatio est et conatio sine ictu*.

13 E's *ctu* seems to be a corruption of the *eta* left when q (or q̇) was
omitted from q̇eta after *a*. E has numerous omissions in fragments ii and iii.
With L's *quieta* this line makes good sense in itself (a very similar use of
inuenire is found, as Courtney p. 174 points out, in Val. Flacc. 4.724–6 *utque
uel immotos Vrsae rigor inuenit amnes/uel freta uersa uadis, hiemem sic unda per
omnem/aut campo iacet aut tumido riget ardua fluctu* and the present *inuenit*
between the futures *minitabitur* and *rigebunt* can be defended from the tenses
in 616–22) but with lightning, strong winds and snow the *arua* are anything
but *quieta*. Hence Courtney transposes this line to follow 15, remarking (in a
letter to me) that '*magis quieta* seems a reasonable correspondence to 14, just
as *rara* in 15 contrasts with *assidue* in 12'. I have accepted this, as the verse
fits nowhere else.

14 uentos 'threatening fierce winds' can be defended from 'threatening
fire' in line 12 (see my note). Grotius conjectured *uenti* for *uentos*. Another
plausible conjecture is *rigebit* for *rigebunt*. But I think the transmitted text
is possible.

15 *Pluuia* does not scan. Grotius proposed *flumina*, but this word is used
nowhere else, as far as I know, by itself to mean 'rain' (cf. *TLL s.u. flumen*). I
proposed, in a seminar at the Institute of Classical Studies, University of

London, either *fulgura* or *fulmina* (and I now find *fulmina* proposed by Le Boeuffle, p. 67), but I can find no place where these words are used with the word *descendunt*; Skutsch objected to them that *descendunt* implies too slow a rate of descent, and his objection is supported by Sen. *Dial.* 5.1.4 *fulmina . . . non eunt sed cadunt* and *N.Q.* 2.13.1 *ignis quem natura sursum uocat . . . non descendit ignis, sed praecipitatur et deducitur.* The only suitable word seems to be Skutsch's own proposal *flamina*, which is supported by Val. Flacc. 7.25 *grataque iam fessis descendunt flamina remis* and 1.686–7 *molli Zephyros descendere lapsu/aspiciunt.*

13 is discussed before 14.

16 frigora durat *Frigora* is treated as something concrete, as in Cic. 58 *de corpore frigus anhelans*, Q. Cic. (= Ausonius 383) 11 *Sagittipotens iaculatur frigora terris* and Lucr. 2. 590 *uoluentes frigora fontes.*

17 As this verse is transmitted, *passus* must be taken as the perfect participle of *patior*, used as a finite verb, as in Verg. *G.* 4.500–3 *neque illum/ . . . praeterea uidit; nec portitor Orci/amplius obiectam passus transire paludem.* The same use of a perfect participle is found in 137–8 and 318–19 in our author. But the aorist is not the right tense after the presents of the previous line, hence I have altered *instabilique* to *instabilita.* *Instabile uestigium* is found in Plin. *Paneg.* 22.4 *locum qui non nisi suspensum et instabile uestigium caperet.* The word *instabilio* is used by Hyginus *de munit. castr.* 54 *angulos castrorum circinari oportet, quia coxas efficiunt instabiliuntque opus ⟨et oppugnationem magis quam⟩ propugnationem tutant* ('You should round off the edges in your camp, for they form "hips" [points where the sides meet, as bones meet at hips] and so weaken the structure, protecting the attack more than the defence'.). I have marked a lacuna after *opus*, which I have filled from Vitruu. 1.5.2 *angulus magis hostem tuetur quam ciuem.* The omission can be explained by the similarity of *et oppugnationem* and *propugnationem.* The change from *instabilita* to *instabiliq.* is especially easy as it is from a rare to a common word and to a case agreeing with the following word. I suggest our author used *instabilita* because the normal *instabilia* does not scan. Goodyear suggested that the author may have written *instabilique gelu* (or *gelus*) *fallit uestigia passu* (taking *gelu* as nom.). In a letter to me Diggle advanced the objections that 'it seems to suggest that it is Frost who is treading unstably' and (to *gelu* nom.) that it 'is inadequately attested'. *TLL* in the introduction to the *gelu* article states that all forms of the nominative and accusative are transmitted in late Latin authors and individual forms in the following authors: nom. *gelus* Cato, Afranius, Accius; *gelu* in the poem *Nux*, line 106 (a work transmitted among the poems of Ovid, but of uncertain date and authorship); *gelum* in Varro (*R.R.* 1.45.2); acc. *gelum* (masc.) in Cato (neut.) in Lucretius. It looks as if the nominative and accusative were avoided in literary works of our author's time. The ablative *gelu* is common. Diggle very tentatively suggested *instabilisque gelu fallit uestigia passus* (taking *gelu* as ablative and taking *instabilis . . . uestigia passus* as 'the steps of an unstable tread'), which he described as 'sense of a sort', expressing, however, grave doubts, which I share, whether this periphrasis is acceptable. I suggest that the *falli passus* which I have printed is used, and not *fallit*, as men slipping is not, like the weather conditions described elsewhere in iii 1–22, something a sign brings, but only something that is liable to, although it does not necessarily, happen as a result of the weather.

22 *Niue moenia durant* seems corrupt, for the sense 'the city walls endure owing to the snow' is absurd. The sense 'the city walls grow hard because of the snow' is open to the objection that it is strange that city walls should be singled out for mention, and the major, and to my mind fatal one, that *durant* has to be taken in the sense *durescunt*. There seems to be only one parallel for this, Aetna 497 *flumina . . . frigore durant*, and this poem has been transmitted in a very corrupt state (so, e.g., *flumina* might be the object of *durant*, the subject being lost in a lacuna). At Verg. *Ecl.* 6.33–6 *ut his exordia primis/omnia et ipse tener mundi concreuerit orbis;/tum durare solum et discludere Nerea ponto/coeperit et rerum paulatim sumere formas* it is perfectly satisfactory to take *mundi orbis* as the subject of *durare*, *solum* then being object, not subject. Conjectures for *moenia* which give *durant* (intransitive) the sense 'become hard' are therefore highly suspect. All that have been proposed are also unsatisfactory in other ways. *Germina* or *gramina* (Kroll *WKPh*): why should these features, any more than *moenia*, be singled out? *Mollia* (W. Morel): what are these *mollia*? *Flumina* (a hand in the British Museum copy of Schwartz's edition): rivers do not become hard because of snow, but because their waters turn to ice. *Nimbi niue durant* (Courtney): falling snow can hardly be said to be harder than rain, and fallen snow does not freeze rain, rain turns the snow into slush (in a temperate climate). *Niueque omnia durant* (which might also be proposed): rivers and the sea do not become hard because of the snow. Moreover, the two clauses comprising 122 are better without *que* joining them. *Que* joined to short e can be partly defended from iv 59 *Virgineque et Libra*, Prop. 3.21.13 *iungiteque extremo*, Tib. 1.3.34 *reddereque antiquo*, 1.6.48 *sanguineque effuso* (all beginning lines). A *que* added to a pyrrhic is found elided in this position in the verse in Verg. *Aen.* 3.156 *nos te Dardania incensa tuaque arma secuti*, 9.273 *corpora captiuosque dabit suaque omnibus arma*, 10.672 *quid manus illa uirum qui me meaque arma secuti*, 10.791 *hic mortis durae casum tuaque optima facta*. Kenney observed that the difficulties of *que* and *duro* used in the sense 'be hard' could be met by writing *nix omnia durat* (the objection to *omnia*, however, remains). It is conceivable that *nix* could have been changed to *niue* to correspond with *grandine* at the beginning of the line. Because of the difficulties in the proposals mentioned above, I believe another approach is required. I suggest *durant* should be *dura est* (*durast*). *Moenia* should be emended to some suitable adjective or participle agreeing with *tellus*. The only one ending in *enus eus inus itus ius* or *ulus* in Gradenwitz's *Laterculi uocum Latinarum* is *condita*, which I have therefore printed. I suggest that *dita* was omitted before *dura* and *niue con durast* emended to *niue moenia durant*. *Niue dura* (hard snow, already fallen) is contrasted with the *niuibus caducis* (falling snow, soft snow) of line 1. Both Pisces and Aries have snow, rain and hail, and both the first and the last line of this passage begin with the word *grandine*.

28 *Mitissimus* is, as Housman p. 36/511 says, an absurd epithet to apply to Saturn, especially after *rigor accedit uentis*. Housman wrote *lentissimus*, stating that '*uentis* absorbed *lentis*' (the gap was filled by an interpolator with the first thing that came into his head). Housman also suggested *tristissimus* and *maestissimus*, remarking that they 'are not so likely'. As Housman p. 36/510 observes, there is no break between iii 28 and iv 1 in sense, hence there is no reason for supposing anything has been lost between the verses. I offer a theory to explain how fragments ii and iii are preserved only in *Z* in section v of the introduction on the manuscripts.

iv 2ff A mention of Aries being missing, and the happenings in 3–6, unlike all the following ones, not being assigned to the presence of Jupiter in any sign, I have marked a lacuna after verse 2, in which a verse such as *et stetit in signo mundi quod continet arcem* was lost. A glance at the surrounding context will show that the lacuna could only have occurred here. The word *stetit* in my suggested supplement is from *sisto*. Cf. my note on iv 35. Manilius calls Aries the sign *mundi quod continet arcem* in 1.262.

6 alto is satisfactory. Cf. Verg. *Aen.* 10.723ff *impastus stabula alta leo ceu saepe peragrans/ . . . gaudet,/sic ruit . . . Mezentius*. Talking of *leporaria* (but he cites a case in which this enclosure was used for pregnant ewes) Varro *R.R.* 3.12.3 says *quis enim ignorat saepta . . . ita esse oportere . . . ut . . . sint alta? . . . ne lupus transilire possit*. Orelli's *arto* could be right.

11 rapidos . . . aestus No need to emend to *rabidos*, with Orelli. Cf. Verg. *Ecl.* 2.10 *rapido . . . aestu* and my note on i 6.

14 Jupiter, not Leo, is the subject of this line, hence, as Housman p. 36/511 says '*incipit*, which is due to *repellit* and *cludit*, must be *incipis*: the return to the third person is managed at 18 by means of a new vocative, "tua, Liber, munera *condit*" '.

soluere uota = 'allow the vows to be fulfilled', as *perficiet* in 292 (*nam neque perficiet cursus et uota breuis lux*) = 'allow to complete'.

16 ante larem primum = 'at the front of the house', as *primos lares* in Prop. 4.8.49–50 *cum subito rauci sonuerunt cardine postes/nec leuia ad primos murmura facta lares*. *Lar/lares* also equals 'house' in Prop. 4.1.128 and 4.10.18. Fixing a *corona* to the doorpost at the front of a house (as a sign of rejoicing or divine protection) is mentioned in Ou. *Met.* 14.733 *postes ornatos saepe coronis*, *Fast.* 1.614 *protegat et uestras querna corona fores*, *Fast.* 4.738 (rem. 32) *tegat ornatas longa (multa) corona fores* and Iuu. 6.51–2 *necte coronam/postibus* and 9.85 *foribus suspende coronas*. The word *larem* in our author also implies honour being paid to the Lares. Our author seems to be imitating Tib. 1.1.15–16 *flaua Ceres, tibi sit nostro de rure corona/spicea, quae templi pendeat ante fores*.

19–20 frigora was conjectured by Housman for the transmitted *munera* (which comes from the preceding verse) in *CQ* 26 (1932), 134; *Classical Papers* vol. 3, p. 1191, article on the *Disticha de mensibus*. The *ae* of *laetae* is the only diphthong (or long vowel) elided before a short syllable in our author (unless *cauda* in 51 is ablative).

23–5 Housman expounds and criticizes the punctuation adopted by editors (a comma ending line 21, a full stop ending 22) as follows (p. 36/511): 'That is: the planet Jupiter causes tempests in Aquarius and Pisces, supposing that he comes to a halt in either (*quocumque* must be *utrolibet*) of these signs. But we have not yet been told what weather he causes there when he does not come to a halt. Then follows the information that he creates thunderstorms in Aries and Leo. But his doings in Aries and Leo have already been related in 3–6 and 12 sq. Therefore the punctuation must be altered'. Housman expounds the text with his punctuation, which I have adopted, as follows. 'In Aquarius and Pisces he causes tempests. Supposing he comes to a halt in any of the twelve signs already enumerated, the result is thunder if the sign be Aries or Leo, wintry weather in every sign without exception. The literal translation of 24 is "he confounds all the signs alike with months of a wintry sort", instead of allowing them to preside over months of seasonable weather: bruma assidua atque alienis mensibus hiemps, in fact. For *quicumque* thus used compare Prop. ii 1 15, Cic. Phil. xii 13'.

29 *Siccatis* being unsuitable (when their rain has fallen, clouds disappear) I have accepted *spissatis*, a word used of *nubes* by Luc. 4.77. *Ss* probably became *cc* under the influence of the following word *caecus*.

32 '*Statio* is στηριγμός, the halting of the planet: Vitruuius uses the same term in the astronomical chapters of his ninth book, while Cicero Tusc. 1 62 translates the Greek by *institio*. "lentos supprimet ignes" means not "quench his fire" but "bring his fiery orb to a standstill", and a *statio* is not *nigra* but *pigra*. So 22 "*statuit* currus . . .*fessos*", ii 19 sq. "nunc *igne citato* (compare *lentos ignis*)/festinare putes, nunc *pigro* sidere somno" ' Housman p. 36–7/511–12.

35 *steterit* is from *sisto*. Cf. Neue-Wagener, *Formenlehre der Lateinischen Sprache*, 3.342–4.

40 In place of *incertus* a word is needed meaning that Mars has entered Cancer, and I have printed what I think the closest appropriate word: *inuectus*. This is suited to Mars, as he is borne in a chariot (cf. *currus . . . fessos* used of Jupiter in iv 22 and the language applicable to one borne in a chariot used of Mars in iv 31–2). If correct, *inuectus* became *inceutus* and so *incertus* by transposition of two letters across an intervening space and further change (on this, cf. Housman Manilius vol. 1 p. lviii, especially the examples under the lemma 'with further change'). *Cancro* could be ablative or dative (*inueho* is followed by the dative of a place into which one goes in Tac. *Ann.* 2.23.1 and Suet. *Aug.* 41.1), the sense coming to the same. An alternative, not as close, is *ingressus* (INGRESSUS could have become INGERSSUS by interchange of letters and so INCERTUS). Here *Cancro* would have to be dative. *Ingressus* is followed by the dative in Verg. *Aen.* 10.148 *castris ingressus Etruscis*, but here the accusative does not scan. I can see no reason why our author should have written *Cancro* instead of *Cancrum* here. *Ingressa* is used of Venus in iv 88 *sin leuis ingressa est spatiosi sidera Cancri*. Iriarte proposed *insertus*, but this implies that Mars has suddenly been placed by some force in some part or between some parts of the Crab (for the sense of *insero* cf. *TLL*), whereas in reality it is his own proper motion (on which cf. ii 6–8) that brings him into it.

42 rimans As the Scorpion has only one tail, the transmitted *primae* cannot mean 'first'; *primae caudae* must = 'of the first part of his tail', i.e. 'of the tip of his tail', as a scorpion's sting is at the end of his tail (cf. 490–1

Scorpion ultima cauda/spicula torquentem, Auien. 682 *telum trahit ultima cauda*).
In Cat. 2.3. *primus digitus* = tip of the finger, Plin. *N.H.* 11.174 *prima lingua*
tip of the tongue, Ou. *Am.* 3.2.64 *primi pedes* tips of the feet. But the end of
the tail is elsewhere called *ultima/nouissima/extrema/ima cauda* (52, 59, 189,
593, 637), the place *qua cauda desinit* (344). *Primae* is the direct opposite of
these. *Summae* is a possible replacement (cf. *tollit* and 393 *Scorpios erecta
torquet qua spicula cauda*); if it is correct, *pri* was omitted and the space filled
by interpolation. But there is a closer word: *rimans,* often used of exploratory
movements (cf. Forcellini-Corradini), and used without any object in
Verg. *Aen.* 7.507–8 *quod cuique repertum/rimanti. Rimans* could have suggested
the far commoner *primas,* later changed to *primae* for the grammar. With
rimans the sense of the line is similar to Plin. *N.H.* 11.87 *semper cauda in ictu
est nulloque momento meditari* ('practise') *cessat, ne quando desit occasioni.* Manilius
uses *rimans* of Scorpius' activity with his tail, although in a different context,
in 4.217–9 *Scorpios armata uiolenta cuspide cauda/qua, sua cum Phoebi currum per
sidera ducit,/rimatur terras et sulcis semina miscet.* While the transmitted *cauda* is
conceivable, as ablative with *rimans,* the transmitted *primae* shows that the
reading *caudae* stood in the text prior to *cauda.*

47 The transmitted *et uentos aut fundet aqua* is plainly corrupt. S has the
conjecture *aquas* for *aqua,* but this contradicts 44 *Martia non illos turbabit
stella . . . imbre.* Hence I have accepted Goodyear's *effundet* (suggested by my
affundet). *Effundo* is followed by the ablative in Verg. *Aen.* 12.276 ⟨*hasta
iuuenem⟩ fulua . . . effundit harena* and used of winds in the passages quoted by
TLL 5.2.222.81ff. *Aqua* = 'the sea' in Cic. *Verr.* 3.36 and 192 and our author
(imitating Vergil) has *instantis aquae mons* of a wave in 302. *Affusis* (which
could be an error for *effusis*) is transmitted in Sil. 17.218–19 *affusis puppes
procedere uentis/ . . . coepere.* The word seems always to be followed by datives
(many examples could be either dative or ablative, but the unambiguous
examples are datives), hence, if it were printed, the further change of *aqua*
to *aquae* would seem to be required.

48 tum The corruption *rim* is anticipatory. A scribe looked at the follow-
ing word *rigor* and wrote *rim* instead of *tum.*

56 As 54–5 describes changeable weather, the missing syllable in this line
seems to be the word *nil. Litore* makes no sense, as there is no shore associated
with the Crab in the sky. The word *Cancri* caused a scribe to replace the
original with the word *litore.* Grotius proposed *sidere,* but this is unlikely, as
sidere occurs in the same place in the verse above. Baehrens proposed *fulgore*
(from *fulgur*), Ellis *limite,* but as neither *fulgur* or *limes* has been mentioned
before in connection with Cancer, *hoc* is not appropriate. I have printed
tempore. Hoc in tempore = 'at that time'. The preposition *in* is found with
tempore (*tempore in omni*) in Manil. 5.719 and (*in tali tempore*) in Liu. 22.35.7;
24.28.1; 25.3.12; 30.37.8; 34.27.6. *Litore* and *tempore* are not dissimilar, and
this could have helped the change.

57 The conjecture *estus* of an ancestor of S is modelled either on iv 11 or 41
(both of which end with *temperat aestus*) or both. Perhaps a scribe omitted
aestus because he accidentally repeated *certum* from the verse above (his eye
slipped from *temperat* to *tempore*) and *certum* was later rightly expunged as a

repetition from the previous verse. τ has the conjecture *annum* (from *temperat . . . annum* in iv 54). This requires a change of *flagrantis* to *flagrantem*. Baehrens conjectured *auras*, but 'burning breezes' is strange.

haec The transmitted *hic* (= 'here', i.e. in Cancer) is inappropriate, as this line talks of Venus' activities in Leo. Transpose 57 and 58 and it might be just tolerable, although it would be otiose. The simplest remedy is to write *haec* after Breysig, ed. 1. The repetition *hoc* (56)/*haec* (57) can be defended from iii 28–iv 1 *lentissimus ille :/Iuppiter est illo laetus magis* and 302 & 304 and the passages quoted on 302 & 304. Grotius conjectured *lucis uis* for *lucens hic*, but 'the force of the light' moderating heat is very odd. Baehrens retained *lucens*, adopting *uis*, but this is an obscure way of referring to Venus (or *Phosphoros* ('light-bearer') as she is called as morning star— cf. iv 73). A better conjecture is *uim* for *hic*, *aestus* and *flagrantis* being its genitive. *Vis aestus* is found in Liu. 25.26.7 *intoleranda uis aestus*, and *flagrantissimo aestu* in Liu. 44.36.7 and Plin. *N.H.* 12.58. Another possibility is Kroll's *tunc* (*WKPh* 1918, 307). But *haec* is closest to *hic*.

60 magis goes with *continua*. In Virgo and Libra the clouds always merely threaten rain, never bring it (*semper pendentia tantum*). They are not, however, *semper pendentia*, they sometimes go, but they are *continua magis*, in contrast with the situation in Cancer, when the clouds are always shifting (*nubila nec diuturna puta* 55).

61–2 *Super*, postponed as in iv 52 *aetherium uenit Taurum super*, governs *Scorpion acrem*. Schmidt, in his edition of 1728 (*teste Breysig*) proposed *Scorpios* for *Scorpion*, but *super* here = 'north of' and the Scorpion is never north of Venus.

64 There is no word *astras*. The *astra* of Aτ is unsuitable, as hail does not fall through the stars. Grotius conjectured *aethram*, but this word, referring to the upper air or at least implying a clear sky (cf. *OLD*) is inappropriate when a thick hail storm is being described. Ellis conjectured *austros*, but when there is rain and thunder everywhere, why does hail only fall in the south? I have printed Housman's *auras*, changed to *astras* because the word *astrum* (found e.g. at the end of line 58 above) was running through a scribe's mind. For *aurae* = 'the atmosphere' cf. *OLD s.u. aura* 4.

66 tendentis spicula signi: cf. 307 *ducentemque ferum sinuato spicula neruo.*

70 The transmitted *ignis* is a repetition from the previous verse.

72 'The subject of *recurrit* is *Cythereius ignis* in 69 and not *Aquarius* in 70: for this negligence compare 17 sq., 100 sqq., 155 sq.' Housman p. 37/512.

73 Phosphoros, Venus' name as morning star, not the transmitted Hesperos, her name as evening star, is required, for lines 49–72 describe the effects of Venus *sub lucem exoriens* (51). *Phos* was omitted before *phor* and *phoros* made metrical by alteration to *Hesperos* (probably suggested by the *hesperos* of 74). **Phosphoros haec tibi signa dabit** seems to be in imitation of Verg. *G.* 1.463 *sol tibi signa dabit.*

Aurora Housman (p. 37/512) suggested the author wrote *lucifera Aurora.* This makes good sense (the adjective *lucifer* suiting *Aurora*: cf. e.g. Verg. *Aen.* 4.584–5 *et iam prima nouo spargebat lumine terras/Tithoni croceum linquens Aurora cubile*) and is very close to the transmitted text. Courtney (p. 140) argues against Housman as follows: 'The few post-Virgilian hypermetric lines, none of them in Germanicus, all end with *–que* (they are listed by J. Soubiran, *L'Elision dans la Poesie latine* 467, where incidentally Hor. *Sat.* i.6.102 should be eliminated as certainly corrupt)'. But the fact that our author has no hypermetric lines elsewhere tells us little about his attitude to them. His extant lines amount to 943½, an insufficient sample. Courtney is incorrect in stating that all post-Vergilian hypermetric lines end in *–que* (Soubiran confined his list to Silius and earlier). Ausonius 371.7 (7.15.7) ends *aureus altero/autumni*. A further objection to Housman's emendation is, as Courtney points out in a letter to me, that, except for the line in Ausonius, no examples of a long syllable at the end of a hypermetric line have been transmitted. Verg. *G.* 1.295 ends with *em*, *Aen.* 7.160 with *um*, but final syllables ending in *m* form a class between long and short syllables. Courtney objects further to the emendation that 'the other elision [of *lucifera*] can barely be defended by 631 *oceanum ortu*, Virg. *Aen.* xii 26 *haec* [*hoc*]*animo hauri*'. A conceivable defence of *lucifera Aurora* would be to suggest that our author may have thought that a hypermetric line added elegance and distinction to a passage (Vergil uses it for special effect in *Aen.* 2.745 *quem non incusaui amens hominumque deorumque*, when he could have written *deumque*). In 262 our author lengthens *que*, as Vergil sometimes does. Cf. my note.

I have not adopted Housman's conjecture, for I feel there is a more likely alternative, namely that *lucifer* is a gloss. Courtney suggests that '*lucifer* was an explanation of *Phosphoros* (cf. *CGL.* vi 657a) before that word was corrupted'. But why should a gloss on the first word of the line have been incorporated into the text here? Far more likely, *lucifer* was written as a gloss on the word immediately below in the next line (*hesperos*) and thus incorporated into the text here. The line became so long or so obviously unmetrical that the last word was either lost or omitted. *Hesperos* is not *lucifer*, but that is no reason why a medieval reader should not have so glossed it. *Iesferos* is glossed as *stella matutina* at *CGL* 4.350.32 by MSS abc (*stella uespertina* by MSS de); the entry at *CGL* 3.242.22 is ὁ Ἐωσφορος, Ἕσπερος *lucifer*.

Courtney suggests that 'the original may have been something like *cum aurora* ⟨*rubescit*⟩. The elision is exactly paralleled at 629 *se ostendere* and probably at 276 *qui illapsus* (Grotius: *lapsus* the manuscripts)'. The present *rubescit* is satisfactory. Cf. Manil. 3.252–3 *haec erit . . . cum . . . /incipiunt* and the variations between present and future in verses 711–16 of our author. Other possibilities are *rubescet* and *rubebit*. *TLL s.u. Aurora* quotes these verbs several times, but no others of the same metrical form.

75 The transmitted *ducere* implies that Venus is falling upon the earth in the same way as night is. *Inducere* avoids this implication. *In* was omitted after the *m* of *noctem*. *Inducet* is used similarly in iv 84 *inducet nubila caelo*.

76 The manuscript variants are corruptions of *haec te*, except the *ecce haec* of Sτ, which is probably based on *ecce*, *haec* being a metrical interpolation.

77 For *comamenalto* Ellis conjectured *torta memento*. To explain how *memento* became *menalto* Housman (p. 27/496) posits the loss of *me* by haplography, the corruption of *n* to *al*, the correction of the corruption suprascript and the

absorption of the suprascript *n* into the text. He expresses this all by
'= ME-ME$\overset{N}{\text{A}}$LTO'. **fulgura torta** = 'jagged flashes of lightning'. Cf. the use
of *tortus* in Plin. *Ep.* 6.20.9 *nubes . . . tortis uibratisque discursibus rupta . . .
fulguribus illae et similes et maiores erant.* Another possible substitute for *coma*
is *crebra*. *Vere cauere . . . fulgura crebra memento* is supported by Plin. *N.H.*
2.136 *uere autem et autumno crebriora fulmina.* *Fulgura* and *crebra* are combined
in Luc. 1.530. Cf. also our author iv 104–5 *crebro fulmine ruptis/nubibus* and
iv 65 *caelum quam saepe sonabit.* For *comamenalto* τ has the conjecture *culmine
ab alto*, Iriarte conjectured *culmine in alto.* *Culmen* is used of the sky (cf. *TLL*
4.1292.55ff), but metaphorically or with *caeli/mundi* expressed or to be
understood from its occurrence in the same sentence. Apul. *Met.* 6.15 has
alti culminis diales uias deserit, but not all that is in Apuleius could occur in
our author. The word *culmine* immediately suggests the meaning for the line
'In spring beware of rain and lightning in your rooftop'. Kroll (p. 308)
conjectured *cum tamen illa.* But line 77 is applicable to Aries, thus there is no
contrast between 77 and 78–81 and *tamen* has no point. Nor is the corruption
of *illa* to *alto* readily understandable. Ellis' *memento* has the further advantage
over these conjectures of requiring no alteration of *cauere.* They require
cauendi or τ's *caueto.* An imperative in this line is satisfactory. Our author also
imparts information in the form of an order in line 343.

78 radiauerit = *si radiauerit*, as *triuerit* = *etsi triuerit* in Hor. *Serm.* 1.1.45–6
milia frumenti tua triuerit area centum,/non tuus hoc capiet uenter plus ac meus.

79 Housman's conjecture supplies the verb necessary for the apodosis.

82–3 Line 83 summarizes lines 84–7, which describe *inconstantia*, hence
Grotius' *inconstantia* is required in 83 in place of the transmitted *constantia.* *In*
was omitted after *m.* From the word *eadem* it is clear that a condition of
inconstantia was described in Taurus (*eadem* cannot refer to conditions in
Aries, for there the weather is uniformly bad). *Vere magis nitido* in 82 prepare
for a description of more favourable weather under Taurus, but this descrip-
tion is given nowhere. *Apponi* could be emended to *nil certum* to give it, but
(1) *nil certum* is very abrupt after the full line introduction (82); (2) *Apponi*
makes good sense with the rest of the line; (3) *Nil certum* is not close to it, nor
can I think of anything suitable any closer. It seems then that there is a
lacuna of one or more lines after 82, in which the weather under Taurus
was described.

86 This sense of *de* is illustrated by *OLD s.u. de* 3.

87 The loss of *uaria* from the sequence *alternauariabit* is readily under-
standable.

90 sidera densa The Crab, which is a moderately large sign with few
stars, and those faint, is called *spatiosus* (88). The other signs of the zodiac
are by contrast *densa* (packed with stars). I do not know of any other passage
where signs are said to reinforce the harmful effects of the sun's heat. The
star Sirius is, however, often said to do so. Cf. e.g. Manil. 5.206ff, particularly
208 *geminatque incendia solis.* Kroll (p. 308) proposed *frigora* for *sidera.* But the
time when the sun has just left the Crab (not long after the summer solstice)
is the hottest in the year. Cold that numbs and weakens bodies would be
inconceivable then.

93 at is used as a particle of transition to a new statement, with no contrast with the previous statement, as in 88, 140, 344 etc. The *ac* of MS 2 is unnecessary.

95 *Plerique* (= 'very many') makes good sense, but the asyndeton is surely impossible. Hence I have printed Grotius' *plenique*. Quint. 11.3.41 calls a low note a *sonus parum clarus nimiumque plenus. Plenus* suits the low rumble of thunder.

96 Cf. the explanation of thunder given in Sen. *N.Q.* 2.27.3 . . . *cum conglobata nubes dissoluitur et eum quo distenta fuerat spiritum emittit. hic proprie fragor dicitur.*

97–9 The transmitted text lacks a mention of Libra and has several other obvious corruptions. Housman restores sense with a few easy changes. *Chelae dum* (= CELEDVM) became *caelum* (CELVM) by the omission of ED after EL. OB is the metrical fillup of a man who minded neither hiatus nor *ob* with the ablative (unless, as Housman suggests, he wrote *ab*, and *ob* is a corruption of this). TE was omitted from the sequence GLACIANTETEPOREM in the next verse. Someone looking at POREM changed it to the Latin word ROREM; then someone else looked at TEROREM and changed it to the Latin word TERROREM. With the loss of the marks of suspension for N and M we have the transmitted *glaciaterrore*. Housman quotes to illustrate the sense Lucr. 6.371–2 *et calor extremus primo cum frigore mixtus/uoluitur, autumni quod fertur nomine tempus.* The collocation *frigore primo . . . glaciante* is unobjectionable. From Kuehner-Stegmann 1.240 I quote Caes. *B.G.* 2.29.3 *locum duplici altissimo muro munierant*, Liu. 2.53.3 *duae potentissimae et maximae finitimae gentes* and 27.22.12 *nauis longas triginta ueteres.* Baehrens suggested *eademque replebit/nubibus assiduis caelum sub frigore primo,/extremum autumni superans glaciante rigore*, but a mention of Libra is required, and *autumni* should be *autumnum.* Breysig modified this text, retaining *superent* and marking a lacuna after line 98. This is conceivable (assuming some such words as *dum Chelae . . . teporem* have been lost in the lacuna), but Housman restores sense without the need to assume a lacuna.

100 caua Cf. my note on 582.

102 ruet is satisfactory, *Venus*, not *Scorpius*, being the subject. For this, cf. the note on iv 72. Venus 'will beat everything flat with storms of rain *sternet sata laeta boumque labores* [Verg. *Aen.* 2.306]' Housman p. 37/513. Schwartz's *ruent* may be right, but it is not necessary.

104–5 crebro fulmine ruptis/nubibus Cf. Verg. *Aen.* 9.670–1 *cum Iuppiter horridus austris/torquet aquosam hiemem et caelo caua nubila rumpit*, 8.391–2 *haud secus atque olim tonitru cum rupta corusco/ignea rima micans percurrit lumine nimbos*, Val. Flacc. 4.661–2 *sic ubi multifidus ruptis e nubibus horror/ effugit*, Petr. 122 lines 122–3 *fulgure rupta corusco/intremuit nubes.*

110 'The sense must be: since you have heard all about Venus, now hear about Mercury. "Veneris stella" is in the preceding verse 109: write then est quoniam certis ea iam tibi cognita signis, = ea tiui iam' Housman p. 38/513. The corruption Housman assumes is that *eaiamtibi* was transposed to *eatibiiam* and corrupted to *ratiuiam. Ea* is unobjectionable. Deferrari's index lists 34 occurrences of the form in Ovid. Morel suggested *dea iam tibi*, which is not quite as close, Kroll (p. 309) *et . . . Paphia est iam (et τ)*, but L. & S. do not quote any example of ἡ Παφία = Venus, or Perin's Onomasticon any of *Paphia*. The forms Παφίη and *Paphie* are quoted (the latter from Mart. 7.74.4 and Ausonius–who has it at 94.3 (= 19.96.3) and 361.21 (= 22.2.21)). Hence the form *Paphie* is to be preferred—and with it *est* can be restored to its transmitted position. The result, *Paphie iam*, was suggested to me by Courtney. PAFIE is not very far from RATIV, and *Paphie* goes well with *Cyllenius ignis* in the next line. But Housman's suggestion seems to me a little closer.

114 pecudis This form is used of Aries in iv 50, 78 and 144. *Dis* was omitted before *uillis*, leaving *pecu*. As *pecus/pecudis* is feminine (except sometimes in early Latin) *auratae* is required.

117 aliqua Schwartz conjectured *alia* for *etiam*, but 'you will notice that different rain is coming in different places' seems merely to state the very obvious fact that the individual particles of water that comprise the rain in one place are different particles from those that comprise the rain in another place. A different remedy is required. I have printed *aliqua* for *alias*, a corruption of a rarer into a more common word, with *s* added under the influence of the next word *pluuias*.

119 affert: *cornibus* = *ad cornua*. Cf. Verg. *Aen.* 3.310 *uerane te facies, uerus mihi nuntius affers*? No need for Kroll's *offert* (p. 309). Taurus is represented as carrying the sun on his horns by Manil. 4.144 *ille suis Phoebi portat cum cornibus orbem*.

120 grandine significat: 'grandine *id* significat. There is an ellipse of *id*' Goodyear. T's *signatur* makes sense, but seems simply to be a conjecture made after the loss of *ific* after *ign* in *significat*.

120 serenti (Schwartz) is better than *serena* (U), for *serenti . . . nautis* is supported by i 13 *nauita quid caueat, quid scitus uitet arator* and, with *serena*, two synonymous expressions (*tranquilla serena* and *placidum caelumque fretumque*) both refer to *nautis*. There is no similar tautology elsewhere in this fragment.

122 A mention of Cancer is missing. As there seems no plausible way of emending the text to introduce it, and the grammar and sense of the clauses transmitted, taken individually, is satisfactory, it seems that a line, whose sense was 'when Venus is in Cancer' has been lost. Baehrens suggested that a line is missing after 122. 122 must have been qualified by this missing line, for it cannot refer to conditions under Gemini, which are *tranquilla* and *placidum . . . caelumque fretumque*. It is equally possible that a line is missing before 122. As it would be misleading to print the text as if nothing were missing, I have printed one of these suggestions, but can see nothing to choose between them.

123 at was omitted before *ar*.

125 Astraei is an adjective agreeing with *ignis*. Quintus Cicero (= Ausonius 383 or 7.25) 10 talks of *flamma Nepai*. Another possibility is Grotius' *Astraeae*, *ignis* then being the subject, and referring to Mercury, called *Cyllenius ignis* in iv 111, *ignis Cyllenaeus* in iv 137.

128 The use of *rumpor* in *rumpuntur fulmina nimbis* is, as Goodyear points out to me, the same as in Verg. *G.* 3.428 *amnes . . . rumpuntur fontibus* ('streams burst forth from their sources').

129 The transmitted *arcus* has arisen from the assimilation of *arcum* to the case of the preceding *cyllenius*.

133 Capricornus is mentioned here and in 130 in the transmitted text, Aquarius nowhere. Hence *Capricornus* here must conceal a reference to Aquarius. How did *Capricornus* come to be written? Perhaps (1) it has taken the place of a word or words whose letters are similar, (2) it is a *perseverationsfehler* from *Capricorni* in 130, (3) a scribe's eye slipped from *Capricorni* in 130 and he wrote *Capricornus*. (2) and (3) are incompatible; (1), (2) or (3) could be the sole cause of corruption, but, more likely, (1) and (2) or (1) and (3) could be operating together. The most likely conjecture is thus the one whose letters most closely resemble *capricornus*. Hence I have printed Housman's *Phryx rorans*. Aquarius is identified with Ganymede in Ampelius 2.11 and Hygin. *Astron.* 2.29 and is called *rorans iuuenis* by Manil. 5.487. If this conjecture is correct, *pricxrorans* probably became *pricarorans* (Housman refers to Gronouius *Obs.* 4.4 for illustrations of the confusion of *x* and *a*); this is gibberish, hence liable to correction, and the first five letters are the same as those of *ca-pri-cornus*. Winterfeld (in *De Germanici codicibus*) suggested *Ganymedes*, but of this only the initial *Ga* bears any resemblance to *Capricornus*.

134 caeli fragores are present, even though the sky is clear (133 *nulla nubila*). 'The phenomenon of thunder in a clear sky, always ominous, often appears in ancient literature' Pease on *De diu.* 1.18 (p. 109), quoting many examples.

137–9 As Housman (p. 38/514) observes, the sense of these lines must be 'since I have told you what Mercury effects as a morning star, now learn what he effects as an evening star'. Ellis' conjecture *quotiens Cyllenius ignis* for the transmitted *ignis quoque Cylleneus* makes good sense, but the trajection of *ignis* away from *Cyllenius*, with which it agrees, and into the middle of the line, is difficult to understand. More probable is Housman's *exoriens ignis modo Cyllenaeus* (*exoriens* changed to the finite verb by someone puzzled by the construction, a hyperbaton, and m̊ confused with q̊; Housman quotes Ou. *Her.* 16.375; *Trist.* 5.3.52; *ex Pont.* 1.8.65; Prop. 2.26.44 as places where *modo* and *quoque* have been confused). He explains *modo exoriens* as 'just risen' and continues 'Thus the close of this passage recalls the opening, 111 sqq. "accipe quid moueat mundo Cyllenius ignis/si *modo* Phoebei flammas *effugerit* axis,/*matutina* ferens solitos per sidera cursus". . . . The construction, as Orelli says, is an hyperbaton, "quandoquidem, exoriens ignis modo Cyllenaeus/quid faceret primo, docui, cum lumine solis,/tempus et, occasu moueat quid, discere, Phoebi" = quandoquidem docui, quid faceret mane, tempus est discere etiam, quid uesperi moueat. In Germanicus, as in most other authors, similar examples can be found: phaen. 595 "Arctophylax, lumine, qui, primo cum Scorpios occidit undis, occulitur pedibus" (qui occulitur cum Scorpios lumine primo occidit), 573 "saepe uelis, quantum superet, cognoscere, noctis" '. More probable than Housman's emendations, is to replace the transmitted *quoque* with *dum*. *Exoritur* with the last syllable lengthened can be defended from Verg. *G.* 3.76 *ingreditur et mollia, Aen.* 1.668 *iactetur odiis,* 2.411 *obruimur oriturque,* 5.284 *datur operum,* all, as here, at the caesura in the third foot. Cf. also *abit* in i 128, with my note. The fourth foot of spondaic lines is usually a dactyl, but in Verg. *G.* 3.276 *saxa per et scopulos et depressas conualles,* it is, as here, a spondee. Aratus 597 ends with κυλληναίη, and a form of *Cyllenaeus* ends Hor. *Epod.* 13.9; Ou. *Ars.* 3.147 and *Met.* 11.304, Auien. 1116 and Cat. 68b. 109. Our author has written a 'Greek' line, with lengthening of *ur* and a spondaic ending.

141 uincet The transmitted *iunget* makes no sense. Grotius proposed *ninget,* but this cannot stand in the middle of the line by itself, nor can *crebro tonitru* be joined to it (it would be strange if *crebro tonitru* were not governed by *exsecrabile* but instead left hanging in a loose relationship with the following verb), nor, as Kroll (p. 309) suggested, can *ninget* govern *florentia rura* (= 'it snows on the flourishing fields'). Kroll stated that *ninget,* like νείφειν, can be used transitively. Forcellini-Corradini give no examples of this (nor can I find any) except Accius (*GLK* 2.504.10–11 Accius in Andromeda: *cum ninxerint caelestium molem mihi*) but the text of such fragments is very liable to corruption; Grotius' *molimine* for *molem mihi* is plausible. The Oxford *Greek-English Lexcion* quotes νείφω with an object only from Philo Iudaeus 1.617 θεὸς νείφει τροφὰς ἀπ'οὐράνου. The object in Philo (and Accius, if the transmitted text is sound) is what is snowed, in our author, according to Kroll, what is snowed upon. In the absence of any evidence that *ningit* can be used this way, I have printed *uincet.* Cf. iv 101–2 *at diris omnia nimbis/ continuisque ruet* and my note there.

143–4 regna Tonantis/ingrediens refers to Mercury's return to visibility at sunset (cf. the use of *exoriens* of Venus as evening star in iv 76 and Verg. *G.* 1.440 *et quae mane refert et quae surgentibus astris* (i.e. *uesperi*)). It does not refer to rising, as these planets are then near the western horizon.

146 *Rapido . . . sidere* = 'with swiftly moving constellation' (cf. Manil. 3.503–4 *sic erit ipse tibi rapidis quaerendus in astris/natalis mundi*), but the Crab moves no faster than any other constellation. *Rapidus* = 'devouring' of *sol* in i 6 and *aestus* iv 11, but here there is nothing to suggest the meaning 'devouring' for *rapido.* Hence I have printed Orelli's *rabido.* Cf. Stat. *Theb.* 4.783 (= 777) *rabidi sub limite Cancri* (where certain mss. have *rapidi*). Of *rabidus* Housman on Manil. 1.396 remarks 'raro librarii intactum relinquunt'.

148 The subject of *ferri* is Mercury, not Taurus. On this cf. my note on iv 72.

149–50 The transmitted *calidus uestigia seruat/hic (hinc) quo dicta Leo saeuisque caloribus ardet* is corrupt. *Vestigia seruare* = 'keep to the footprints', in i.19 *axis at immotus semper uestigia seruat* by remaining immobile and so always in one's own footprints, in Verg. *Aen.* 2.711 *longe seruet uestigia coniunx,* by treading in someone else's. No sense of *quo* is suitable here. The sense 'at the place where' is appropriate, but it appears that, by itself, *quo* cannot have this meaning (cf. Forcellini-Corradini). *Qua* is an easy change. *Hic qua* = 'where'. *TLL* calls this *hic* 'hic praeparatiuum' and illustrates it with examples at 6.3.2762. 37ff. Of *hinc qua* (= 'where') it gives only one example

(6.3.2806.34), from the late Latin Avienius (*Orb. terr.* 1232), and here there is a *hinc . . . hinc* contrast. Thus I have preferred *hic* to *hinc*. The text with *qua* can be taken to mean (omitting the corrupt *dicta*) 'He is hot when he stands where the Lion . . . and burns with cruel heat'. A verb is required to complete the sense, and no trochaic form of any verb will suit. One remedy would be to assume a lacuna either before or after *dicta*, but our author would hardly spend two lines saying 'where the hot Lion is' (Avienius might). Sense is restored by transposing the second half of 149 with the second half of 150 and emending *dicta* to *ficta*. *Ficta* = *fixa, ficta uestigia* being in imitation of Lucr. 3.3–4 *inque tuis nunc/ficta pedum pono pressis uestigia signis*. *Que* in 150b = 'but', as in other places after a negative (cf. Housman on Manil. 1.877 and *L & S s.u. que* VI. Our author uses *que* in an adversative sense in iv 9). Mercury is described as causing heat by being hot himself. Cf. iv 57 (of Venus) *placide lucens haec temperat aestus*.

152 'Write *iusta* . . . The Virgin is Astraea or Iustitia and is called "iustissima uirgo" phaen. 137. *Tendenti* is altered by Iriarte and subsequent editors into *metenti*: it is at once easier and more pointed to write *tenenti*; the Balance is not at odds with the goddess who carries it, Astraea or Virgo. Ancient coins and calendars sometimes put Libra in the hand of a male or female figure, the latter apparently Iustitia: see Thiele, Antike Himmelsbilder p. 71' Housman p. 38/515.

154 Cessare ab is illustrated by *TLL* 3.962.54ff.

159 *Rapidis* is possible, but *rabidis* more probable. Cf. Auien. 2.1693 *duri . . . Euri*, 3.847 *qua lene Notus spirat, qua perstrepit Eurus*, Ou. *Met.* 15.603 *ubi trux insibilat Eurus, Ep.* 11.9 ⟨*Macareus*⟩ *multo . . . suis truculentior Euris* and 14 *imperat et pennis, Eure proterue, tuis*, Verg. *G.* 2.441 *quas* ⟨*siluas*⟩ *animosi Euri assidue franguntque feruntque*, 2.107 *nauigiis uiolentior incidit Eurus. Rabidis* is also supported by the following word *horrebit*. Of *rabidus* Housman on Manil. 1.396 notes 'raro librarii intactum relinquunt'.

Fragment v

This fragment, found only in A, was first published by Baehrens in *RhM* for 1877, p. 323. Breysig, ed. 2 declared it spurious, on the grounds that an expression such as *humeris uirtutis* = *humeris uirtute praeditis* does not occur before Minucius Felix (preface p. xxviii). It seems, however, that these words are merely a textual corruption for *numeris uersutus* (cf. note on line 2). Thus there is no reason for supposing the fragment spurious.

1 The *astrorum globos* are mentioned by Cic. *Rep.* 6.17 *nouem tibi orbibus uel potius globis conexa sunt omnia*. Cf. also my notes on i 530 and ii 10.

1 & 6 Atlas . . . Aeolus Cf. Plin. *N.H.* 7.203 *adiecit . . . astrologiam Atlas Libyae filius . . . uentorum rationem Aeolus Hellenis filius*.

maximus Atlas This clausula is also found in Ou. *Met.* 6.174; Verg. *Aen.* 1.741; 4.481 and 8.136.

1 & 4 Atlas . . . Tyrii Vergil (*Aen.* 1.741ff) talks of Iopas, *docuit quem maximus Atlas*, singing of astronomy to *Tyrii* (747).

2 numeris uersutus is strongly supported by Vitruu. 6.7.6 *Atlas enim formatur historia sustinens mundum, ideo quod is primum cursum solis et lunae* *siderumque omnium uersationum rationes uigore animi sollertiaque curauit hominibus tradenda.* A reader, not knowing that Atlas taught astronomy, but well aware that he supported the sky, changed these words to *humeris uirtutis.*

4 Tyrii, not *Syrii, uiri* were famous for seafaring. Cf. i 41 *Phoenicas Cynosura regit,* Manil. 1.300–1 ⟨*Cynosura*⟩ *iudice uincit/maiorem Tyrio,* Val. Flacc. 1.17–20 *neque enim Tyriis Cynosura carinis/certior aut Grais Helice seruanda magistris,/tu si signa dabis; se te duce, Graecia mittet/et Sidon Nilusque rates* (*Nilus:* cf. *Pharii* in our author).

6 Cf. Manil. 2.684 *in partis diuisi quattuor orbis.*

7 'For *quo* Baehrens conjectures and Breysig accepts *qua,* quite wrongly. *quo* matches *unde* just as *premeret* matches *attolleret,* and *premeret,* like *attolleret,* governs *imbres*: "whither Boreas drives the rainclouds down and whence Notus drives them up", i.e. what is the direction of the winds called Boreas and Notus. The north wind is said *premere* and the south *attollere* because the north pole is overhead and the south pole is underfoot' Housman p. 39/515.

8 The war of the four winds is described by Verg. *Aen.* 1.84–6.

Fragment vi

As Tiberius, who either wrote this poem or had it dedicated to him, objected to the excessive use of Greek words in Latin (Suet. *Tib.* 71), the original sense of this fragment must have been, as Housman (p. 39/515) says, 'I do not see why I should not use the word *triangula* instead of the Greek τρίγωνα'.

Graecia is vocative, hence *te* is required before *diuite lingua.* It would be awkward if it did not come immediately before, but there seems no particular reason why it should have fallen out after *cur.* Moreover, if *cur* is right, the author must have written something meaning 'this is the reason' or 'there is a good reason' before it, in which case it would seem that he defended his practice before or after this fragment. It seems more probable that this fragment was simply a parenthesis in a passage about *trigona* (on which in astrology cf. Manil. 2.274ff). Hence I have accepted Housman's *quidni te diuite lingua. dnite* could easily have been absorbed by *diuite* and *qui* changed to *qur* (which *TLL* in the introduction on *cur* says 'legitur CORP 1. 1454, praeterea saepissime in codd. manusc.', giving examples).

INDEX

The references in items 1 to 6 are to pages of the commentary, in 7 to lines of the text.

1 : Imitations of earlier writers

Apollonius Rhodius, 101
Attalus, 83
Catullus, 96
Cicero's Aratus, 83, 85, 87
Hesiod, 93, 96
Homer, 100, 113–14

Lucretius, 138
Ovid, 96
Tibullus, 128
Vergil, 80, 81, 82, 84, 87, 96 (twice), 97, 111, 131

2 : Imitations by later writers

Avienius, 93 (twice), 120, 123
Hyginus, 93

Statius, 98

3 : Conjecture made to the text of another author

Hyginus (*de munit. castr.* 54), 126

4 : Words treated

a + que, 107
abrumpo, 82
abs, 107
agnoscere & cognoscere, 80
assulto, 96
Auster & Austri, 92
axis & orbis, 81
bellus, 111
crinita stella & crinis, 85, 117
cui postponed, 94, 95
est & sunt understood, 80, 83, 87, 94–5 (three times), 126
flecto habenas, 86
gelu, 126
in & ad, 80
instabilio, 126

is, ea, id, 81, 134
iuba, 108
laeuus & scaeuus, 84
lunatus, 113
mi & mihi, 103
penso, 85
que lengthened, 93; with short *e*, 127; adversative, 138
qui postponed, 95; *see also* cui
quis & qui after si, 107
rapidus & rabidus, 80, 96, 116, 128, 137, 138
scaeuus & laeuus, 84
tamen, 98
ue, 113

5: Textual errors

alteration of meaningless to Latin words, 86, 94, 113, 119, 125, 134

alteration to commoner word or to regularize construction, 93, 95, 105, 109, 126, 128, 130, 135

alteration to restore construction, 85

alteration to 'restore' sense, 115, 139

anticipation, 98, 129

assimilation, 81, 83, 92, 100, 101, 125, 126, 136

change under influence of context, 124, 130, 131

deliberate alteration by excerptor, 88

dittography, 83

doubling of a letter, 81, 98, 135

error due to use of abbreviations, 96, 125, 136

false word division, 94

glosses, 107, 132

incorrect incorporation of matter into text, 94, 111

interchange of words, 106

interpolation, 88, 107–8, 108 (twice), 111, 113

metrical interpolation, 105, 107, 119 (twice), 120, 132

omission due to similarity (generally with subsequent alteration), 80, 81, 82, 83, 89, 91 (twice), 92, 94, 95, 101, 103, 106, 108, 109, 110 (twice), 115, 120, 121 (twice), 125, 127, 128, 131, 132, 133 (twice), 134 (twice), 135 (twice), 139

replacement of original by adjacent words or letters, 85–6, 102, 104, 111, 113, 117

spurious verses, 112

transposition, 94–5, 108, 110, 120, 129, 136

6: Index of other subjects

alliteration, 82, 105

elision, 82, 85, 128

hiatus, 109

hyperbata, 95, 136

hypermetric lines, 131–2

lengthening of last syllable of word, 87, 122, 137

repetition of words, 82, 97, 131

romanizing of Aratus, 81, 86 (four times), 89

sense pauses near the end of lines, 90

short open vowels avoided before sc, sp, 84, 103

7: Index of proper names

Achillis, 422

Aegoceros, 286, 483, iii 16, iv 104; ~i, 381, 597, iv 69; ~o (ab), iv 158

Aeolus, v 6

Agenorei (m g), iv 145

Alcides (nom), 544

Alcyone (nom), 262

Ales (=Aquila) (nom), 316, 607, 689

Altaria (=Ara), 691

Amnis (=Eridanus), 617, 644; ~em, 362, 363

Andromeda (nom), 201, 640; ~an, 200, 357; ~ae (g), 207, 208, 232, 247, 463, 661

Anguis (=Draco) (g), 192; (=Serpens) (nom), 79, 88, 467, 672; (g), 84, 508, 592

Aquarius, 285, 387, iv 70, 107, 159; see also Hydrochoos, Phryx

Aquilam, 509
Aquilonis, 700; ~e, 23, 492
Arae (d), 420
Aratus, 1
[Arcitenens (nom), 566]
Arctophylax (nom), 91, 594
Arctos, 226; ~on, 55; ~oe, 25, 63
Arcturus, 625; ~um, 95, 395
Arcus (constellation), 312, 491, 551;
    ~um, 306, 669, iv 129; ~us (g),
    674
Argoae (g), 345, 621, 683
Ariadnaeo (m ab), 71
Aries (nom), 8, 224, 239, 361, 501,
    502, 532, 703, iii 1, iv 26
Asterope (nom), 263
Astraei (proper name), 105; ~ae (g),
    iv 125
Athos, 584
Atlantida, 322
Atlas (nom), 264, v 1
Atthide, 157
Auem (=Cycnus), 275
Auguste, 558
Auriga, 169; ~am, 686; ~ae (g),
    157, 174, 180, 462
Aurora (nom or ab), iv 73
Auster, 293, 360, 404; ~um, 241;
    ~o (d), 492; ~os, 241, 327, 380,
    482, 701; ~is (d), 394

Bacchus, 72; ~i, 91
Belliger (=Mars), iv 32
Belua (nom), 362, 383
Bootes, 139, 598, 624; ~n, 718
Boreas, iv 48, v 7; ~n, 242, 325,
    380, 413, 459; ~ae (d), 359, 482
Bos (=Taurus), 182

Cancer (nom), 469, 484, iv 146;
    (voc), 545; ~um, 6, 147, 428, 476,
    589; ~i, [565], iii 8, iv 55, 88; ~o
    (d), iv 10, 40; (ab), 151, 524, 605,
    iv 149; (d or ab), 471
Canchli, 665
Canis, 333, 341, 621, 681; (g), 344,
    488, 611

Caprae (g), 167, 685
Capricornus, 523, [567], 686; ~um,
    321, iv 38; ~i, 7, 289, iv 130; ~o
    (ab), iv 120
Carinae (=Argo) (g), 374
Cassiepia, 193; ~am, 252, 662
Celaeno (nom), 262
Centaurus (Australis), 671; ~um,
    427; ~i, 415, 490; (=Sagittarius),
    iv 103, 129
Cepheida, 240, 704
Cepheus, 184, 314, 643, 680; ~os,
    189, 191, 282
Cereri, iv 3
Chelae (nom), 89, 233, 632, iv 27,
    98; ~as, 416, 507, 549, 623
Chion, 652
Chiron (constellation) (nom), 421,
    637, 669, 675; ~a, 695
Colchis (nom), 534
Corona (Australis) (nom), 391, 692
Corona (Borealis) (nom), 71, 636;
    ~ae (g), 590, 667; ~a (ab), 87
Coruus (constellation), 430, 431;
    ~i, 505
Corybantes (nom), 38
Crater (constellation) (nom), 429,
    431; ~a (a), 505
Cresia (f nom), 32, 44
Cretaeo (m d), 539; ~ae (g), 167;
    (nom), 24
Creterra (ab), 620; see also Crater
Cycnus, 276, 466, 615, 639, 690;
    ~um, 278; ~i, 679; ~o (ab), 280
Cyllenaeus, iv 137
Cyllene (nom), 584
Cyllenius (adj), iv 111; (sub), iv 129
Cynosura (nom), 39, 41, 45, 54, 313;
    ~an, 51, 187
Cynosurida, 189
Cytherea (nom), iv 76
Cythereius (adj), ii 2, iv 69

Dea (Virgo), iv 152; ~am, iv 38
Delphin (nom), 321
Delphinus, 613, 691
Deltoton (nom), 239; (a), 235

Deucalion (*nom*), 562
Dictaeis (*n ab*), 38
Dis: Ditis, iv 13
Doridos, 666
Draconis, 58, 273; *see also* Anguis

Electra (*nom*), 262
Equus (=Pegasus): Equi (*g*), 209, 284, 465
Ericthonius, 158
Eridanus, 367, 603; ~i, 374, 722; *see also* Padus
Eurus, v 8; ~os, 425; ~is (*ab*), iv 159
Europe (*nom*), 537

Fauoni (*g*), iv 123

Ganymeden, 318
Gargaron (*nom*), 585
Gemini (constellation) (*nom*), 148, 540, iv 26, 146; ~os, 461, 720, iv 10; ~orum, 163, [565]; ~is (*d*), iv 83; (*ab*), 379, 433, 716, iii 6, iv 54, 120, 149
Gorgonis, 218
Gradiuus (=Mars), ii 16
Graecia (*voc*), vi 2
Grai (*nom*), 22, 335; ~is (*d*), 40

Haedi (*nom*), 171; ~os, 169, 713
Haemus, 243, 584
Helice (*nom*), 39, 40, 42, 147; ~n, 51, 90, 141; ~s, 53, 60
Helicone, 218
Hellen, 533
Hesperos, iv 74
Hippocrenen, 221
Hippodamian, 162
Hyades (*nom*), 178
Hydra (constellation) (*nom*), 619, 626; ~am, 698; *see also* Hydros
Hydra (Lernaean); ~am, 543
Hydrochoos, 382, 693; ~on, iv 21; *see also* Aquarius
Hydros (constellation), 426, 432, 668; ~i, 505, 609; *see also* Hydra

Iasides (*nom*), 184
Iason (*nom*), 351
Icarus, 92
Ides, 585
[imbrifer (=Aquarius), 567]
Iuno (*nom*), 545; ~nis, 351
Iuppiter (*nom*), 166, 185, 319, 410, ii 5, iii 4, iv 1, 63; (*voc*), 689; Iouem, 556; ~is, 35, 39, 166, 265, 277, 316, 317, 365, 420, 607, 714; ~e, 1, 251
Iustitia (*nom*), 104

Lanigeri (*g*), 240, [565], 706; ~o (*ab*), iv 23
Larem, iv 16
Latiis (*f ab*), 15
Latonia (*voc*), 646
Ledae (*g*), 276
Ledaeos, 542
Leo (*nom*), 468, 547, [566], iii 9, iv 12, 150; ~nem, 149, 427, 469; ~nis, 604, iv 23, 26, 94, 124
Lepus (*nom*), 610, 683; Leporem, 341, 343; ~is, 373, 488
Liber (*voc*), iv 18
Libra (*nom*), 8, iv 17, 126, 152; ~ae (*g*), iii 11; ~a (*ab*), iv 59
Luna (*nom*), 78, 194, 230
Lycaonis, 226
Lyra (*nom*), 270, 274, 279, 614, 679

Maia (*nom*), 263
Mars *see* Gradiuus, Mauors
Martia (*f nom*), iv 44
Mauors (*nom*), ii 3, iv 25; *see also* Gradiuus
Mercurialis (*f nom*), 279
Mercurius, ii 4, 16; ~o (*d*), 270
Merope (*nom*), 262
Minoae (*g*), 590; ~a (*ab*), 692
Musaeos, 220
Musas, 552; ~is (*d*), 444; (*ab*), 15
Myrtilos, 160, 181, 183, 711
Myrtoas, 159

Nemeaeus, 547; ~i (*n g*), iv 58

Neptune, 323
Nereia (ƒ nom), 356
Nereidas, 705
Nereus: Nerea, 409
Nili, 235
Notus, v 7

Oceanus, 590, 696; ~um, 396, 581, 631; ~i, 23, 63, 569; ~o (d), 182, 667; (ab), 43, 171, 287, 522, 624, 675, 720
Oenopioni (d), 652
Olympus, 585; ~on, iv 132; ~i, 32
Ophiuchus, 75, 592, 676; ~um, 80, 508; ~i, 719
Orion (nom), 314, 329, 601, 658, 682, 724; ~a, 504, 645; ~is, 233, 368; ~e, 343, 550

Padus, 617; see also Eridanus
Palladia (ab), 518
Panopes, 666
Paphie (nom), iv 110 (conjecture mentioned in apparatus)
Pegasus, 222, 510, 638; ~on, 283, 694; see also Equus
Pelopis, 162
Perseida, 462
Perseus, 685, 707; ~a, 708; ~os, 249
Phaethonta, 363
Phaethontides (nom), 366
Pharii (nom), v 4
Philyra (ab), 634
Phoebe (nom), ii 2, 10, 14
Phoebei (m g), iv 112; ~os, 630, iv 25; ~is (n ab), 553
Phoebus, 497, 576, ii 18; ~i, 150, 275, 653, iv 139
Phoenicas, 41
Phosphoros, iv 73; see also Venus
Phrixeae (g), iv 78
Phrixum, 533
Phrygium (m), 318
Phryx, iv 133
Pierio (m ab), 218
Piscis (g), 246; ~es, 241, 361, 365,

[567], 699, 704, iv 43, 109, 163; (a), 700, iv 21; ~ibus (d), 284, 369; (ab), 181, 379, 702, iii 19, iv 72, 136
Piscis (Austrinus), 384, 591
Pistricis, 717 see also Pristis
Plaustra (nom), 26
Pleiades (nom), 256; see also Plias
Plias (nom), 266, 708; Pliada, iv 9; see also Pleiades
Poeni (m g), iv 23
Pristis (nom), 356, 487, 640; ~in, 360, 361, 381; ~is (g), 371, 390, 661, 721 see also Pistricis
Procyon (nom), 433, 610, 688
Puppis (=Argo) (nom), 626; (g), 345, 407, 489, 620, 687

Romani (adj) (n g), 25

Sagitta (nom), 315, 614; see also Telum
Sagittiferum (m), iv 19; ~i (m g), 392; (n g), iv 157; ~o (m d), 551; (m ab), iii 15
Saturnia (ƒ nom), 545
Saturnus, ii 5; ~o (ab), iii 25
Scorpios, 81, 311, 393, 548, [566], 595, 632, 645, 660, iii 12, iv 42, 100, 127, 155; ~on, 490, 655, iv 18, 61
Serpens (nom), 49, 86, 677; ~ntis, 54, 61, 69; see also Anguis
Serta (nom), 85, 667; (a), 590; ~is (ab), 73
Sidoniam, 47
Sirius, 610, iv 41; ~on, 335
Sol (nom), 6, 43, 289, 492, ii 10; ~em, ii 11, iii 21; ~is, 336, 357, 531, 575, 582, ii 1, iv 1, 138; soles (nom), iv 89; (a), iv 45, 84, 85; ~ibus (ab), iv 93
Sonipes (=Centaurus), 418; (= Pegasus), 207, 618; see also Centaurus, Pegasus
Spica (nom), 97
Syriae (g), 563

Tartara (*a*), 540
Taurus, 174, 501, 536, iii 3; ~um, iv 52, 147, i 177, 255, 328, 503, [565], 709, iv 8, 37, 82, 119, 145; ~o (*ab*), 182, 717
Tauros (people), 533
Taygete (*nom*), 263
Telum (=Sagitta) (*nom*), 690; *see also* Sagitta
Tethys (*nom*), 589
Threicium (*m*), 242; ~as, 247
Titan (=Sol) (*nom*), 306, 476
Titania (*a*), 554
Tithonidos, 588
Tonas: ~antis, iv 143; *see also* Iuppiter

Troia (*nom*), 320
Turibulum (*a*), 394, 402, 707; ~i or ~o (*d*), 397; *see also* Ara
Tyrii (*nom*), v 4

Venus (*nom*), iv 50, 74; ~eris, iv 109; ~i, ii 15; *see also* Hesperos, Phosphoros
Virgo (Diana) (*voc*), 646
Virgo (constellation) (*nom*), 468, 547, [566], 621, iii 10; ~inis, 96, 140, 612; ~e, 418, iv 14, 59, 95
Vrsae (*g*), 164; ~a (*ab*), 225; ~ae (*nom*), 25; ~is (*ab*), 460

Zephyrus, v 8; ~is (*ab*), 156